W9-AEQ-384

Praise for *The Cradle of Thought*

'Brilliant . . . a groundbreaking book, one that can, and should,
be read by psychologists, parents, and laypersons alike'
Dr Suzanne Zeedyk

'We are in rare company here. Hobson's intelligence,
elegance of expression and wide-ranging learning have given
birth to a body of work that is nothing less than a vision
of how we come to be what we are'
Dr Charles Fernyhough

'What is so special about this book is the excitement with which
Hobson communicates his ideas. He is a consummate story-teller . . .
This book rates with the very best of popular scientific writing'
Jeremy Holmes, Royal College of Psychiatrists

'There is much to admire in this immensely readable book . . .
Hobson is both an outstanding scholar and passionate
about his subject'
Professor Simon Baron-Cohen, Nature

'An admirable book . . .
philosophically sophisticated in a real sense'
Professor David Hamlyn

The Cradle of Thought

Peter Hobson is Professor of Developmental Psychopathology at the Tavistock Clinic and at the department of Psychiatry and Behavioural Sciences at University College, London. He works clinically as a psychotherapist, with adults, as well as being Director of the Unit for the Study of Lifespan Development. He is author of many original research publications and has written one previous book, *Autism and the Development of Mind.*

PETER HOBSON

The Cradle of Thought

*Exploring the Origins
of Thinking*

PAN BOOKS

First published 2002 by Macmillan

This edition published 2004 by Pan Books
an imprint of Pan Macmillan Ltd
Pan Macmillan, 20 New Wharf Road, London N1 9RR
Basingstoke and Oxford
Associated companies throughout the world
www.panmacmillan.com

ISBN 978-0-330-48828-0

A CIP catalogue record for this book is available from
the British Library.

Typeset by SetSystems Ltd, Saffron Walden, Essex
Printed and bound in Great Britain by
Mackays of Chatham plc, Chatham, Kent

Visit www.panmacmillan.com to read more about all our books and to buy
them. You will also find features, author interviews and news of any author
events, and you can sign up for e-newsletters so that you're always first to hear
about our new releases.

To two wonderful colleagues, Beate Hermelin and Anthony Lee, and to my late father Bob Hobson.

Contents

Picture Acknowledgements

La Pensée by Auguste Rodin (© Photo RMN – R. G. Ojeda; Réunion des Museés Nationaux); '*Do you have something for the human condition?*' Cartoon by Mel Calman (© S. & C. Calman); *Ceci n'est pas une pipe* by Rene Magritte (© ADAGP, Paris and DACS, London 2002; Bridgeman Art Library); *Madonna con il Bambino* by Giovanni Bellini (Accademia Carrara Di Belle Arti); *Andrieu d'Andres* by Auguste Rodin (Museé Rodin); *Akhnaten and Nefertiti* – Egyptian altar relief from 1345 BC (Bildarchiv Preussischer Kulturbesitz); *Steam-Boat off a Harbour's Mouth* by J. M. W. Turner (© Tate, London 2002); *The Duke of Wellington* by Francisco de Goya (© National Gallery, London); *Woman Crying* (study for Guernica) 1937 by Pablo Picasso (© Succession Picasso / DACS 2002; Museo Nacional Centro de Arte Reina Sofia, Madrid / Bridgeman Art Library).

Preface

Ever since the seventeenth century, when Aristotle's distinction between knowledge and desire was elaborated into a threefold division of mental activity involving cognition (thought), conation (the will) and affect (feelings), we have had a terrible time trying to piece Humpty Dumpty together again. The best and perhaps the only way to heal these rents in our picture of the mind is to study early development. If we can start with babies, and follow how babies act and feel and perceive things, then maybe we shall see how thinking is distilled out of infant-level ways of relating that are imbued with feeling and action.

That is the primary aim of this book: to begin with the mental life of babies and to end up with a story of how thinking – or to be more precise, the kind of creative, flexible and imaginative thinking that characterizes humans – emerges in the course of early development. In order to arrive at an accurate story, we also need to see what happens when human development is deflected from its usual path. How is thinking affected in individuals who face serious emotional or social difficulties early in life, for example? How do conditions such as autism or congenital blindness or early profound deprivation alter the development of thinking? It turns out that perspectives from atypical development force us to make radical changes in our customary ways of thinking about thinking.

Already, then, we have two ways in which we can begin to integrate what has been split asunder: we can examine the psychological abilities of children and adults through the lens of infancy, and we can study normal and abnormal development alongside each other. With these approaches, if we are lucky, we may also achieve two further kinds of conceptual integration: the bodily with the mental, and the individual with the social.

When we watch a baby interacting with her caregiver, are we merely watching her body, or do we see her mental state? When a baby watches or listens to us, does she see our bodies and hear our voices much like she sees other objects or hears other noises? If not, then what does she experience? These rhetorical questions may seem a long way from our topic, but the infant's growing awareness of what it means to have a subjective perspective, that is, what it is to be a human being with a mind, proves to be critically important for the development of her own thinking. So we shall need to understand how infants forge this link between seeing bodies and apprehending minds.

Tied up with the body–mind issue is the relation between the individual and society. Most of us think of thinking as an individual affair, something we do in our own heads. This must be right in some sense, otherwise what are we doing as we sit in an armchair contemplating the meaning of life? Yet the fact that we become able to reflect in such an abstract way, all by ourselves, does not mean that it was all by ourselves that we acquired the ability to think in the first place. Nor does it mean that the psychological mechanisms by which we think – the tools of thought, as it were – are things that arose in our own brains by some individualistic process like gene-determined brain growth. I shall be arguing that on the contrary, the tools of thought are constructed on the basis of an infant's emotional engagement with other people. To put it bluntly, if an infant were not involved with other people, then she would not come to think.

It may help to highlight the far-reaching nature of this claim by considering scientists' recent attempts to replicate human thinking on computers. There is nothing wrong in modelling aspects of thinking on computers, just as there is nothing wrong in talking of a human being computing a mathematical equation. The problem arises when the computer is supposed to be doing the thinking for itself. Here computer enthusiasts face the disconcerting fact that only humans, and not computers 'themselves', make sense of the input and output data. Computers don't understand anything, nor do they care. They do not find meaning, because they do not have the necessary kinds of linkage with the world that surrounds them. Any thinker, whether human or merely humanoid, needs the appropriate kind of body and capacities to feel and act in order to connect with the world that contains the objects of thought. Then there is the other devastating limitation that consigns computers to thoughtlessness. It is not just that computers do not have the right kind of relations with the things around them – it is also that they do not have the right kind of relations with each other. If computers want to think, they had better get a social life.

There is a final batch of 'integrations' that I am trying to achieve in writing this book, and these are more personal. As a medically trained psychiatrist, I have great respect for the mixture of clinical science and concern for the individual, both as a person and as a unique 'case' for understanding, that characterizes the psychiatric approach to patients and mental disorder. As an experimental psychologist, I find it a bracing challenge to identify a focus of controversy or a critical unknown about the abilities of a given group of children or adults, and design an experiment to test what is really the case. It may sound romantic, but at its best this is like coaxing nature to reveal itself – and it is especially exhilarating when nature surprises or teases you with the unexpected. And finally, as a psychoanalyst trained at the Institute of Psychoanalysis in London, I am convinced that the disciplined approach of listening to individuals and discerning patterns of relationship in the here and now of patient–therapist exchanges is one that yields rich dividends in understanding the depths and subtleties of the mind.

So the personal element is that for the first time in this book, I have brought these professional strands together. I hope it will seem natural to have done so. Yet it has been a struggle to keep hold of them all in my own working life. I recall a senior figure in psychiatry telling me that I needed to choose between being a proper scientist and being a psychotherapist (a term he used with a mixture of disdain and indulgence); and when I finally dared to present my experimental research on autism at the Institute of Psychoanalysis, I heard afterwards that some of the audience had felt my stance was anti-psychoanalytic. I hope what I have written will show why I needed to follow the route that I have, in order to arrive at the perspective that I have.

There are a couple of other ingredients added into the mix. I was drawn into the study of autism not only by my fascination with human mental development, but also by my interest in philosophy of mind. When I was an undergraduate at Cambridge University reading medicine and then psychology, I sometimes attended philosopy lectures when I should have been channelling my interests elsewhere. Many years later I had my first encounter with someone who had autism. Immediately it struck me that here was someone who had a quite different 'form of life' (a phrase coined by the philosopher Ludwig Wittgenstein), and I seized the chance to pursue a kind of practical philosophy through the study of autism. I was especially taken with the idea that Wittgenstein's philosophical account of how we understand other minds through perceiving and responding to expressions of feeling might explain autistic children's severely limited understanding of other people — and beyond this, might explain their restricted creativity in thought. In addition, all this seemed to point to the distinctiveness of human mentality, and to suggest something important about the evolution of the mind.

These, then, are the themes of the present book. Now to a comment about style. My first book, entitled *Autism and the Development of Mind*,[1] was so dense and laden with references that only a few academic stalwarts managed to read it from cover to cover. Several sympathetic colleagues and friends told me they had dipped into it, and would one day return, but that was just kindness. So this time, I have tried to say what I have to say as directly as I can, and have included only the most pivotal references to the work of others. I hope that any fellow psychologists who feel neglected will look back to my previous work for citations of their research. In broadening and deepening the scope of my argument, I have tried to keep to essentials. To the extent that I may have done so, and in more or less readable prose, has much to do with the patient and firm advice I have received from my editorial advisors Georgina Morley and Peter Robinson ('Don't lecture!'), and especially from the detailed and penetrating comments on the manuscript offered by two special people, Linda Young and David King. To these individuals I am very grateful.

I need to explain two points about the text. Firstly, I have referred to the individual child with autism as 'he', for the reason that males with this condition substantially outnumber females. I have referred to the individual infant as female, to balance the equation. In general I have referred to a caregiver as 'she', because most of the research on relations between infants and their caregivers has been conducted with mothers. I have also referred to the adult with borderline personality disorder as 'she', both because this reflects the preponderance of females in this group and also because our own research in this area has been exclusively with females. I trust that readers will be aware that no sex discrimination is implied, and that I employ these devices only to avoid cumbersome alternatives. Although there are important scientific issues that have to do with special characteristics of each gender with respect to the conditions (such as autism) and roles (such as parenting) discussed, I have not dealt with these matters. Secondly, I have not only disguised all clinical material so that individuals are unrecognizable, but also I have integrated quotations from different sources so that any given case description amounts to a 'composite' person, not any particular person. I hope that this necessary distortion of reality has not compromised the representativeness of what I have written.

The early research on children reported here was undertaken at the Department of Child and Adolescent Psychiatry in the Institute of Psychiatry, London, where Michael Rutter was a major influence, and at the MRC Developmental Psychology Unit under the tolerant and supportive leadership of Neil O'Connor. The more recent body of research and clinical work was conducted in the Adult Department of the Tavistock Clinic and in the Department of Psychiatry and Behavioural Sciences, University College, London. Colleagues and myself are indebted to a number of organizations that have provided financial support for the research, and in particular to the Medical Research Council, the Wellcome Foundation, the Baily Thomas Charitable Foundation, the Hayward Foundation, the Joseph Levy Foundation, the Mary Kitzinger Trust, the Winnicott Trust, the London Clinic of Psychoanalysis, the US National Institute of Health, the Office of R&D for Health and Social Services NHS Cymru, Wales, and the National Health Service R&D funding system. The Tavistock Foundation, chaired by Nick Temple, has also given our Unit vital assistance.

The work that underpins the book was conducted in collaboration with a group of gifted colleagues whom I name in the text, and to each of whom I am deeply indebted. Yet above all, it has been my mentor and long-standing friend Beate Hermelin, with her extraordinary mix of originality and incisiveness — unfailingly generous, consistently unpredictable, often breathtakingly direct, and ever a source of wonder and delight — who has inspired and sustained me over the last two decades. To Beate and my fellow researcher Tony Lee, the most sensitive and disciplined tester of children I know and a 'salt of the earth' man if ever there was one, I dedicate this book. To them, and to my late father Bob Hobson, whose thoughts and feelings are woven into the fabric of this vision.

ONE

Just Think...

Just think ... and you will realize how remarkable thinking is. In thinking about thinking, or even (on a simpler level) in thinking about whether to read on, you are doing something no other species but ours can do. This book is about the nature of that uniquely human skill. More than this, it is about how humans, as babies, acquire the skill of thinking in the first place. By following the story of mental development over the early months of an infant's life, we shall reach down to the very roots of human thought. For even two-year-olds are such good thinkers that they have far transcended the mentality of non-human creatures. It is not just that they have begun to speak and to understand the speech of others. They have also begun to think *about* things, and have entered the realm of the imagination. They have taken their place in human cultural life.

It has been said that culture is roughly anything we do that monkeys don't. If we can trace the origins of thought in the mental life of human infants, then perhaps we shall also discover how it was that our primate ancestors evolved into thinking and talking members of the species *Homo sapiens*. If we can understand how babies become able to think, maybe we shall stumble across the source of human culture.

This issue for evolutionary theory — how humans became unique among animals in their capacity to think — provides a suitable starting point for our journey, just as its return in the final chapter will herald the close of the book. For a start, it confronts us with the challenge of defining what *is* unique about the human mind. To be sure, there are ways in which animals other than man may be said to think, yet such thinking is a faint shadow of the imaginative and creative thought that has come with the emergence of *Homo sapiens*. More important still, the evolutionary tack is one that exposes us to the critical developmental question: How could evolution on the one hand, or a baby's experiences on the other, shape humans who have the capacity to think out of creatures lacking that capacity?

The difficulty with the evolution part of this question is that, by and large, evolution proceeds in a series of small steps. All the time, small changes happen in the genetic constitution of organisms. Sometimes these changes confer advantages on an individual so that it tends to leave more offspring than its competitors. Little by little, the changed feature becomes widespread within the population: an evolutionary advance has occurred. But how could this have happened in the case of imaginative thought and language? Here we encounter a problem that is still unsolved by those who stress the specifically human innate endowment for language: where did the endowment come from? If we have a language instinct, how was this particular instinct added on to the other instincts we share with our non-human kin in the animal kingdom? Or, again, out of which earlier psychological abilities was imaginative thought built? The fact is that we have not yet been able to trace the steps that gave rise to the momentous changes which signalled the dawning of human mentality.

Those psychologists who believe that humankind became unique by acquiring language are not altogether wrong. But they are not altogether right, either. Before language, there was something else — more basic, in a way more primitive, and with unequalled power in its formative potential, that propelled us *into* language. Something that could evolve in tiny steps, but suddenly gave rise to the thinking processes that revolutionized mental life. Something that (unfortunately) no fossil remains can show us. That something else was *social engagement with each other*. The links that can join one person's mind with the mind of someone else — especially, to begin with, emotional links — are the very links that draw us into thought. To put it crudely: the foundations of thinking were laid at the point when ancestral primates began to connect with each other emotionally in the same ways that human babies connect with their caregivers.

Social engagement is what provides the foundations for language. Not only does it serve as a motive for language to appear in the first place, but, in the structure of what is exchanged between one person and another, it also provides enough – just enough – to begin to shape grammar.

In my view, then, it was a change in the nature of primate social engagement that led to the kinds of thinking and language that are the hallmark of human beings. The solution to our conundrum about evolution – how can thinking arise from anything less than thinking – lies in subtle but profound changes in the commonplace face-to-face interactions that occur between one creature and another. Thinking does not arise from anything *less* than thinking; it arises from something *different* from thinking. Our human pre-*sapiens* ancestors differed from their chimp-like peers in the primate world by virtue of their deeper connectedness with each other. It was this that gave them thought and the leg-up into language. And, startling though it may sound, it was through minute changes in emotional interchanges and relationships that the wonderful transformation took place.

This radical suggestion needs justifying. It also needs to be connected with what can be observed in infant development. If evolution has dealt human beings a strong hand for developing a sophisticated mind, it is still the case that each and every baby has to develop thought and language for herself. Such wonderful abilities do not just appear like an instant meal pre-packed by our genes. What genes give us is the equipment to benefit from experience in such a way that language and thought become possible. There is still the question of what kinds of experience need to be available if a baby is to fulfil that potential. We also want to know how the mental equipment is applied to experience to manufacture thought.

My hope is that once we see how a baby develops thought through her interpersonal exchanges with others, and once we have noted the critically important features of those exchanges, we can then turn back to the evolutionary questions about how such exchanges became possible. In other words, our work in tracing the development of thinking in the individual human baby should direct our search for evolutionary changes that have made human babies so special.

I want to move on and say something about the tactics that we shall employ to make progress in this difficult terrain. But there is a further intellectual stumbling block that we cannot simply bypass, so may as well reckon with from the outset. I have said we are going to 'see' how babies develop in relation to others, but our task is to grasp how *the human mind* emerges as a result. We shall be gathering observations of behaviour, which is bodily, in the hope of finding out about thinking, which is mental. How can we cross the bridge from the physical world, so definite and tangible, to the insubstantial world of the imagination? It would be bad enough if the problem were merely this, a matter of dovetailing our own empirical methods with our theories. But the problem goes deeper. What about *the baby's* need to grasp the mental dimension of human beings through her bodily anchored relations with others? If this is critical for her own mental development – as I shall argue – then we have no choice but to address the mind–body problem that has long bedevilled psychology and philosophy. We do not need to explain everything about how the mind relates to the body, thank goodness, but we do need to understand how human beings come to find out about minds through their bodily interactions with others.

So, consider the two pictures below. The one on the left shows a chimpanzee. The one on the right is a sculpture by Rodin, entitled *Thought*. When you look at them, steadily, what *kinds* of difference do you discern? Suppose someone were to say that there is greater depth

to the woman in thought – would there be any difficulty in understanding this statement? And, a question we cannot answer, but need to ask: If we generously allow that a chimpanzee might find any meaning in these representations, would that chimpanzee see (or feel) the difference in depth between the face of its peer and the person of its human cousin?

If the story of evolution is merely a subtext of this book, then how is the principal story about human development going to unfold? By and large, I shall be looking at the path of 'normal' (i.e. typical) development through the lens of abnormality. By studying children who seem to be following a different pathway of development as they grow up, we stand to learn a great deal about what happens in healthy and optimal development. Some things about children become so familiar to us that we lose sight of how remarkable they are – and lose sight, too, of how little we understand the processes that underlie developmental achievements. What happens when we turn to the abnormal case is that suddenly we are confronted with aspects of mental life that are failing to develop or that seem to be developing in unusual ways. In trying to understand what is happening, we are compelled to examine exactly how and why the steps in development deviate from normality – and this in turn reveals how poorly we understand the step-by-step changes in the usual case. Sometimes our most cherished assumptions have to go.

Especially startling insights into typical development have come from a condition of childhood that was first described in the 1940s: early childhood autism. Centrally and critically, autism reveals what it means to have mutual engagement with someone else. It reveals this by presenting us with the tragic picture of human beings for whom such engagement is partial or missing. The autistic child's lack of emotional connectedness with others is devastating in its own right, but also it has quite startling implications for the child's ability to think. These implications are what enable us to see how thinking itself is born out of interpersonal relations.

So what is autism? Autism is what we call a syndrome, which means nothing more nor less than a collection of clinical features that cluster together. It is a rare condition, affecting fewer than one in a thousand children and around three times as many boys as girls. The abnormalities it presents are these: a profound and characteristic impairment in social relations; a severe limitation in communication with other people, often including abnormalities in language; an impoverishment in imagination, including play; and unusual repetitive preoccupations and rituals. The challenge for psychologists is surprisingly simple to state and remarkably difficult to meet: to explain why these things are found together.

The answer would be straightforward enough if there were one part of the brain that was needed for normal social relations, communication, imaginative thought, and so on. In that case it would be plausible that damage to this area is what causes autism. But there is no such part of the brain. Many able scientists have looked for it, with conspicuous lack of success. This is not to say that the brains of people with autism are working perfectly well. On the contrary, there is plenty to indicate that their brains are malfunctioning. It is just that there does not seem to be a simple relationship between what is wrong with the mental processes of people with autism, and what is wrong with their brains.

The solution to the problem will come from seeing how the syndrome of autism emerges *over the course of early development*. Our first task will be to determine what is basic to autism. Here we seek an abnormality or abnormalities in psychological functioning that are always present from the onset of the condition and not the side effect of some other problem. Then we shall need to explain how the basic abnormalities give rise to the other features of the disorder as the affected child grows older. This means we shall have to draw upon an adequate theory of development – which may prove something of a problem, given that we do not have a theory of development which works when applied to the case of autism. This leads to justified unease that perhaps our theories of normal development are in need of revision.

It is not that scientists have returned from their researches into autism empty-handed. They have uncovered genetic causes of autism, they have identified some infections of the nervous system that can cause autism, and they have located parts of the brain that seem abnormal in a few children with autism.[1] It is just that investigations of individuals with autism seem to throw up a variety of causes that apply in some cases and not in others, and that seem to explain only fragments of the clinical picture. Even researchers who have recognized the need to trace the cascading effects of abnormality over the course of development have failed to construct a unifying theory of autism.

I think there is a reason why we feel so near to understanding autism, yet so far away. It is the same reason why we seem to understand a lot about thinking in human beings, yet are largely baffled when we seek the roots of thought in children's early development. The reason is that we are preoccupied with explanations that focus on individuals in isolation. We imagine that we shall identify a particular cause of pathology within each individual with autism, for example. Or, in the case of typical babies, we suppose that by examining the individual child's abilities to categorize things or act upon objects in increasingly complex ways, or by conducting ever more penetrating brain scans so that we can see how the individual child's nervous system is developing, we shall understand how thought becomes possible. These expectations are not going to be fulfilled.

A new approach is required. We need to realize that one of the most powerful influences on development is what happens *between* people. Or, in the case of autism, that one of the most harmful things that can affect development is when certain kinds of interaction fail to happen between people.[2]

We shall never be able to capture what happens between people in a brain scan. To be sure, we may see patches of colour that betray all kinds of neurological goings-on when individuals relate to one another. These events in the nervous system are a necessary part of the story. Yet they amount to only one small piece of a much broader picture. It is a picture that involves another person, and each person's experience of the other. The roots of thought are embedded here, in what happens by virtue of one individual's experience of someone else. And the roots of autism are to be found in what fails to happen between people. There may be a variety of different childhood disorders that prevent a given child from experiencing vital aspects of interpersonal relations — and autism may result. Or conditions in the child may conspire with deficiencies in what his environment provides by way of interpersonal contact — and autism may result. Or, in the most extreme circumstances, autism may even arise because a child is subject to the most terrible privation and receives almost nothing by way of sensitive care. In each case, we shall understand autism only if we grasp how the lack of certain forms of interpersonal experience has a profound impact on the developing mind.

Autism will be my most important example from developmental psychopathology (which is the scientific term for considering normal and abnormal development alongside each other), but it will not be the only one.[3] Autism is revealing because of what children with autism lack on the one hand, and what abilities they possess on the other. Some other conditions are revealing for what affected individuals display with unusual prominence. For example, some disturbed adults suspect other people of harbouring grudges against them, or of manipulating or abusing them. Sometimes, of course, the suspicions are justified, but often they are not. It would be easy to dismiss such ideas and experiences as crazy, beyond the pale of normality, were it not that similar suspiciousness and feelings of persecution also seem to be present in shadow form in adults who are not disturbed. They appear under conditions of stress, for example, and they crop up in dreams. This being the case, we are faced with the disquieting possibility that perhaps abnormality betrays a feature of normality writ large.

If this is so, then why do some people feel these things more strongly than others? And why do people with such disturbed, night-marish forms of experience seem to have disturbed relationships? Should we think in terms of an individual developing these abnormal ideas because of bad experiences in childhood? Or do they arise because of a lack of good experiences that can tame something potentially abnormal within us all? Or are the conditions genetically caused, and unconnected with particular kinds of care? These are questions that excite heated controversy. Many psychologists find it inconceivable that the development of thinking might be so dependent on feelings; many psychiatrists find it preposterous even to speculate that normality arises out of what we call abnormal. So perhaps it becomes evident why the study of developmental psychopathology may give us novel insights into the deepest issues of human mental development. Truly we may discover things that have not been discovered before.

There is a second reason why this may be so. We now have unusual depth and variety to the methods of investigation at our disposal. This is my next topic. I realize that the prospect of having to read even a couple of pages on 'methods of investigation' must be as welcome as the kiss of death. All I can say is: the effort will be worthwhile. It is a bit like having to learn a foreign language. That, too, begins as a labour, but can end up enlightening, satisfying, and extremely useful for managing in a strange land. So here goes . . .

The first approach I want to deal with is the clinical method. I am using this term in a rather loose sense, just as Jean Piaget, the father of modern child psychology, did when he spoke of '*la méthode clinique*'. I mean careful descriptions of individual cases, whether these are clinical in the sense of applying to people who attend a psychiatric clinic, or clinical in the sense of being formulated with all the searching attention and probing techniques of the clinician. There is no better way to begin to understand people, whether 'normal' or disabled, whether adult or child, than to observe and examine a few individuals very closely.

There is no doubt that methodical observation of infants, abnormally developing children, adults with mental disorders of one kind or another, and chimpanzees and gorillas (among other non-human species) can reveal a great deal about the mind and its development. For example, detailed case histories of particular individuals with abnormal conditions can alert us to the perplexing varieties of human psychology. One such case history appeared in the film *Rain Man*. Dustin Hoffman's deft and sensitive portrayal of an adult with autism opened the eyes of thousands to the extraordinary mix of abilities and disabilities that may feature in this condition — and, in so doing, prompted them to re-evaluate human nature.

We can stay with autism to see what the clinical method can achieve. My illustration comes from the paper of 1943 in which the American psychiatrist Leo Kanner first described the syndrome. Here are edited excerpts from Kanner's description of one of the eleven children in whom he recognized 'autistic disturbances of affective [i.e. emotional] contact':

Case 9: Charles was brought to the clinic at the age of four and a half years, his mother complaining how 'the thing that upsets me most is that I can't reach my baby'. As a baby, this child would lie in the crib, just staring. When he was one and a half years old, he began to spend hours spinning toys and the lids of bottles and jars. His mother remarked: 'He would pay no attention to me and show no recognition of me if I enter the room. The most impressive thing is his detachment and his inaccessibility. He walks as if he is in a shadow, lives in a world of his own where he cannot be reached. No sense of relationship to persons. He went through a period of quoting another person; never offers anything himself. His entire conversation is a replica of whatever has been said to him. He used to speak of himself in the second person, now he uses the third person at times; he would say, "He wants" – never "I want" ... When he is with other people, he doesn't look up at them. Last July, we had a group of people. When Charles came in, it was just like a foal who'd been let out of an enclosure ... He never initiates conversation, and conversation is limited, extensive only as far as objects go.'[4]

In this moving account by a mother who felt she could not reach her baby, we can register the force of Kanner's suggestion that autistic children 'have come into the world with innate inability to form the usual, biologically provided affective contact with people'. The sense of emotional connectedness that we feel when relating to other people – whether the people are infants, children or adults – seems to have been tragically lacking in this mother's relationship with her own son. Charles was inaccessible to her. For his part, Charles seemed not to attend to his mother or to other people, nor even to recognize them as beings with whom he could become emotionally engaged: 'it was just like a foal who'd been let out of an enclosure'. Where was the meeting of hearts and minds that this mother yearned for with her child? There even seemed to be something lacking in the boy's sense of his own self, in that neither his presence nor his conversation conveyed self-assertion or self-expression: 'He walks as if he is in a shadow ... He would say, "He wants" – never "I want"'.

If it is true that children with autism miss out on the experience of meeting the hearts and minds of others, what might their idea of other people be like? Perhaps the most succinct and striking account is that provided by an intelligent young autistic adult interviewed by the psychiatrist Donald Cohen. This man described how the first years of his life were devoid of people: 'I really didn't know there were people until I was seven years old. I then suddenly realized that there were people. But not like you do. I still have to remind myself that there are people . . . I never could have a friend. I really don't know what to do with other people, really.'5

So, even when the person with autism realizes that there are people, he still finds it difficult to relate to them *as* people. Only slowly does it dawn on him that persons are a special class of thing with their own feelings, thoughts and beliefs about the world; and even when he achieves such understanding, in so far as he does, still he lacks the natural ability to engage on a personal level.

The above clinical descriptions have helped us to get a feel for autism. Nothing is more important than the 'feel' for our understanding of this rare and strange condition, and for our grasp of what it can teach us about normal human development. For all their richness, however, observational studies can reveal only so much. There is such a lot that is particular to any one case that it is usually impossible to tease out what exactly causes what in the individual's development. So many events and seeming idiosyncrasies fall under suspicion as sources of mischief – from untoward events early in life, to the effects of vaccines, to the inevitable bumps on the head sustained in the rough and tumble of growing up. Even when observational studies are directed at a group of individuals with a given condition such as autism, so that one can see what is characteristic across particular individuals, it is still not possible to be sure whether one aspect of the clinical picture underlies or is the result of another. Moreover, the essence of the condition may be obscured by the variety of abnormalities present. For example, it is no easy task to distil out what is truly unique to autism and what is more a reflection of the mental retardation that often accompanies autism. Is the child's unresponsiveness to subtle emotional signals a feature of general slowness in the development of all mental capacities, or is there something unique to autism here? In order to examine such issues, experimental studies are invaluable.

The idea of an experiment is disquieting to some people, and for good reason. It conjures up the idea of an experimenter doing something to a person or an animal – often something unpleasant. It can even suggest experimenting 'on' someone. I am using the term in a different, more technical, sense (although it is also true that one has to be very careful in designing and conducting studies so that those who take part are not exploited). What I am talking about is a simple but powerful way of setting up a study so that one can pinpoint exactly how one group of individuals differs from another. This can enable us to say what is special and specific to a condition such as autism.

In essence, the method is very simple. First, you establish two groups of individuals. Within each group you have a certain type of individual. To continue with the example of autism, you might have fifteen children with autism in one group, and roughly the same number of children without autism in the other group. If you now give some kind of task or test to these two groups, it becomes possible for you to detect things that had simply not struck you before. It is almost like coming to see those hidden creatures in trees depicted in childhood comics.

There are two ways in which this happens. On the one hand, you notice ways in which the children within each group are similar – for example, how they find particular things about a task easy or difficult. On the other hand, your attention is drawn to how there are differences between the groups, and how those with autism differ from those who do not have autism. It is this combination of seeing similarities and differences that enables you to analyse what makes autism 'autism', for example.[6]

The situation is a bit more complicated than this, however. In a way, you need to make things as difficult as possible for yourself in order to get the most out of the experiment. For a start, the two groups need to be similar as well as different to each other. This may sound paradoxical, but the point is that if they differ in a lot of respects, and if they then perform differently on a task, one cannot tell what is responsible for the pattern of results. Suppose, for example, children with autism are compared with children who do not have autism, but the two groups differ in the ability to understand language. Suppose, too, the children with autism seem to find more difficulty than the comparison group in, say, sorting pictures of faces into those showing positive and negative emotions. We cannot tell whether this group difference is due to autism, or whether the children with autism are less able to understand what they are being asked to do, or perhaps less able to think because they lack language. So one needs to compare children with and without autism who are similar in the ability to understand language, as well as similar in a number of other respects such as how as old they are. Then any differences between them cannot be due to differences in using language or in their ages. This is the importance of testing a matched 'control group' of non-autistic children.

A complementary procedure is to include control tasks. Let us continue with our example. Suppose we find that the children with autism have difficulty in sorting pictures of faces. We still do not know whether there is something about faces that presents them with a problem, or whether there is a much more general difficulty with seeing how things fall into classes. We do not know, for example, whether they might also have found it difficult to sort pictures of animals or furniture. If we were to launch into some theory about the children's particular inability to recognize emotions in faces, then we might have missed the point. In the most extreme case, *any* conclusion about their ability to recognize meaning in faces would be unjustified. It is conceivable that the autistic children were unable to recognize pictures as pictures, rather in the way that household pets fail to see pictures as representing anything. It might be that their ability to recognize emotion in real-life faces was perfectly normal – it was just pictures of faces (like pictures of anything else) that presented a problem. In this situation, of course, one would have been in danger of drawing completely false conclusions from the results of the experiment.

The way to ensure that one does not fall into this trap is to include control tasks in the experiment. These are tests to ensure that, if one does find group differences, these differences are indeed differences in what one is trying to test. In the above example, one might include tests of sorting pictures of animals into sea creatures and land creatures. The critical thing is that the children with autism would need to demonstrate that on the control task they were just as good as the children without autism. Then and only then could one conclude that it was specifically for children with autism and not children in the control group, and specifically on the task of sorting faces and not on the control task, that unusual difficulties were encountered.

A further, and vital, element in designing a satisfying experiment is that one should start out with an issue that needs to be investigated and with a hunch (an hypothesis) about what is going on. Preferably, your own hunch should be different from someone else's, so that the two explanations compete with one another. Then you set up an experiment that addresses the problem. You design the experiment so that you predict the results will turn out one way and your competitor predicts they will turn out another. This can be the most exciting and nerve-racking way to do science, because you can easily spend six months proving your own hypothesis to be wrong. But then at least you have the consolation that it was you and not your competitor who demonstrated the fact.

Here is an example of an experiment in action. The experiment concerns one of my principal topics, the social impairments of children with autism. It was designed to test an hypothesis. Behind the hypothesis there is a theory that what is central to autism is an impairment in emotional aspects of interpersonal relatedness. The simple idea behind this complex statement is that there is something badly wrong with the children's ability to connect emotionally with other people. As one manifestation of this, the hypothesis goes, children with autism do not react to the emotional expressions of other people like the rest of us do. Someone else's smile or delighted voice does not seem to give them a feeling of warmth; a fearful face or gasp does not induce fear; and so on. To put it more strongly, the child with autism may not perceive a smile *as a smile* but as a contorted face; he may not perceive a gasp of fear as a fearful expression but as an unusual sound.

One of the grave difficulties in trying to test such ideas through experiments is that the natural and alive quality of emotional expressions is easily lost. Even lifelike photographs or recorded voices are far less evocative than real live people who are expressing genuine feelings. It is also difficult to assess to what extent emotional expressions are meaningful to the children. After all, one might learn to attach the word 'happy' to a face with an upturned mouth without having much idea what happiness really means. The way my colleagues, Janet Ouston and Tony Lee, and I tried to examine this in the study I am going to describe was to see whether children were able to tell which emotionally expressive faces corresponded with which emotionally expressive voices.[7] Our prediction was that, because they have difficulty in picking up the emotional meanings of expressions, children with autism would find this task more difficult than other children. Competing theories suggesting that autism is *not* primarily about difficulties in understanding the meanings of emotional expressions would not predict this result, because they would posit no reason why such expressions were any more difficult to interpret than the appearances and sounds of non-personal objects.

Although in other experiments we have presented videotaped faces in order to retain the aliveness of the expressions, in this case we used photographs of expressive faces. This meant that we could ask children to choose which photograph went with which audiotaped sound. Six photographed faces (of which three are shown below, by permission of Paul Ekman) were laid out in front of the child.[8] These showed the same person showing happiness, sadness, anger, fear, surprise and disgust, respectively. The task was to select which one of these was the right one to go with each voice we played from the audio tape. On some occasions the voice took the form of a grunt, gasp, moan or other expressive sound; on other occasions it took the form of a short passage of speech spoken with feeling. After each response, the chosen photograph was put back in its place and the next voice was played.

Now there was the challenge to design a control task, that is, a test of matching non-emotional sounds and pictures, so that we could determine whether it was specifically the emotional content of the task that was critical. The problem here was that there is nothing else like a face. In a face, small changes in expression can signify huge changes in emotional meaning. But if you try to look at the photographed faces in a dispassionate way, without allowing yourself to be emotionally moved, you will find that there is really surprisingly little difference between a sad face and an angry face. On the other hand, if you now allow emotions to enter the picture, suddenly there is a very big difference between perceiving sadness and perceiving anger in someone's face. In addition, changes in feeling are coupled not only with changes in the face but also with corresponding changes in the voice. In each case, changes that occur in the expression of a face or a voice are potentially reversible, as one expression changes to another and then back again.

We simply had to accept that there is nothing else outside emotions that parallels these properties of emotional expressions. This meant that there was no way we could construct a single control task that was just like our emotions task except that it was non-emotional. So we had to be satisfied with the best we could do. This was to present a series of tasks involving photographs and sounds of non-emotional events and objects. For example, we presented photographs of six states of a single substance, water – a stream, a waterfall, a lake, a shower, a fountain and the sea – each of which corresponded with a BBC recording of the typical sounds of each. Or we presented photographs of a person engaged in different kinds of 'walking' – running downstairs, walking on shingle, walking on a pavement, walking on rubble, running on a pavement and walking on snow – and again there were recordings of what each of these sounded like. (The single person who did the walking was actually myself, and it was early one chill February morning that two dedicated scientists could be seen hurrying off with a camera to find the last sizeable patch of melting snow.) Other materials comprised photographs and sounds of six kinds

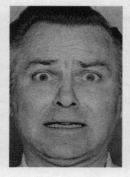

FIGURE 3

of bird (these are shown overleaf), six kinds of electrical appliance (including a refrigerator, which emits the most boring sound you can imagine), six kinds of vehicle (a milk float sounds pretty dull too), and six kinds of garden tool (I shall leave that one to your imagination). The rationale was that if the children with autism were as good as the non-autistic children at choosing photographs to match each of the recorded sounds of these objects and events, but were less good at choosing photographs of expressive faces to match the recorded voices, then we could conclude there was something specific to their difficulty in recognizing emotional meanings in bodily expressions. In a second part of the study, we also asked children to name each of the emotion-related and non-emotional photographs and sounds.

That is all that needs to be said about the design of our experiment, except to add that we tested children and adolescents who fell into two groups — one with autism and another without autism — who were similar in age and in their ability to complete a standard test of language. The principal results can be stated succinctly: in over 75 per cent of the twenty-one matched pairs of autistic and non-autistic children we tested, those with autism scored relatively less well in the emotion than in the non-emotion versions of the sound–picture matching tasks when compared with the children who did not have autism. In other words, three-quarters of the children with autism had specific difficulties with making emotional judgements. And, in an additional test of naming the photographs and sounds, these children with autism did reasonably well on non-emotional naming but were substantially worse at naming photographed faces and sounds of emotion.[9] They were good at identifying the birds, for example, so they were able to produce names for quite complex categories of thing (or, in this case, animal). It was in naming emotions that they were specifically at a disadvantage compared with the non-autistic children.

These results take us just one step towards pinpointing a problem in autism to do with making sense of others' emotions. It is only when we have taken a succession of steps through further experiments like this, and through further case descriptions, that the evidence will become compelling.

FIGURE 4

*

I now turn to the third of my methods of investigation. This is far more controversial than the other two. It is the technique of psychoanalysis.

The approach of psychoanalysis is not what many people suppose. It is not essentially a matter of delving into a person's past in order to dig up evidence of early traumatic happenings. It is not even a matter

FIGURE 5

of explaining the present in terms of the past. And it is certainly not a matter of tracking down how sexuality is at the bottom of everything. No, the method is much simpler than that. What the psychoanalyst does is somewhat like what the experimenter does. He sets up an unusual situation that allows him to observe things that would otherwise remain hidden. In this case, what is set up is not an experiment with its control group and control tasks, but instead a standardized arrangement in which a patient comes for regular meetings with the analyst and talks about things that come to mind. The standardized arrangement is important here, just as it is in experiments.

Sessions begin at a certain time – or at least it is the analyst's job to be present and ready to begin at the set time, even if the patient has not turned up – and they end at a set time, usually after fifty minutes. Typically, the patient lies down on a couch facing away from the analyst, and the analyst waits and attends carefully.

The patient now has to deal with an analyst about whom he knows very little. Moreover, this takes place under conditions that mean the patient is dependent on the analyst to be respectful, neither intrusive nor withdrawn, and at the same time to analyse the patient's problems – whatever that means. These conditions mobilize very deep anxieties, expectations and beliefs in the patient, especially anxieties that have to do with forming intimate relationships with someone else. Is this person trustworthy? Does he know what he is doing? Is he only out to impose his ideas? Is he strong enough to weather my fierce criticisms? Has he got any room in his mind for me? Not all of these anxieties are conscious, at least not at first, and the patient has his own specific ways of trying to deal with them. For example, the patient who is afraid of being abandoned by his analyst may assert his independence; the patient who is afraid of his own aggression may be placating or over-controlled; the patient who is suspicious of the analyst's motives or doubtful about his abilities may try to convince himself that this particular analyst must be all right because he is so famous ... and so on.

The theory behind psychoanalysis is that the patterns of relation-ship that emerge in relation to the analyst are of deep and general significance, in that they colour and shape all the patient's intimate relationships. These include the patient's relationship with himself, which may also be untrusting, aggressive and self-punitive, idealizing, and so on. Analysts talk about the transference, because they take the view that what are transferred on to the person of the analyst are these deeply ingrained patterns of anxieties and defences – patterns that often but not always originate in earlier life. What the patient felt towards his parents or his siblings or other figures from the distant or not so distant past are now felt towards the analyst; and the patient's ways of trying to deal with those feelings, and trying to manage those relationships, now shape the transactions between patient and analyst (the transference).[10] The crux is that the patterns of relationship are relived now, in the present, in this current relationship with a specific person, the analyst. A principal aim of psychoanalysis is to make the patterns manifest.

This usually means that the analyst has to work very hard. His job is to arrive at judgements about what is happening between the patient and himself at the present moment in any analytic session. In order to do this, he has to be able to register not only how the patient appears to be behaving, but also how this behaviour has a specific emotional impact on the analyst himself. What kind of relationship is the patient trying to establish? What kind of feared relationship or feared events is the patient trying to avoid? What role is the patient giving to or with-holding from the analyst? Instead of responding in a reflex way to the pressures that are being brought to bear on him, the analyst has to think about what is happening. Among other things, this often means he has to withstand some difficult and at times anxiety-provoking feelings in himself. Instead of reacting to the patient – for instance, by defending himself against criticism or hitting back or being accom-modating and reassuring – the analyst needs to contain his own feelings and those of his patient, and to digest what is happening so that it can be thought about. It is through this new approach to thinking about the patient's ways of relating to and affecting the analyst that the patient's problems become understandable.

Before I give a specific example, I should explain why all this is important for my central theme about the origins of thinking. There are two reasons. The first is that, just as the experimental method is simple but powerful, so the psychoanalytic method is simple in principle but far-reaching in what it reveals. Anyone with the right kind of training and skills can conduct an experiment, and anyone with the right kind of training and skills (including emotional skills that not everyone can acquire) is able to conduct an analysis. In other words, there is nothing mystical or mysterious about either approach. On the other hand, what emerges from applying the method of psychoanalysis is sometimes even more surprising and disconcerting than what comes out of experiments. We find that the mind works in ways that are more complex than common sense or even experimental psychology would suggest. In particular, there are ways of thinking and relating to people that appear to be more primitive and less rational than we might suppose. These styles of thought and feeling need to be encompassed by any account of the origins of thinking. In this way, psychoanalysis adds pieces to the explanatory jigsaw depicting the development of mind. At times the findings of psychoanalysis show that we have been trying to fit the pieces together in the wrong way.

The second reason why psychoanalysis is important for studying the nature and origins of thinking is that it casts light on a particular aspect of mental functioning. This is the close connection that exists between what happens *within* an individual person's mind and what happens *between* one person and another — a central theme of this book.

We are accustomed to thinking of thinking as happening in the individual. What we tend to overlook is that the individual's capacity to think may be strongly affected by the influence of other people. Here I mean not only the contributions that other people may make to a person's ability to see reason or to think more correctly or more deeply. I also mean the ways in which someone else's emotional presence may strengthen or weaken an individual's capacity to think at all. Perhaps especially if you are in a state of anxiety or conflict, the presence of a steady, attentive person can enormously increase the chances that you will be able to think things through. This may be the case even if the person holds back from giving advice, and simply registers and understands your emotional struggles.

This simple fact assumes enormous importance when one considers the developmental dimension. We need to reckon with the potential impact that a caregiver's emotional care and sensitivity may have on a baby's developing ability to think. Note that I say 'ability to think'. We are considering more than the child's thinking in a given situation: we are considering her ability to think at all, or perhaps her ability to think whenever anxieties or conflicts are stirred. We shall see that psycho-analytic research has alerted us to how important the role of the care-giver may be.

So to my example of what is involved in analysing the transference. I have selected the most straightforward of illustrations. The patient was a man in his mid-twenties whom I saw for an assessment interview many years ago. He was referred to the hospital where I was working because of recurrent difficulties in his relationships, and for some physical symptoms which were not explicable in medical terms and from which his consultations with physicians had brought little relief. He filled out a questionnaire before the interview itself, so that I knew quite a lot about his background. The interview was conducted in a health-service setting, with the patient sitting up and facing me rather than lying down on a couch.

I am going to cover only the first ten minutes of the interview. The man arrived and we shook hands as I introduced myself and explained that the meeting would last for ninety minutes. The patient said that was fine, and paused expectantly. He said he wondered what I wanted him to talk about, and then seemed to realize that, instead of my asking questions, he might need to take the lead in saying what he thought was relevant and important. What he did was engage with me as though I had been both solicitous and encouraging towards him. It was as if I was already a confidant. He talked with some animation and feeling about how he had seen a range of other doctors, but nothing had really helped. As his account unfolded, it appeared that not only were the treatments ineffective, but also the doctors he had seen were in various ways inadequate or unprofessional. He seemed to be conveying to me how I might succeed in helping him, where everyone else had failed.

Yet it did not *feel* to me that this man had any confidence in what I might achieve on his behalf. For example, he had been speaking non-stop for ten minutes, and at no time did he seem interested in my view of his story. I felt that I might as well have been a fly on the wall, and I was very pessimistic that he would pay any attention to me if I tried to offer a comment. In the end I decided to interrupt what appeared to be an increasingly elaborate and entangled account to say, 'I wonder if I might stop you for a moment there. You are speaking to me as if I had been very helpful to you at the beginning, and as if you have confidence in me and what I might offer in this interview. Yet I wonder what is really going on.'

At this the patient looked dumbfounded, then exclaimed, 'You mean you want me to be honest?' I said yes, I wanted him to be honest. What subsequently emerged was that, far from having confidence in me, this patient was already convinced that I, too, was unprofessional and inept and the last thing he expected was that I would be able to do anything worthwhile.

Then it was possible to address how what had been happening in the interview was actually quite typical of this man. When he came into a dependent relationship with someone else, he would convince the other person and even himself that all would be well, but underneath there was suspicion and mistrust. In relation to me as a psychotherapist, he was repeating a familiar storyline, one in which he began as compliant and ended up disillusioned and frustrated by those who should have been taking care of him. Yet, because I did not join him in living out the customary succession of events, we were able to *think about* the recurring patterns in his attitudes and behaviour. We could examine in detail what was shaping the current interview and could pinpoint what he was feeling and doing right then and there in relation to myself. Together we could identify what was actually going on. We could do so because it was possible to track how the patient felt and then deal with his feelings, moment by moment. And we could see that what was going on had far-reaching importance for the patient's complaints and for his emotional life.

This example is mainly intended to illustrate what it means for a psychoanalyst to focus on his work of analysing the transference (although you may note that I was doing much more feeling and thinking than talking to the patient). It also illustrates how a situation may arise where one individual's ability to think about, rather than avoid, emotionally important issues is affected by the stance of someone else. In the case I have described, the patient was at least partly aware of what he was doing, even though he was not so aware of how it represented a pattern that was relevant for his difficulties. Sometimes patients are much less aware of what is happening. And sometimes what is happening is more complicated and disturbing than this. Psychoanalytic findings take us beyond everyday observations and show us how many-layered the mind is. Most importantly for our present purposes, they give us insights into the role of interpersonal experience for the development of thinking.

I have been stressing the importance of thinking, and it is obvious that thinking out loud has a special place in psychoanalysis. Psychoanalysis and related psychotherapies are sometimes referred to as 'talking cures'. One of the ways in which psychoanalysis works is by enabling someone to understand himself better through expressing things in words. Once a person can think about what he is doing and feeling — that is, once a person has insight — then he has more control over his life.

When strong emotions hold sway, thinking and talking with someone may hold the secret to mental health. When Macduff was reeling with the anguish of hearing that his wife and babes had been savagely slaughtered on the instruction of Macbeth (Act IV, scene iii), Malcolm enjoined him thus:

> Give sorrow words. The grief that does not speak
> Whispers the o'erfraught heart and bids it break.

The ability to think and to speak in words (a form of symbol), and the ability to communicate with someone else who registers what you convey, may keep your heart from breaking. In other circumstances, it may even keep your mind from disintegrating. If this early-rooted ability does not develop properly, there can be serious consequences later in life.

I have just alluded to the emotional significance of thinking in symbols. The intellectual significance is even greater. The ability to symbolize is the hallmark of human thinking. The origins of thinking are intimately bound up with a person coming to appreciate what symbols are and what symbols can do. Therefore I need to conclude this chapter with a few reflections on symbolizing.

As a first approximation, a symbol is something that stands for something else. It is something that anchors meaning. For example, the symbol 'pipe' stands for an actual, real-life pipe. The symbol may or may not pick out a particular pipe, but it stands for 'the kind of thing that a pipe is' or, if you like, for an object with the property of pipeness. If I talk about a pipe, then, you know that what I have in mind is the kind of thing that *you* bring to mind in connection with the symbol 'pipe'.

This may sound convoluted, but bear with me. For what I have just described is how an idea gets transmitted from my mind to yours. It gets transmitted by means of my communicating the symbol for the idea. This is a wonderful achievement. And it is an achievement that is

FIGURE 6

enormously amplified when I combine the symbol of 'pipe' with other symbols, as in the statement 'I smoke my pipe too much' (which I do).

Magritte's famous picture of a pipe brings out the ambiguity of symbols. The statement it makes in words – which we cannot help but assume *is* a statement directed at us – can be understood as saying, 'What you see is not a real pipe, but a picture of a pipe.' But the layers of meaning go deeper than this, because one can equally question whether the squiggles that read '*Ceci n'est pas une pipe*' – 'This is not a pipe' – really amount to a statement that claims to be true of 'This' (is it the picture frame that decides what 'This' refers to?). The squiggles themselves need to be interpreted a certain way, as words in a sentence, if they are to have meaning. More specifically, they need to be taken as having been intended as words by the artist, and, moreover, intended to communicate something to us.[11] Without hesitation we make the assumption that each of these symbols is intended to mean something, as we look at the picture.

Even in this example of a painting-with-words, we find that language is a specially elaborated and a specially powerful system of symbols. At the same time, of course, the picture of a pipe stands for an object in the world, or at least for a potential object. When a child uses something to represent something else, as when she uses a box to serve as a doll's bed in play, she too is performing the mental operation we call symbolizing. She is choosing to make this stand for that. She creates a symbol out of something that would otherwise be meaningless or have some other meaning. A squiggle such as 'pipe' is just a squiggle until it is used to carry meaning, when it becomes a written word; a box is just a box unless someone gives it the role of symbolizing something else such as a bed.

Here is another example. When is a cloud not merely a cloud, but also a symbol? Consider this short excerpt from Act III, Scene ii, of *Hamlet*:

HAMLET: Do you see yonder cloud that's almost in shape of a camel?

POLONIUS: By th' mass, and 'tis like a camel indeed.

HAMLET: Methinks it is like a weasel.

POLONIUS: It is back'd like a weasel.

HAMLET: Or like a whale?

POLONIUS: Very like a whale.

HAMLET: Then I will come to my mother by and by.

Hamlet could have treated the cloud as a symbol for anything, and Polonius could have followed him through every twist and turn – but, once their minds turned elsewhere, the cloud was no longer a symbol at all. Nothing is symbolic but thinking makes it so.

If understanding and using symbols is integral to specifically human kinds of thinking, then we stand a good chance of finding the origins of thinking in the conditions that promote early symbolizing. Following the drift of the argument thus far, we shall be looking for evidence that an infant comes to understand and use symbols through her interpersonal relations with others. Not only this, but, according to the 'social origins' theory of symbolizing, severely restricted experience of interpersonal relations should lead to difficulties in using symbols flexibly and creatively. We shall need to discover whether this expectation is fulfilled.

That completes our preparation for the journey. We know what we are looking for: something that prefigures thought in human infancy but is absent from all other species — perhaps something in the quality of the baby's social relations. We know how we shall find our bearings: a mix of clinical psychiatry, developmental psychopathology, psychoanalysis and just a little comparative research with chimps. And we know our ultimate aim: to understand how nature dovetails the human infant's innate capacity for social engagement with what a caregiver provides, and thereby creates an interpersonal cradle for the growth of symbolic thinking.

TWO

Before Thought

W e need to begin at the beginning – before thought. It is only because of what happens before thought that thought becomes possible.

Scientists and philosophers sometimes write as if thinking arises from nowhere. There is a contemporary version of this approach, which maintains that some aspects of thinking or some mechanisms of thinking must be innate. This is a perfectly reasonable claim. It is reasonable because some components of mental functioning are innately given to humans, and almost any aspect of the mind will depend on innate abilities in some way or other. The challenge is to discover which abilities underpin which other abilities, and to map the developmental processes that lead from the one kind to the other.

It is in these respects that claims for the innateness of thought may provide a cloak for ignorance. They may disguise our failure to understand how intellectual abilities come into existence. They may even discourage further enquiry about the origins of the abilities in question: they are taken to be innate, built into our minds by our genes, so no further explanation is required. But this is a mistake, because a lot more explanation is required. Thinking is something that develops, and the challenge is to discover how that development takes place. I am going to begin my account by describing some innate social abilities that seem (but only seem) to have little connection with thinking.

The place: Heraklion, Crete. The setting: a maternity hospital. A baby has just been delivered. Standing by is a psychologist by the name of Giannis Kugiumutzakis. Not all psychologists can be said to be warm and engaging, but Giannis certainly can. I think it would be difficult for anyone to resist the charm and openness of his manner, the expansiveness and colour of his personality. These facts are not irrelevant for what I am about to describe – an experimental study of imitation in newborns.[1] For Giannis is about to model actions in front of a baby no more than forty-five minutes old. Truly a newborn.

With the agreement of relatives, who watch the unfolding events on a TV screen, Giannis either places the baby on a special baby-bed or holds the baby in his arms, depending on where the infant seems most comfortable. He has arranged a mirror to reflect his own image at the same time as a camera captures the behaviour of the infant. He is wearing a black shirt so that his face is the brightest thing in view, and he has adapted the room's lighting so that the infant's eyes are open. When the infant is calm and motionless, Giannis does one of four things, up to five times in succession: he either sticks out his tongue, slowly and deliberately; or he opens his mouth wide and then closes it again; or he closes his eyes and then opens them again; or he makes sounds. After each event he pauses for a ten-second period and presents a calm face so that the infant can respond.

I have described all this in the present tense because there is real drama here. Babies less than an hour old are being asked if they are interested in someone else and interested in doing something utterly remarkable: to perceive the person's actions and to react by copying them. In order to do this, they need to see something in the facial behaviour and expressions of someone else, and then do something with their own mouths or eyes, which of course they cannot see.

So (now assuming the past tense) how did the babies respond? No one will be surprised that quite a lot of babies (being babies) never achieved the sought-for state of alert calmness. In these cases, the infant's crying or drowsiness or general thrashing-around meant that the experiment could not proceed. This in no way perturbed Giannis, for whom a first priority was to ask the baby's permission to take part in the study. He simply accepted that some babies would decline the invitation. In fact to collect a sample of babies who were happy to participate – and he eventually collected 170 of these – Giannis would have to invite a whole lot more (412, in fact).

I will not go into the checks that were made to ensure that the

FIGURE 7

videotapes of the interactions were rated in an unbiased manner. Suffice it to say that frequently the infants were rated as showing the kind of behaviour they had just witnessed in Giannis. When Giannis had shown tongue protrusion, the baby would often thrust her tongue forward beyond her lips and then withdraw it again into the mouth; when he had opened his mouth, the baby would often separate her lips widely and form an O; when he had closed and then opened his eyes, the baby would often close and open her eyes in a clear blink; and, when he had made an 'aa' sound, the baby would often do the same. The babies were imitating.

Now in any field of scientific research one is always very cautious about giving too much weight to the findings from a single study. This is especially so when what is being studied is as delicate and transient as a baby's facial movements. Yet this kind of experiment has been conducted with tiny babies in the United States and in several other countries, often with similar results.[2] These studies have shown that even facial expressions of emotion can be imitated. For example, infants under two days old have been presented with a person making surprised, happy, and sad faces. In response to the surprised face, they tended to show widened eyes and mouth opening; in response to the happy face, they showed widening of their lips; and when they saw a sad expression, they tightened their mouths, protruded their lips, and furrowed their brows. It was almost as if expressions were being transferred from the faces of the adults to those of the infants.

On the other hand, there are also researchers who have found it difficult to elicit the kinds of reaction I have described. Others again have felt that what we witness in these babies are automatic reflexes triggered by stimuli that are not specific to human beings. A pen protruding from a box might elicit the reaction just as well as a tongue protruding from a mouth (which would also be pretty amazing). Who is to say whether the infants are really copying someone else? One way to address these doubts is to look more closely at *how* babies imitate. So back to Heraklion ...

Giannis Kugiumutzakis has given us the following details about the behaviour of the infants when they imitated faces. First, the babies showed two patterns of attending to the adult. The most frequent pattern was that they made clear efforts to inspect the moving part of the face, often with signs of interest and frowning. Or, in the case of listening to sounds, the babies might show head turning and eye widening, with their brows held high. So this first pattern of attention seemed to indicate intense concentration. The second pattern was quite different. Here the infants would look at the face hastily and then reproduce the facial action immediately.

Then there were three ways in which the babies made their responses. Some performed an immediate imitation, often with surprising accuracy. For example, 75 per cent of the babies who imitated mouth-opening produced full mouth-opening on their first attempt to copy the model. This seems to indicate that they had registered what they were aiming for even before they had begun to react. Other babies produced a succession of imitative responses, each time getting closer to the model. In these cases, a baby's first efforts to copy tongue-protrusion might involve preparatory movements of the tongue inside the mouth. The third group of babies made successive attempts, but these grew less rather than more successful each time.

These are remarkable observations. It seems that infants have abilities to perceive actions and expressions in another person and then translate what is perceived in the other to plan for their own actions and expressions. They then make strenuous efforts to copy the other person. Giannis concludes that infants have a basic drive to match the behaviour and in a way the mind of another person, because they are endowed with a 'motive system that is seeking another emotional being with whom to play together a cooperative, complementary, intersubjective game'.

For many scientists this is going too far. Justified scepticism is a worthy hallmark of the scientific endeavour, and here is a case where scepticism is understandable. There is a wide gap between observations of an infant's imitation of someone else and claims about the infant's motives to seek engagement with another emotional being. Besides, there is only so much we can say with confidence on the basis of studies of imitation alone. So we need to look elsewhere to corroborate or contradict the idea that infants engage in cooperative and complementary relations with others. Let us turn to studies of slightly older infants, when they are two or three months old, and see what we find there.

Over two decades ago, in 1974, the American paediatrician Berry Brazelton and his colleagues decided that they should film infants interacting with a person on the one hand and with an object on the other.[3] This might reveal whether human infants are pre-wired to relate to other people in ways that are special to people. What they did was to film four-week-old and slightly older infants as they engaged with their mothers in relaxed face-to-face contact. In a separate testing procedure, they filmed the infants as a small toy monkey suspended on a string moved just within reach and then withdrew again.

What happened in the case of the toy monkey was as follows. The babies' attention was captured by the approaching object — almost hooked on it, in fact — so that they stared at it fixedly, with small jerks of the face and limbs. As the monkey came within reaching distance, they opened their mouths as if about to mouth it, and those who were already six weeks old made jerky hand movements towards it. A state of intense, rapt attention built up gradually to a peak that suddenly ended as the infant turned away and flailed her limbs. Only in older infants, those from about four months old, were these abrupt transitions from attentiveness to withdrawal replaced by less jagged patterns of responding.

Now to the infant's behaviour when interacting with her mother. Here the cycles of attention and withdrawal were quite different. There seemed to be smoother and shorter spans of attentiveness and looking away. For example, the infant's eyes and face would brighten as she looked at and extended her extremities towards her mother. As the mother responded, the infant's face showed fleeting smiles, grimaces and vocalizations, as well as smooth movements of the hands and feet. There was often enhanced bodily activity leading to vocal sounds, and smiling increased when the mother smiled in unison. There might be a brief period of excitement followed by a gradual waning of this state, when the baby looked away to modulate the stimulating encounter. During all of this, a sensitive mother modified her own behaviour to fit in with these cycles of engagement and disengagement.

There have been many more recent studies documenting the specialness of a mother's interactions with her young infant. Just as a two-month-old baby often appears to be striving to communicate with her mother, so the mother adjusts her own mode of interaction to fit with her baby's needs. The following account by Colwyn Trevarthen illustrates this well:

> As soon as a mother begins to talk to the baby her movements become regular and subdued. She speaks more quietly and more gently and becomes highly attentive, spending as much time waiting and watching as speaking. The form of speech is changed in consistent ways towards the regularity, repetition and musical, questioning intonation known as 'baby talk'. Alternatively, the mother may become active and playful, or teasing, making rhythmical and exaggerated movements of her head, trunk and whole body, or reach to touch the infant ... close imitation of the infants by the mothers is characteristic ... In summary: mothers' responses to two-month-old infants are stimulating, attentive, confirmatory, interpretative and highly supportive.[4]

Thus a responsive mother may dovetail with her infant in such a way that 'the two behave in complete concert as if dancing together'.[5] Here Trevarthen is attempting to characterize intersubjectivity between infant and mother and to show how the experiences of one are linked to the experiences of the other: not only does the infant's behaviour express her own consciousness and purposes, but these expressions are coordinated with the behaviour and experiences of another person. Patterns of bodily expression involving gestures of the trunk and limbs may convey states such as disgust as well as pleasure which a mother picks up and interprets. By the age of six weeks, the infant's ability to sustain eye contact with someone is a strong draw to interpersonal engagement.

It is important to appreciate that here we are dealing not with isolated bits of behaviour but with coherent patterns of relatedness between infant and adult. As Edward Tronick and his colleagues described in an early account of face-to-face interactions between three-month-olds and their mothers, such prolonged exchanges involve a typical succession of episodes.[6] Things might begin with an initiation – for example, with the mother attracting attention by moving her face into the infant's line of vision and calling the baby's name repeatedly, or with the infant vocalizing. Then there is a phase of mutual orientation when the infant is neutral or bright-faced in expression and the mother shifts to smoother vocalizations and smiling. Then there is a greeting, where the baby smiles and moves her limbs and the mother becomes more animated. Next is a phase of play dialogue, when the mother talks in brief bursts interspersed with pauses, the infant vocalizes, the mother responds with changes in facial expression or with further talk, and so on. Then, as the final episode in this sequence of waxing and waning involvement, the infant looks away with a neutral or even sober face. The affective engagement has been broken – until the next initiation.

There has been vigorous debate among developmental psychologists about the respective roles of infant and mother in these social exchanges. At one extreme is the view that the infant means to communicate from the start, and has the intention of involving the other person. This is the position of Trevarthen and Kugiumutzakis, among others. At the other extreme is the view that the mother's activity gives us the impression of there being a dialogue, but in fact the communicative traffic is one-way. The infant is not playing an active role, except to behave in a manner that the mother can interpret as socially meaningful. In no way is the infant trying to achieve or adjust to interpersonal engagement. For myself, I am persuaded by the account of Tronick and his colleagues, who deftly express their perspective as follows: 'Never is one partner *causing* the other to do something. One musician does not cause the other to play the next note. In the same manner neither the mother nor the infant causes the other to greet or to attend. They are mutually engaged in an activity.' The thrust of this account is that both participants in the exchange modify their actions in accord with the feedback they receive from their partner – and so the interchange is genuinely reciprocal.

Some of the most persuasive evidence that there is more than the appearance of mutual interchange comes from situations which interfere with the seamless patterning of adult–infant interaction. One way to create such a situation is to disrupt the normally fluent to and fro of mother–infant exchanges. Here we can continue to follow the pioneering work of Ed Tronick, because it was Tronick and his colleagues who embarked on intensive study of the most striking of disruptions: the still-face challenge.[7] This is an experimental procedure that involves three phases. In the first phase the mother interacts normally with her infant, face to face. In the second phase she follows an instruction to assume a still or poker face and to remain unresponsive to her infant. In the final phase she returns to a natural social interaction. Typically, each phase lasts for two or three minutes. The interaction is videotaped, so that careful ratings of the infant's behaviour can be made by independent judges who ensure that the observations are accurate.

The still-face procedure has been used with infants ranging from two to nine months in age. Even in two-month-olds, the results are often dramatic. When a two-month-old is faced with an unresponsive mother, the infant sobers and looks uneasy. She stares at her mother, gives her a transient smile, and looks away from her. She may then alternate brief glances towards her mother with glances away, apparently monitoring her mother's behaviour. She occasionally smiles warily, but seems to become less and less convinced of her ability to get the interaction back on track. As her attempts fail, the infant withdraws, orientating her face and body away from her mother with a hopeless expression. At this point the infant gives up and stays turned away. The second of the two videotape stills shown below illustrates how the two-month-old infant of a sensitive mother in our own research reacted to the still-face procedure.

Here, then, Tronick describes the infant as showing a sequence of sobering, wariness, checking, repeated attempts to bring the mother out of her immobility, and eventual withdrawal. The infant plays an active

FIGURE 8

role in modifying her own communicative displays in response to the feedback (or non-feedback) provided by her mother. She *is* seeking and expecting a personal engagement; she *is* registering when the engagement is not happening; she *is* trying to re-establish contact and then having to deal with the unpleasant feelings stirred by an apparently inviting but steadfastly unresponsive mother.

In recent work, researchers such as Nina Kogan and Alice Carter have turned their attention to the ways in which infants differ in the final recovery phase of the procedure.[8] Evidence is emerging that four-month-old infants of sensitive mothers may re-engage smoothly following the still face. The child remains orientated towards the mother and her now-welcoming behaviour.

By contrast, infants of less sensitive mothers tend to turn away from or seemingly reject their mothers when the still-face phase has ended. They are much more easily put out and put off. So it seems that infants' attempts to regulate their own emotions depend on the emotional availability of their mothers. This may point to a more general truth about the influence of parenting on infants' ability to manage feelings. When it is necessary for infants to keep a check on excitement or anxiety or aggression, or to find ways to balance impulses to explore and impulses to withdraw, they may need help from a caregiver. One result is that babies of sensitive mothers remain flexible and open even in the face of stress, whereas those who are not supported in this way tend to be affected more negatively.

Yet, for all this, we should not idealize the sensitive mother, father, grandmother or whoever. Life is not easy, and interpersonal relations are rarely smooth for long. As Tronick himself has emphasized, it is commonplace for interpersonal interactions to become disjointed, and what is critical is how successfully misalignments can be repaired.[9] We have seen how in the still-face situation, infants may try to get their mothers engaged and then show negative emotions and regulate their feelings in a self-directed manner by looking away and self-comforting. More subtle attempts to soften the impact of social faux pas are probably happening all the time in the everyday social life of the infant. The question is whether repeated and more serious failures of reciprocity between infants and their caregivers may lead to lasting and potentially harmful effects – perhaps especially if infants cannot find help in managing distress and conflict.

Now one failure of reciprocity is when something goes wrong with the way things are timed. The dancers tread on each other's toes; the musicians miss the beat. There is an unsettling joke which begins with one person asking another, 'What is the essence of comedy?' Just as the respondent is about to offer a suggestion, the questioner blurts out, 'Timing!' The joke works because bad timing is disconcerting and potentially disturbing. We have seen how, in the still-face procedure, a disturbance is created when one person is totally unreactive to another in a two-person exchange. Poor timing, too, can disrupt an infant's social interactions with others.

To explore this, Lynne Murray and Colwyn Trevarthen sat individual two- and three-month-old infants in front of a television.[10] The screen showed the infant's mother live on television, looking towards the infant. The mother herself was facing a camera, sitting in another room. Not only this, but the mother too was watching a television, so that she could see the live image of her infant facing her, relayed over a two-way link-up. This may sound a highly artificial arrangement, but mother and baby were able to engage with each other over video in a surprisingly natural and fluent way. Until the disruption was introduced, that is. In this case, what perturbed the interaction was a delay of just thirty seconds between events at the two ends of the video link. Now when the baby acted and watched the video monitor, what the baby could see was the mother responding to her actions of thirty seconds ago. It was not that the mother's earlier responses were unpleasant in any way. It was just that they were suited to a different moment, and not in tune with what the infant was expressing now. The effect of introducing the delay was considerable infant distress. Often the infant would turn away from the mother's image and then dart brief glances back at the screen – a quite different set of reactions from those that occurred when the mother merely looked away to one side. Therefore it was not simply that the infant felt unattended to or even unresponded to – it was that the interactions were not in tune, and disturbingly so.

We may conclude that infants do not live in the blooming, buzzing confusion envisaged by the psychologist William James. Even very small infants have an organized mental life, and this mental life is expressed in behaviour that is innately fashioned to coordinate with the social behaviour of other people.

A final example of such coordination highlights a particular component of social life – the significance of emotional coordination between one individual and another. The following study may seem rather contrived in comparison with some of the observations of mothers and infants already described, which were also charged with feelings. Yet for this very reason it brings into focus how infants have certain abilities that make mutually sensitive social exchanges possible. More specifically, it illuminates how even young infants both perceive and react to expressions of emotion in other people.

The study was conducted by Jeanette Haviland and Mary Lelwica, and was one in which ten-week-old infants were observed reacting to their mothers.[11] The mothers were asked to show different emotional expressions in the course of face-to-face interactions with their babies. When the mothers showed joy in their faces and voices, their infants reacted by increasing their own joy and interest and lessened their mouthing. When the mothers showed sadness, the infants were more subdued and increased their mouthing. When the mothers showed anger, the infants also showed increased anger and a decrease in their movements. So what emerged was that infants of only ten weeks old reacted to the emotional expressions of their mothers with emotional states of their own.

Even in early infancy, then, to perceive emotion is also to react to emotion. If the infants had shown no reaction, we would have concluded that they were unable to perceive emotion at all. The emotional reactions seem to reveal that babies have a perception *of* feelings that prompts feelings. This simple observation has far-reaching implications for our view of what creates the bridge between the mind of one person and that of another. And, far from being restricted to interpersonal exchanges of joy or sadness, such feeling-imbued perception is a pervasive aspect of an infant's interpersonal engagement — as Bellini's painting *Madonna with the Pear* illustrates beautifully.

Young infants soon grow up into older infants. It will serve the purposes of this chapter to follow the story up to the age of eight or nine months, no further. By then we shall have taken the first step in a three-step process that leads from intimate interpersonal engagement between infant and caregiver in the earliest months of life to the revolution in thinking that takes place in the middle of the second year.

Let us see where infants of six months or so have got to in their relations with other people. We still find that there is a contrast between the infant's relation with things on the one hand and with people on the other. There are even times when the infant seems more interested in banging and sucking and otherwise exploring the world of things than in engaging with people — sometimes to the hurt or chagrin of a parent who seeks attention. But of course the infant is still very much engaged with her caregiver. Experimental studies involving disruptions in interaction show that it continues to matter that the interactions are dynamic (still faces are still not popular with infants), that they occur with someone who is familiar (an infant is more willing to tolerate unusual behaviour from her mother than from a stranger), and that the adults' interactions are well coordinated with the infants' own.

There also continues to be evidence that infants are affected by the emotional expressions of the person with whom they are interacting, so, for example, they smile less when that person is sad. Once again, experiments have defined more precisely some of the abilities that underpin such reactions. To give just one example, Arlene Walker tested five- to seven-month-olds for their ability to recognize emotions.[12] The technique was to present two films side by side, and to broadcast a sound from between the two films. The films were

FIGURE 9

of animated and emotionally expressive faces, and the sounds were of human voices. For example, one film showed a woman speaking continuously with a happy face, while the other showed a woman who was also speaking continuously but with a sad face. When a happy voice was played from between the two faces, the infants tended to look at the happy face; when a sad voice was played, they tended to look at the sad face. This preference was not seen if the faces were presented upside-down and so appeared meaningless from an emotional point of view. Therefore the infants recognized the emotional meaning that was common to a happy face and a happy voice, and so on. This is something that proves difficult for children with autism, as we have seen already.

So what are infants doing with these remarkable abilities to perceive and respond to the behaviour of other people in one-to-one interactions? If all is going well, they are developing increasingly rich and pleasurable forms of mutually sensitive interpersonal engagement. I shall concentrate on just one specially interesting and instructive form of engagement – structured play. By 'structured play' I do not mean play with formal rules, but rather play that has a certain pattern to it. Familiar examples are peekaboo, ring-a-ring-o'-roses, and 'This little piggy went to market'. The American developmental psychologist Jerome Bruner has drawn attention to the fact that such games operate according to a format with demarcated roles, and with a place for accompanying gestures and sounds that dovetail with the action.[13] In a way, the games provide a kind of framework for early to-and-fro communications between infant and caregiver. They feature regular and predictable sequences of actions and events – for example, involving the disappearance and then reappearance of objects – that allow the infant to adopt a progressively more active role. Eventually, towards and beyond the end of the first year, the infant begins to switch roles with the adult.

Thus, in the period around six to eight months, infants are becoming attuned to the regularities of games. These regularities provide a structure within which babies can take certain events for granted and anticipate the familiar moves in the game – *and* communicate and share pleasure with the adult playmate. In addition, the regularities allow variations on a theme. In peekaboo, for example, mother's disappearance may be orchestrated in novel ways, and the build-up to her reappearance may be filled with anticipatory sounds and tantalizing gestures. The games embody some important features of communication, and in due course they provide a kind of scaffolding for the introduction of language itself. Although infants this young cannot comment on a shared topic, they can be involved in a game and look up at their mother and smile – which, as Bruner suggests, is like a comment ('This we are sharing') – before the next step in the game proceeds. It is only because adult and child are attending to the game together, are acting together and are sharing an emotional engagement with each other in a regulated context, that this is possible. Together, infant and mother are preparing the way to language.

There is, therefore, no doubt that, from the earliest months of life, infants are highly attuned to other people – to their parents, their siblings, their grandparents, their other caregivers, and even to adults who are strangers. They have an active social life right from the start. More than this, it is a social life that deepens so swiftly that it serves the eight-month-old as a fountain of pleasure, a reservoir of reassurance, and a well-spring of mischief. It also swirls that same infant into a whirlpool of pulls, pushes and other emotional currents that, as we shall come to see, wrest the infant from a kind of self-centredness and liberate the very processes of thought.

But suppose for a moment there were babies who were built differently – babies who were not so socially attuned nor so hungry for social engagement. Children for whom another person's expressions of emotion were not especially arresting and resonant with meaning, and for whom the dance of human gestures and sounds had far, far less allure than for their peers. What would such babies be like? And in what ways would their development differ from that of anyone else? I have already indicated that perhaps there are such babies, and that the effects of their limited interpersonal engagement are more far-reaching than one could have imagined. These are babies who will come to have early childhood autism. As we return to autism, we find the qualities of normal infants' social exchanges thrown into sharp relief.

In saying that there are babies 'who will come to have early childhood autism', I chose my words carefully. For there is something odd about the picture of autism. This is that autism is rarely diagnosed in the first year of life. There is even disagreement among the experts as to whether all children who are later recognized to be autistic were abnormal as babies. Certainly there are cases where there seems to have been little cause for concern in the early months, and sometimes it seems that some major catastrophe such as a brain infection or other disease has changed a normally developing child into someone who has lost the ability to engage fully with others. In other cases, however, we simply do not know why the derailment occurs.

Yet, despite this, I believe that what underlies autism is something lacking in just the kind of person-with-person engagement that is so characteristic of typically developing infants and their caregivers. In other words, the abnormality is of a kind that could be described in terms of infant-like abilities that are missing or awry – especially things that have to do with emotional connectedness and communication before language. I do not know why the disorder is not more striking in infancy, but I believe that nearly always it is there. And, if one looks closely enough, there are signs that subtle but ominous pointers are already present by the second year of life.

I have a colleague, Dawn Wimpory, who is a clinical psychologist with a special interest in music therapy, and someone with a heightened sensitivity to the significance of the earliest and most deeply rooted patterns of bodily rhythm and exchange between one human being and another. Dawn interviewed parents of very young children who were referred to her Child Development Centre with noticeable difficulties in relating to and communicating with others.[14] Such difficulties have many sources, including general mental retardation, and only a small proportion of the children turn out to have the collection of clinical features that justify the diagnosis of autism. The important thing was that the interviews were conducted with parents when their children were between thirty-two and forty-eight months old, and before a diagnosis had been made. This meant that, when the parents were asked about the children's behaviour in the first two years of life, they did not have to recall events which had taken place very long ago (the range was from six to twenty-four months), and their memories were not distorted by what they had read from books after a diagnosis had been made. In addition, the form of the interview was that they were asked in a friendly way about the achievements as well as the difficulties of their children in infancy, and the interviewer assisted their memory by asking what the infant would do in specific contexts. When enquiring about the nature of the infant's social engagement during play, for example, the interviewer might ask, 'Would he be happy for you to join in his play with toys or would he regard that as an intrusion and prefer to play alone?' After the parent had replied, the interviewer might ask, 'Would you need toys in order to play with him? Could you amuse him without toys, if, say, you were together on a bus or in a doctor's waiting room where no toys were available?'

The parents' reports indicated that infants later diagnosed to have autism were substantially less engaged with other people than infants of similar age and ability who did not have autism. And, sure enough, there were abnormalities in the area of person-to-person non-verbal communication and interpersonal contact. *Not one of the infants with autism* but at least half of the infants without autism showed frequent and intense eye contact, and were said to engage in turn-taking with adults and to use noises communicatively. There were also fewer infants with autism who greeted or waved to their parents, who raised their arms to be picked up, who directed feelings of anger and distress towards people, or who were sociable in play. In each of these respects there were clear limitations in their one-to-one interpersonal engagement.

Recall how rich is the patterned interplay between the typically developing infant and her mother or father, and how finely tuned and emotionally expressive are the transactions and mutual adjustments of action, gesture and vocalization. Only against this backdrop can one see how much is limited or absent in infants with autism; and it is especially against the backdrop of autism that one can appreciate what infant social engagement usually entails.

Very recently, some observational studies have appeared that provide direct evidence that even young children with autism have a lack of emotional responsiveness to others. In a study of twenty-month-olds by Tony Charman and his colleagues, an investigator joined with the child in playing with a toy hammer and plastic object to pound.[15] At a point when the child was actually touching the object, the investigator pretended to hurt himself by hitting his thumb with the hammer. He stopped touching the object and for ten seconds he cried with pain and displayed facial expressions of distress. Then he sobered and showed the child that his finger did not hurt any more. This sequence of events was videotaped, and ratings were made of whether during the first ten seconds of the procedure the child looked to the investigator's face, or looked to his hand, or stopped playing with the object. The child's face was also scrutinized for any sign of concern or upset. The ratings revealed that not a single one of the ten children with autism showed any facial concern. This compared with four of the nine children with developmental delay and thirteen of the nineteen normally developing children. Moreover, six out of the ten children with autism did not even look to the investigator's pained face, despite his evident distress. This was in marked contrast to the behaviour of the children in the other two groups, every one of whom looked to the adult's face. Whereas half the non-autistic children stopped touching the object and looked to the investigator's hand, most of the children with autism continued to touch the object and only two bothered to look at his hand.

These two sources of evidence — recent parental reports and direct observation of twenty-month-old children with autism — complement one another perfectly. The quality of interpersonal, emotionally charged contact that is typical of normally developing and non-autistic developmentally delayed infants and very young children seems to be weak or missing in many children with autism. All this is going to be very important when we come to analyse whether thought is constructed on the basis of social engagement, because we shall see what happens to thought when the foundations for its development are not in place.

Before we move on to the development of thinking, however, we need to achieve a clearer sense of what it means to have social engagement, and especially those forms of sensitivity and emotional exchange that are a feature of human relations from the cradle to the grave. We need more than descriptions of behaviour: we want to get 'inside' the phenomena, as it were. It may seem odd to try to do this by considering older children and even adolescents with autism, but it turns out that here we can find not only a graphic picture of the underlying processes that normally link one person and another — processes that are present in humans of all ages – but also an indication of some of the mechanisms by which those processes work. In what follows, we are going to encounter a fresh and startling perspective on infant-level forms of interpersonal engagement, precisely because we shall see what happens when these forms of engagement are lacking, and moreover lacking in individuals well past infancy. It is an approach reminiscent of those speeded-up films made by anthropologists that show humans bobbing their heads and limbs as they converse, or scurrying like ants in crowded city streets. In each case, it is the very unfamiliarity of the viewpoint that reveals what is otherwise too familiar to be found striking.

Take the most important element of personal engagement: the linkage between the subjective experiences of one person and the subjective experiences of another. Here is a second description from Kanner's original account of autism. It concerns six-year-old Frederick, attending Kanner's clinic for the first time:

> He was led into the psychiatrist's office by a nurse, who left the room immediately afterward. His facial expression was tense, somewhat apprehensive, and gave the impression of intelligence. He wandered aimlessly about for a few moments, showing no sign of awareness of the three adults present. He then sat down on the couch, ejaculating unintelligible sounds, and then abruptly lay down, wearing throughout a dreamy-like smile ... Objects absorbed him easily and he showed good attention and perseverance in playing with them. He seemed to regard people as unwelcome intruders to whom he paid as little attention as they would permit. When forced to respond, he did so briefly and returned to his absorption in things. When a hand was held out before him so that he could not possibly ignore it, he played with it briefly as if it were a detached object.[16]

It is very, very unusual for a human being to be so unengaged with others. No wonder that a number of writers have described how the child with autism seems to treat other people as if they were pieces of furniture. No wonder, because that is what it can feel like – that one is little more than a table or a chair. As in Frederick's treatment of the human hand, the child with autism often seems to relate to a person as a thing. The distressing possibility is that the child *experiences* other people rather like things. This is to paint an extreme picture, and we shall come to see that children with autism are aware that people have some special properties. Yet, when we consider what the world seems to mean to Frederick, we are struck that other people seem so insignificant.

For most of us, the kinds of person-to-person exchange that are already finely tuned in infants continue to underpin human social relations throughout the lifespan. There is a universal body language, more basic than the language of words, that connects us with other people *mentally*. It is a mechanism for interpersonal engagement that operates before thought, or at least before the kind of symbolic thought that allows us to think about things in an imaginative way. For individuals with autism, this body language does not seem to work properly.

I have said that the psychological processes we are considering happen before thought. This is true in a number of senses. They occur before thought develops in the individual, in that they emerge in the first year of life before creative symbolic thinking has begun. They also happen before thought in the sense that even in adults they seem to occur in a rapid and automatic way, without the need for premeditation. They even appear before thought in the animal kingdom: it is possible to communicate with species that cannot think symbolically, for instance with our pet dogs. In general, these processes of communication are heavily dependent on the functioning of the older and deeper parts of the brain, rather than those more recently developed outer layers of our brains (the neocortex) that seem specialized for more sophisticated mental operations.

One might wonder, therefore, why we need to be bothered with this so-called infant level of communication. Why all this fuss about what happens before thought? Surely our aim is to explain human-type creative thinking – precisely the kind of mental process that depends on the more recently developed areas of the brain. True, but this leaves out a critical dimension: how a young child comes to *use* those recently developed areas of the brain for symbolic thinking. If a child fails to experience interpersonal engagement, the elaborate circuitry of the neocortex proves to be about as useful as computer hardware working with inadequate software. The computer can still do fancy things of a rather humdrum kind, but it cannot support creative symbolic thinking. Crudely put, this is what autism shows us.

There has been a difficulty in arguing this case. There are many who are sceptical that failures in personal relatedness are really so fundamental to autism. In order to provide evidence, one needs to *measure* psychological connectedness, or what I am calling intersubjective engagement, in a manner that is scientifically objective. Yet the only measuring instrument for detecting interpersonal contact is a subjective (and supposedly non-objective and therefore unscientific) human being. A person can *feel* that there is something missing when relating to someone who is autistic – it is as if one is in the presence of a changeling, someone from a different world – but this escapes the net of scientific methods.

My colleague Tony Lee and I tried to address this problem. In 1998 we published a paper entitled 'Hello and Goodbye: A Study of Social Engagement in Autism'.[17] I mention the title because there is a story behind it – one that illustrates how easy it is for science to squeeze out the subjective, personal dimension of life in the quest for objectivity, and to wrench what is physical away from what is mental in human communication. I shall return to the story after I have described the study itself.

What we did was to set up a situation in which we could videotape children and adolescents greeting an unfamiliar person (me, in fact, since I had not visited the schools in a long time) and later taking their leave. We were aiming to capture aspects of human exchange that happen before thought in the sense that they usually occur from early in life (recall that the non-autistic retarded infants in Wimpory's study were reported to greet and to wave), and happen without the need for premeditation. Here is what happened with Susan, a mildly retarded adolescent who does not have autism.

The sequence began with Susan entering the room with Tony, who introduced me. Immediately Susan met my gaze and smiled spontaneously, with an unprompted 'Hello, Peter.' In fact she maintained both the eye contact and the smile all the way across the classroom, until she took her seat opposite me across the table. She also checked my gaze just before sitting down. Then, when it was time to end the session, Susan initially half turned away awkwardly, seeming a little unsure what to say, and gave a brief 'Thank you' to me before placing her chair beneath the table. She was already turning away when I said 'Goodbye', and, although she replied with her own 'Bye', she did not bother to turn round again. In response to my final farewell as she left the room, Susan turned, smiled, said 'Bye', and gave a brief wave.

Now here is Marilyn, a person of the same age and level of ability who has autism. Marilyn gave only the briefest glance towards me as she entered, and then looked away. As Tony said, 'This is Peter', she continued to look away for about a second, then looked towards me without changing her rather set facial expression, and gave a brief and toneless 'Unn' in acknowledgement of my presence. Then she looked away to one side, and maintained the lack of eye contact as she walked across the room with her hands linked together in front of her body. She sat down without looking at me. Once seated, she did not look up at me across the table. She fixed her gaze towards her lap. Throughout the sequence, she gave little sense of any emotional contact with either Tony or myself. Then, when she was told that our session was over, Marilyn stood up rather abruptly without making eye contact with me, and made some gesture towards me only when I said my first, rather insistent, 'Goodbye' as she turned to leave. Even then, the gesture was to flap her left hand behind her vaguely in my direction – a wave that hardly seemed like a wave, especially since she was still looking away from me – and her only remark was a rather nasal and flat 'Bye'. My final 'Goodbye' was met with the faintest of head turns, another quiet and hardly expressive 'Bye', and what seemed like a stiff extension of her right wrist behind her body, which might have been a further wave. Although she had seemed aware of my presence, I felt this involved little sense of me as a person.

There was something else that was noticeable in the videotapes: how I behaved. I was trying to be as natural and consistent as possible. Yet, despite my best efforts, I did not do very well. Towards Susan, for example, there was a looseness and energy to my own voice and gestures, and one could see how the contact between the two of us had a kind of vibrancy and reciprocity that seemed to carry the exchange forward. With Marilyn, on the other hand, there was a deliberateness to my own gestures and actions. I was less outgoing and more hesitant in my efforts to make contact, and my 'Goodbye' seemed forced. It was clear that I was doing my best to be relaxed and engaging, but I did a poor job when I did not have an engaging partner. The lesson is: interpersonal engagement is just that – *inter*personal.

Overall, compared with the other children and adolescents, only about half as many of those with autism gave spontaneous expressions of greeting in the 'Hello' episode. A substantial proportion of those with autism failed to respond even after prompting. All twenty-four of the young people without autism made eye contact, but a third of those with autism failed to do so; no fewer than seventeen of the former group smiled, but only six of the twenty-four with autism. In the farewell episode, half the individuals without autism but only three of those with autism made eye contact and said a goodbye. And not only were there fewer than half as many autistic as non-autistic individuals who waved in response to my final prompt, but also their waves were strangely uncoordinated and limp. The really important thing, however, is not that the participants with autism lacked certain bits of behaviour – there are plenty of other ways to make emotional contact with others – but rather that these abnormalities expressed something deeper about their limited intersubjective experience of others. So when we first submitted our paper for publication, it carried the title 'Hello and Goodbye: A Study of Interpersonal Engagement in Autism'.

The journal editor who dealt with our manuscript disliked this title, and favoured something more neutral about the greeting and farewell 'behaviors' of the children we studied. Fortunately, we had done something else when we came to rating the videotapes. We had also asked our judges to look at the greeting episode up to the time the child sat down at the table, and to rate the degree of personal engagement with myself. It turned out that different judges who made these ratings independently were in good agreement with each other. The results were that fourteen non-autistic but only two autistic children were judged to be in the most strongly engaged category, and only two non-autistic but thirteen autistic children in the least engaged category. This meant we were now in a position to insist that one should not reduce the observations to recordings of behaviour. The behaviour observed was an expression of something less accessible to scientific measurement but more important for our understanding of the nature of human relations and the impairments in autism. Out of respect for the editor's concerns, we suggested a somewhat less provocative title that refers to social rather than interpersonal engagement. At least we didn't have to call this a study of 'behaviors'.

Really, it takes only a moment's thought to realize that the study is about more than behaviour. What about the children's *perception* of another person? The children with autism did not seem interested in the stranger; they often did not look to him, they did not seem to react with feelings to his presence and his orientation towards themselves. Do children with autism even perceive other people *as* people whose behaviour expresses feelings? Or, to put this another way, do individuals with autism see beneath the skin, and apprehend the feelings that lie behind expressions of emotion in other people?

At this point it is worth emphasizing that feelings and other aspects of mental life are expressed in more than the face and the voice. Nowhere is this more powerfully illustrated than in the sculptures of Rodin, who has already given us Thought in bodily form. Sommerville Story describes how Rodin had a number of nude models in his studio, moving or reposing. 'He was constantly looking at them, and thus was always familiar with the spectacle of muscles in movement ... and learned to read the expression of feeling in all parts of the body. The face is usually regarded as the only mirror of the soul, and mobility of features is supposed to be the only exteriorization of spiritual life. But in reality there is not a muscle of the body which does not reveal thoughts and feeling.'[18] Rodin's set of studies for the *Burghers of Calais* could hardly be more eloquent testament of this fact.

For a final time in this chapter, we can turn to autism in order to address issues that have immediate relevance for understanding processes that are basic to human social functioning – in this case, perceptual processes that lead to emotional contact between people. In the present instance, we can test whether people with autism share our sense of the feelings behind gestures like those of Rodin's sculpture. Autism promises to reveal some really interesting and hitherto unexplored things about forms of human perception that operate from infancy onwards.

My colleagues Derek Moore and Tony Lee and I presented

FIGURE 10

children and adolescents with videotape sequences of people depicted merely by dots of light.[19] I show four stills taken from a live walking sequence in the figure below. What we had done was to attach reflective patches to the limbs and torso of a person, and to film that person doing things under reduced illumination. This meant that all one could see were dots of light moving as the person moved. When the person walked, the dots of light on the legs 'walked' too, and those on the arms swung in concert. The still images only hint at a person walking, but the actual videotape sequence is compelling.

FIGURE II

There is a curious thing about this kind of moving-dot display. It is something that was demonstrated by a Swedish psychologist called Gunnar Johansson in the early 1970s.[20] The curious thing is that, when you watch the dots, you hardly see dots at all. What you see *through* the moving dots is a person. There is no doubt about it – you are watching a person doing things. Johansson demonstrated that we need only very brief exposures of a moving-dot display to see that a person is being depicted. It is not slowly and with effort that one comes to realize that a person is represented – it happens quickly and automatically. This seems to suggest that the displays are both unnatural, in that in everyday life one never sees human beings taking the appearance of moving pin-points of light, and in some way natural, in the sense that the human perceptual system is tuned in to some abstract combination of pattern and movement characteristic of people and captured (amazingly enough) in these artificial stimuli. It is as if the displays home in on a brain mechanism that detects people. No need to think, no need to go through a conscious process of judgement – one simply sees a person.

This should make us wonder whether the brain mechanism is there from early in life. Perhaps it is something built into our nervous system, so that babies, too, can perceive people without having to think about it. Which would be just as well, if they need to perceive people *before* they are able to think. It is therefore revealing to find that experiments have been done in which displays of this kind have been shown to infants.[21] The technique is to see whether infants prefer to look at one moving pattern of dots rather than another. If they do, it may indicate that they find something interesting and meaningful in the preferred display. The experiments showed that five-month-olds preferred to look at videotapes of point-light people walking than to look at randomly moving point-lights. On the other hand, if the point-light people were presented in such a way as to make the displays appear meaningless – for example, upside-down – this preference disappeared. So it does seem that very young humans tune in to the movements of people.

This was why we decided to use moving-dot displays to examine how individuals with autism perceive aspects of people. Our aim was to see whether they do so in the way that seems natural for everyone else. All being well, the unusual form of the displays would confound judgements that might have been based on less natural and perhaps more intellectual appraisals. We decided that we would pit children's abilities to perceive emotions and other attitudes against their ability to perceive actions such as digging or pushing. This was especially ambitious, given that we did not know whether individuals with autism would perceive *any* meanings in point-light displays. Some theories suggest that children with autism are unable to integrate patterns, so that they tend to see things in parts rather than perceive them as wholes. It was entirely possible that the children with autism would not be able to see people at all in our moving dots, in which case we had no hope of showing that they could see some (but only some) more subtle aspects of personal meaning.

Happily, the initial part of our study showed that almost all the participants in each group were able to recognize people in the point-light displays. Those with autism were as good at this as the non-autistic participants of similar verbal ability. Many of the children needed exposure times of as little as one-fifth of a second to tell that the dots were stuck to a person. There was therefore no doubt that, in this very basic aspect of person recognition, the children with autism could read our moving dots without difficulty.

Then we presented separate five-second sequences of the point-light person (without accompanying sounds) enacting in turn the gestures of surprise, sadness, fear, anger and happiness. In the surprise sequence, the person walked forward and suddenly checked his stride and jerked backwards with his arms thrown out to the side, and subsequently gave a sigh of relief. In the sad sequence, the person walked forward with a stooped posture, paused, and sighed; he raised his arms slowly and allowed them to drop to his sides; and he seated himself in a slumped manner and put his head in his hands. The frightened sequence showed a person starting and quaking; the angry sequence showed him gesturing in an irritated manner with his arms and stamping; and the happy sequence showed him dancing and skipping. In each case, adults who saw the videotapes were 100 per cent accurate in judging the expressions. Four stills from the 'sad' sequence are shown below.

The children were told, 'You're going to see some bits of film of a person moving. I want you to tell me about this person. Tell me what's happening.' We took care to phrase the instructions and any prompts we gave in terms of what was happening and made no reference to feelings or actions. Our prediction was that individuals with autism would differ from the non-autistic individuals in remarking on the actions, rather than the emotional attitudes, of the point-light person depicted.

The prediction proved to be correct. All but one of the non-autistic children made a spontaneous comment about the person's emotional state for at least one presentation, and most referred to emotions in response to two or more of the five sequences. In contrast, ten of the thirteen children with autism *never* referred to emotional states, whether correctly or incorrectly. This was not because they failed to respond at all. On the contrary, all children in both groups saw meaningful content in each and every presentation, and commented on this. It was just that, in the case of the children and adolescents with autism, it was the person's movements and actions rather than feelings that were reported.

The responses by the children and adolescents with autism betray how gestural expressions of emotion appear to them. (Remember that

FIGURE 12

dots-of-light people do not have faces.) The sad figure was described as 'walking and sitting down on a chair', 'walking and flapping arms and bent down', and 'walking and waving his arms and kneeling down ... hands to face'. The scared figure was said to be 'standing up and moving backwards', 'standing on tiptoe ... walking backwards', and 'moving backwards ... sort of jumping'. The angry figure was 'dancing to some music ... clapping a little bit', 'walking and jogging and shaking his arms', and 'walking and nodding'. Almost none of these responses were wrong. There is nothing wrong in noticing and commenting upon a person's actions rather than the person's emotional attitudes. Indeed, the non-autistic as well as the autistic participants made frequent references to the actions depicted. The thing that distinguished the groups was that the non-autistic participants also remarked upon some of the feelings expressed. Very few of the individuals with autism seemed to notice the emotions at all.

A final task was designed to explore how accurately the children and adolescents could name actions and emotions when explicitly asked to do so. Here we were studying what made sense to the children. We were testing which actions and emotions they could recognize in the point-light displays when pressed for a specific answer, rather than testing what they noticed for themselves. For this part of the study we added five new emotionally expressive sequences to the five already described: these showed the point-light person in states of itchiness, boredom, tiredness, cold and hurt. When these sequences were shown, one by one, we said, 'I want you to tell me what the person is feeling.' Alongside this test involving emotions and other attitudes, there was a test for the recognition of non-emotional actions: lifting, chopping, hopping, kicking, jumping, pushing, digging, sitting, climbing and running. Here the instructions were: 'I want you to tell me what the person is doing.'

Before we analysed the results, we needed to adjust the tasks so that any items that were too easy (so that everyone got them right) or too difficult (so that no one did) were excluded. It turned out that recognizing kicking and jumping fell into the former category, and recognizing surprise and boredom into the latter. When these items were excluded, the two sets of items – of emotional and other attitudes

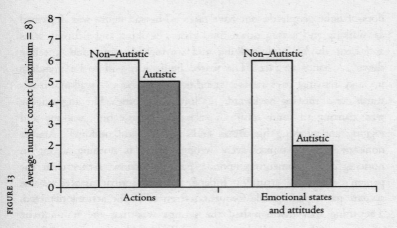

FIGURE 13

on the one hand, and of actions on the other — were equally difficult for the non-autistic participants. This is apparent from the above graph, where you can see that their average score was 6 out of 8 for each type of sequence.

The figure also shows that the participants with autism were not significantly different in their scores on the actions task: they had an average of about 5 out of 8 correct. On the emotions and attitudes task, on the other hand, their performance slumped. They scored only 2 out of 8 correct, on average. They seemed to have real difficulty in reading the subjective states of the person depicted — a difficulty that did *not* extend to their judgements of actions. For example, when one autistic child was asked what the 'itching' person was feeling, he said, 'Scratching ... lots of fleas.' This captures the action component of what was happening, but the emphasis is on the 'scratching', not the feeling that might have prompted the person to scratch.

We have come a long way quite quickly. We have seen how early in life babies become engaged with other people. The engagement is intense, and it is highly emotional. It happens because babies are built to perceive and react to what they see in the behaviour and expressions of people, and because they are ready to take their role in the communicative dance of interpersonal exchange. From the first months of life, they relate to people *as* people. They do more than show coordinated patterns of behaviour with other people; they are emotion-ally connected with them.

The situation is different for children who have autism. As we have seen from studies of infants as well as older children and adolescents with autism, there is something profoundly lacking in their orientation towards people, in their interest and responsiveness to others, and, perhaps most strikingly of all, in their emotional engagement. It is as if we are looking at a negative image of what nature provides to ensure vital and energetic interpersonal linkage and exchange.

To be emotionally connected with someone *is* to experience the someone else as a person. Such connectedness is what enables a baby, or indeed an older child or an adult, to differentiate people from things. I don't just mean that it is used to classify people as one type of thing and objects as other types of thing. A baby could do this on the basis of a number of physical features such as size, the presence of arms and legs, spontaneous motion, and so on. I mean something deeper. It is through emotional connectedness that a baby discovers the *kind* of thing a person is. A person is the kind of thing with which one can feel and share things, and the kind of thing with which one can communicate.

> Can I see another's woe
> And not be in sorrow too?
> Can I see another's grief,
> And not seek for kind relief?
>
> Can I see a falling tear,
> And not feel my sorrow's share?
> Can a father see his child
> Weep, nor be with sorrow filled?
>
> Can a mother sit and hear
> An infant groan, an infant fear?
> No, no! never can it be!
> Never, never can it be!
>
> William Blake, *Songs of Innocence*,
> 'On another's sorrow'

Blake insists that we cannot watch someone else's feelings and fail to react with feelings ourselves. We have a basic human response to expressions of feeling in others — a response that is more basic than thought. But just suppose one lacked this responsiveness to others. And further suppose that the lack existed from very early in life, just as one might lack vision from very early in life. Would one experience people *as* people? If one lacked this direct access to the mental life of others, how would one arrive at an understanding that people have minds? How much would thinking be affected? I have stressed several times that there are forms of interpersonal engagement that happen before thought. Could it be that such engagement also provides the *basis* for thought?

THREE

The Dawn of Thinking

The previous chapter gave us a picture of an infant intensely involved with others. The next chapter will dwell on what thought is, and in particular how we think about things. We can think about the Prime Minister, for example: we can judge him to be sincere, or a master of spin-doctoring, or perhaps someone with both of these qualities. The important thing in thinking *about* him is that we can fix the idea of the Prime Minister in our minds, and then characterize him this way or that. The challenge we face here is to explain how thinking of this kind is sculpted out of an infant's emotional exchanges with other people.

The explanation is contained in this Egyptian altar relief from 1345 BC, where Akhnaten and Nefertiti's three children look into the face of either their mother or their father, and point. They are sharing experiences of the world with their parents.

Clearly, personal relations are not just about exchanging smiles and coos and other endearing or not-so-endearing gestures with someone else. They are also about sharing experiences of things. Personal relations are about connecting with someone else and making reciprocal emotional contact, but also about exchanging points of view, or agreeing and disagreeing about this or that, or sharing jokes. If we can clarify how infants engage with someone else so that communication is *about* a third object or outside event, then we may draw closer to seeing how they come to think about things.

The first signs of a broadening and deepening in the way an infant relates to others occur in the months around a baby's first birthday. Colwyn Trevarthen called it the stage of secondary intersubjectivity, because it follows the primary stage of person-to-person intersubjective

FIGURE 14

connectedness.[1] The terms are a bit clumsy, but their emphasis is exactly right: the link between the infant's subjective experiences and those of another person. Trevarthen portrays the link in just the right way, too: as an emotional link. The defining feature of secondary inter-subjectivity is that an object or event can become a focus *between* people. Objects and events can be communicated about. Or, to put this another way, the infant's interactions with another person begin to have reference to the things that surround them. The baby starts showing her mother dolls, she gestures in request for a sweetie, she refuses to hand over the keys, she is affected by her mother's reactions to things, and so on.

These events reveal that the infant is no longer restricted to a focus either on an object or on a person, but instead may be sensitive to a person's relation to an object. This means that the infant's experience of the other person has expanded. She registers that the other person is connected not just with herself, but with objects and events in the world. She is becoming aware of the other person's awareness of things, conscious of the other's consciousness. She is interested in and responsive to what the other person does with things and feels towards things.

A brief note of caution here. We must not over-interpret this behaviour. We should hold back from supposing it amounts to the infant understanding or *thinking* that another person has a mind and experiences of her own. What we see is the infant relating and reacting to the other person in new ways. This is quite impressive enough.

It is also important not to focus too narrowly on the 'thing' that is being shown, requested or withheld in the interactions. In this period towards the end of the first year there may be a more gradual and subtle shift in the infant's awareness of what another person is aware of. This may be illustrated by the research of a former student of Trevarthen, Vasu Reddy. Reddy is interested in how infants tease and muck about with their caregivers.[2] One example she gives is of nine-month-old Shamini, who was engaging in give-and-take exchanges with her father. Suddenly Shamini looked intently to her father's face and offered an object as before, but then, as her father's hand stretched out, her eyes crinkled and she drew the object back. Turning away, she gave a broad smile. Then she looked back. Her father laughed and, acknowledging the tease, said, 'You, gimme, gimme, gimme' as he stretched out his hand further. This led to a repeat of the same sequence.

As Reddy observes, Shamini is making a kind of pretend offer. She seems to understand what her father expects her to do, and playfully confounds his expectation. In this kind of teasing, the infant shows not-for-serious intentions. She appears to be offering something, but is not. As in the infant's new-found pleasure in showing off and clowning, we can see that she is aware of another person's attention towards her actions, and she revels in it.

But I wonder if that way of putting it – 'she is aware of another person's attention towards her actions' – is quite right for the nine-month-old. It is certainly the way many psychologists would describe the situation. My concern is that the words 'awareness' and 'attention' are too bland and abstract for what we need to say. What we see in Shamini and other nine-month-olds is a new kind of emotional engagement with the attitudes of others. The infant enjoys making sounds to elicit a reaction of amusement, and she delights in provoking a response by cheekily and provocatively embarking on some prohibited act. She is captivated by another person's emotional response not just to herself but, more specifically, to what she is doing. In so far as Shamini is aware of another person's attention, this is part and parcel of an intense engagement that is physical as well as mental. So we should think twice before describing infants in terms that are more applicable to grown-ups. Otherwise we may mistake what our grown-up experiences grow out of.

To begin with, then, the infant registers that an adult is attuned to herself. Such awareness is present from two months at least. Next the infant becomes aware that an adult is orientated to what she is doing, as in the case of Shamini. Then the infant begins to relate to an adult's actions and attitudes towards something quite separate from either herself or the adult. It is this achievement which shows that the infant has reached the stage of secondary intersubjectivity.

My colleagues and I have recently begun to study the changes that occur at the end of the first year of infancy. We are tracking how the baby understands the physical properties of things, a form of understanding she can probably acquire all by herself, alongside her ways of relating to people and things together.

By way of illustration, here is a delightful little girl, Annie, whom we first tested at the age of just under eight months. The testing session began with Annie seated in a high chair at a table with her mother to one side and our research worker, Rosa, sitting opposite. Rosa's opening bid, 'Are you ready to play with me?', prompted Annie to look up and smile. Rosa dangled some large plastic keys on a string in front of Annie but out of her reach, and said, 'Look what I have here.' Annie looked at the keys, smiled, held her arms out away from her sides, and then slapped both her hands on the table in anticipation. Rosa put the keys down on the table near herself, and draped the string across the table so that this was just within Annie's reach. Annie used her right hand to hit the table next to the string, tried to grasp it, and gave a brief glance to the keys. Then she brought both her hands down on the string and with some difficulty managed to get hold of it in her left hand. Quite deliberately, she pulled the string so that it brought the keys within reach. Immediately she took hold of the keys and shook them. Laughing, Rosa said 'Wow!'. Annie's mother smiled proudly.

As Rosa had indicated, it is not always that babies of eight months can use something as a means to getting something else – in this case, using the string to pull the keys within reach – but it sometimes happens. Next we tested whether Annie was aware that an object continues to exist when it is covered. Rosa waved a colourful soft toy before Annie, and placed it out of her reach on a towel. Then Rosa covered the toy with a cloth. She pushed everything towards Annie so that the towel but not the hidden toy was within reach. At first Annie had been excited by the toy, but once it was covered over her interest waned abruptly. Despite her success in the string-and-keys test, she did not use the cloth as a means to pull the covered toy within reach.

In another non-personal task, Rosa turned two plastic cups upside down on the table and introduced a small toy bunny. Annie watched the bunny with interest as Rosa waved it before her. Rosa said that the bunny was going to hide, and placed it under one of the cups. She then pushed both cups together towards Annie, saying, 'Where is he?' Once again to our surprise, Anne's rather clumsy reach went first to the cup under which the bunny had been hidden, and she retrieved the toy successfully; but, even when the bunny was placed under the other cup, Annie continued to choose the cup she had first selected, and it was not clear that she understood where the hidden bunny really was. She could not keep track of the bunny's existence under a particular cup.

In a second version of this task, Rosa put a marble in a box and shook it to make a noise. Then Rosa surreptitiously removed the marble, and gave Annie the box. Annie took it, twisted it in the air, then began to chew it. She did not examine it further. If the marble had continued to exist where it was put, then it should still have been in the box – but this was something that Annie did not seem to follow. A rerun of the procedure had the same result: no searching for the missing marble.

The social tasks were very different. The first was a bubbles task. Rosa opened a bubble tube and dipped in the circular end of the bubble stick. Annie watched intently. Rosa turned up and away to one side and blew a small cluster of bubbles. Annie was riveted. She followed the bubbles as they floated down and, with an expression of wonderment, she leaned forward and extended her arms out to the side. When the bubbles had passed away, she looked slighly deflated and fixed her eyes on the bubble stick, held motionless in Rosa's hand. She looked away briefly, then back at the bubble tube and stick, and then in a half-hearted way slapped the table twice. Then she looked away to the floor. There was no attempt to get Rosa to blow more bubbles, despite the pleasure this had given a few moments previously. After a brief pause, Rosa blew another cluster of bubbles, and Annie responded exactly as before.

The second test for Annie's ability to make a request involved a toy merry-go-round. Rosa positioned this out of Annie's reach and activated it by pressing a knob on the top. Annie beamed and threw her arms out to the side. She also leaned forward towards the toy as it slowed down, and one of her hands twisted forward and back. She gazed at the toy intently for two or three seconds after it had stopped, but then looked away. She smiled at her mother briefly, fixed her eyes on the toy once more for a second or two, and then looked away. Having established very clearly that Annie was not going to make a request, Rosa restarted the merry-go-round and gave it to Annie. Annie played with it happily.

Next Rosa engaged Annie in friendly eye contact and, turning her head to the left and fixing her eyes on a picture on the wall, said, 'Look at that!' She looked at Annie again and repeated the sequence. Annie's response was to maintain her gaze on Rosa's face. Finally Annie cast her eyes down at the floor on the side to which Rosa had been directing her looks, but there was no sign of her trying to look where Rosa had been looking.

Later in the procedure there was a second version of this test. Rosa gained Annie's attention to her face, and then looked to the right and, extending her right arm and finger into a point, said, 'Look at that!' Annie shifted her gaze as far as Rosa's extended wrist, held it there for a moment, and returned her look to Rosa's face. Then she lost interest. There was no sign that she might follow the point into the shared surroundings.

Another social task involved a hand-sized rubber ball. Rosa rolled this from one of her hands to the other and, looking towards Annie, said, 'Do you want to play with me?' Annie met Rosa's eyes and slapped the table. Rosa rolled the ball to her, and Annie gathered it up in both hands. It then rolled over her arm and out to one side. Rosa retrieved the ball and again rolled it gently to Annie. Annie gathered it up, and Rosa held out her hands in a request. Annie seemed to let go of the ball for a moment, then took it again and briefly looked at Rosa's outstretched hands – but that was all. Rosa took the ball and tried again, but Annie never tried to pass it back.

The social tasks ended with a play session between mother and child. In the course of this, a Chinese bell chimed from a corner of the room. Annie paused and smiled and raised her eyes from the toys, but only to look in front of her. Annie's mother could not stop herself from saying, 'What's that?', but Annie herself resumed her play without further ado.

Finally, Annie was carried to the floor from her high chair and settled at play with a toy. Her mother got up from the floor and seated herself in a nearby chair. Out from a hiding place on the floor, a remote-controlled car emerged and sped towards Annie, then moved back and forth in front of her. Annie's response was to look at the car intently, only to resume her play in a slightly distracted manner. Her one look towards her mother was when her mother adjusted her sitting position. At no point did Annie check with her mother whether the car was threatening or innocent.

We were able to test Annie again when she was just thirteen months old. Although some of the developments we shall observe had been present for some time, we can see from her behaviour just how much has changed over the months since her last visit.

Annie was sitting at the same table as before, looking very grown-up in her blue dress. Her face had thinned out, and her blonde straight hair was swept back from her face. Rosa dangled the plastic keys from the string, and immediately Annie's left hand extended towards them. Rosa stretched the string across the table to Annie. With a single hand Annie took hold of the string and pulled the keys to herself. She contemplated them for a few moments – and then offered them back to Rosa. In the hidden-toy version of this task, Rosa again shook the soft toy at a tantalizing distance before placing it upon a towel and hiding it beneath a cloth. She then slid the towel to within Annie's reach. Annie glanced to where the toy was hidden, looked up at Rosa's eyes, and then, with a deliberate motion, pulled the towel so that the hidden toy was brought closer and lifted the cloth that was hiding it. Without Annie noticing, the toy slipped on to the floor beside her and she seemed bewildered that it was not beneath the cloth as it should have been. When the whole procedure was repeated and Annie discovered the toy beneath its cover, she grasped it with delight.

Annie was clearly aware that objects continue to exist when out of sight. When Rosa hid the bunny under one cup, Annie very deliberately placed her hand on the correct (hiding) cup, looked up at Rosa, lifted the cup, and retrieved the bunny. When the bunny was hidden under the other cup, at first Annie seemed more interested in Rosa than in which cup to lift, but on a subsequent occasion she chose correctly. The next test involved the marble in the box. When Rosa had surreptitiously removed the marble and handed the box to Annie, Annie took this in her hands, looked up at Rosa, and then peered inside it inquisitively. When she found the marble was not there, she appeared surprised, looked up at Rosa's eyes, looked at the table under the box as if seeking the marble, and finally returned her gaze to Rosa and handed back the box.

When Rosa took up the bubble tube, Annie showed close interest. She watched the blowing of the bubbles in a rather sober way this time, and when Rosa did not immediately repeat the bubble-blowing Annie looked a bit expectant, smiled at her mother, and then looked back at the bubble tube and then up at Rosa's face. Rosa hesitated, then blew the bubbles again. Annie watched them float out of sight and, once they had gone, looked up to Rosa's face again and chuckled self-consciously, seeming to share the moment with Rosa. Then she looked again towards the place where the bubbles had disappeared, glanced at Rosa, and sighed. For whatever reason, she did not actively make a request for more.

In the second version of the task, however, the exchange in which Rosa activated a toy merry-go-round, Annie made clear requests. The first way in which this happened was that Annie leaned forward with her left arm outstretched and pointed at the merry-go-round with her index finger. Then she withdrew her hand and stretched out her right arm towards Rosa (this time without a point, but with fingers splayed), and looked up to Rosa's eyes in request. When Rosa did not respond, she withdrew with a look of disappointment, glanced at the mery-go-round again, and tried to reach it herself with her left hand. When this failed, she turned towards her mother on her right and tried to reach her mother's hand. Annie's mother offered her hand, and Annie tried to pull it over towards the merry-go-round, and then looked at Rosa. After two unsuccessful pulls, Annie looked up to her mother's face, and was finally given the toy.

Then there was the test of gaze-following. When Rosa turned to her right and looked up to a teddy bear on a high shelf, saying, 'Can you see that teddy bear? Look at that!', Annie at first fixed her eyes on Rosa's face. Rosa repeated her action, and now Annie turned in a clear movement to look to her far right, in the direction of Rosa's look – although not upwards to see the teddy. After a moment's hesitation, Annie also stretched out the forefinger of her hand to make a point, and looked straight back to Rosa.

Later came the test in which Rosa pointed to her right. Annie first fixed her gaze on Rosa's outstretched hand, then looked back to Rosa's face. But, at the moment that Rosa withdrew her hand, Annie spontaneously looked to the side once again to a location close to the target of Rosa's point, well beyond the hand itself. While Annie was still looking in that direction, Rosa pointed again and Annie adjusted the focus of her eyes to coincide with the trajectory of Rosa's point. One could see how she moved her eyes back and forth between the target and Rosa's outstretched finger. Then Annie herself made what seemed like a half-point in the same direction.

In the ball-passing game, Annie received the ball from Rosa in both hands, looked up to Rosa's face and at Rosa's request for the ball, looked at it again, and thrust it forward towards Rosa. Rosa returned it to Annie, and with a playful laugh Annie pushed it back again.

Then there was the episode of mother–infant play and the chiming of the Chinese bell. On the first occasion the bell rang, Annie gave no reaction at all. The second time, she interrupted her play by looking

FIGURE 15

towards the source of the sound, vocalized with a distinctive light 'aah' sound (as if making a comment) and, immediately after, lifted her right hand with outstretched fingers as if to point, withdrew her arm while still looking, and then resumed her play. On this occasion, she did just about everything except look up to her mother to share the experience.

Finally there was the episode of Annie playing on the floor. When Annie's mother sat her on the carpet next to the toys, Annie took hold of a doll. With her gaze fixed upon the doll in her hands, Annie stood herself up. At this point, the noisy remote-controlled car sped across the floor. It was meant to be driven up close to Annie, but because of the erratic driving skills of the operator it drove on by. Annie looked up at the noise, glanced at the car for just a moment, and immediately turned to look at her mother's face. Annie gave a brief smile and an 'Oh' which seemed to express interest and mild surprise, and her mother reflexly echoed with her own 'Oh'. By this time, just a fraction of a second later, Annie had already returned her eyes to the car. As it resumed its movements, Annie cast away the doll and, first walking unsteadily and then crawling determinedly, headed off in pursuit.

What have we learned from these observations of Annie? The eight-month-old happily engages with the person of the experimenter and, in parallel with this, becomes involved in examining and acting upon the objects around her. What she does not do is share her experiences of the world with another person. When she wants something, she does not turn to someone else and request help; when she seems to be enjoying something, she does not look to someone else to share this enjoyment; when she is confronted with something novel, she does not seek out her mother's reaction to what is happening. She does not follow the adult's attempts to share experiences with her or to draw her attention to something by pointing. Nor does she engage in the simplest kind of 'you do it and then I do it' which is needed for passing a ball back and forth between herself and someone else.

By the time she is twelve or thirteen months of age, on the other hand, much has changed. Now she can request someone to do things for her, she offers things and points things out, and she follows someone else's looking or pointing. She engages in reciprocal to-and-fro games. She can also look to someone else not only to share her experiences, but also to check whether something is threatening. Our testing procedure has managed to capture elements of this transition from primary to secondary intersubjectivity, but it does not cover everything. As we shall see, around her first birthday there are other indicators of big changes in the way an infant relates to other people. And along with these developments, *through* other people, fundamental change is occurring in the infant's relations with the non-personal world.

Here I want to highlight the infant's new-found ability to detect and respond to another person's emotional responses to things and events in the environment. It is something vividly demonstrated in a study from Colorado that employed an apparatus called a visual cliff.[3] A visual cliff is a flat surface that looks a bit like a frozen paddling pool. It is constructed so that one half looks like a solid surface to crawl on, but then there appears to be a sudden drop (like a cliff) halfway across. In fact the transparent surface is still perfectly safe as a support. In the study in question, infants of twelve months were placed on the obviously solid side of the apparatus. Beyond the cliff, a few metres away, the infant's mother was standing with an attractive toy.

A number of infants set off towards mother and toy, but when they came to the edge of the cliff they hesitated and looked to their mother's face. When the mother put on a happy face, fourteen of these nineteen infants crossed to the transparent side; when the mother gave a fearful expression, not one of the infants ventured across. When the mother gave an angry expression, only two out of eighteen infants proceeded across the cliff, and fourteen actively retreated by moving back towards their starting point.

The infants not only sought out their mother's attitude to what was happening, but also were able to connect her feelings with the situation that confronted them. Then they reacted accordingly in feeling and action. The infants recognized that their mother's expression of feeling had meaning in relation to a shared situation, and this affected the meaning that the situation held for them. One might say that they were responding to the world according to someone else. If the visual cliff was alarming to their mother, it was alarming for them too.

From just this study, one might doubt that description of what is happening. For example, the adult's feelings might be altering the infant's general mood state, and not being interpreted with reference to anything in particular. But there is something more specific here. There is an impact on the infant's feelings towards the object or event at the focus of the adult's attitude. It is not just that the infant becomes confident or scared or subdued. It is also that she picks up what the adult's feelings are about, and then changes her own feelings towards that particular something.

This becomes clear from the following study by Robin Hornik and colleagues, again with twelve-month-olds.[4] The set-up was that infants were shown a series of three toys one by one. In each case the mother displayed a different feeling. By facial, vocal and gestural expressions, she showed positive feelings towards the toy, or showed negative feelings of disgust, or took a neutral stance. The infants' responses were influenced by their mothers' attitudes towards particular toys. Children played less with the toy towards which the mother showed disgust, for example, even though there were no significant effects on play with other toys in the vicinity or changes in the infant's general mood. Then, when the three toys had been presented and reacted to, a second round of testing took place with the same toys but with the mothers showing neutral expressions towards all of them. The children continued to avoid and played less with the toys towards which their mothers had previously shown disgust. The infants seemed to understand that the messages in the first testing session were specific to those toys. A similar finding emerged from another study in which infants of ten to thirteen months spent more time touching a toy towards which a parent had expressed positive feelings than a toy in relation to which the parent had communicated a fearful attitude ('What a scary toy!').[5]

I hope it is becoming evident what it means to say that infants are learning *through* other people and are responding to the-world-accord-ing-to-someone-else. The child starts out by reacting to the world in her own terms. She finds a toy alluring, for example. She then perceives her mother relating to that toy with disgust or fear. According to the mother's reaction, the toy is not so alluring. What then happens is that the toy loses its appeal for the child herself. Its meaning has changed because of what it means to someone else.

These findings are really important. We are witnessing the begin-ning of a Copernican revolution in infants only twelve months old. Copernicus discovered that the earth is not the centre of the universe, as humans had fondly believed: our little world is but one small planet that revolves around the sun, and what we apprehend is but a narrow and partial perspective on a greater reality. Twelve-month-old infants are discovering the same. The world is not simply a world-for-me, a world that has meaning because of what I feel about it or what I do with it. The world also has meanings for others, and the meaning for someone else can affect the meaning it has for me.

I say this is the *beginning* of a revolution, because at the beginning the infant does not know in an intellectual way that the world has a meaning for others. The discovery is a discovery in action and feeling, rather than a discovery in thought. I believe that it is only because the infant finds herself reacting in these ways – identifying with others and being affected by others' reactions to things – that in due course she arrives at a true understanding of her own position relative to that of others. The initial role-taking in terms of action and feeling establishes a route by which the infant arrives at the painful but exciting insight that she, too, is not the centre of the universe. It will take a few months yet for the penny to drop, and for her to understand and be able to think that this is so – but when the penny does drop, every-thing will be changed.

What else is developing at the end of the first year? Consider how the infant plays her part in games such as rolling a ball back and forth with someone else. She has become able to switch roles from being the receiver to being the giver. The exchange has become reciprocal. She can also take the lead in such interactions. In his detailed description of the game of peekaboo as it evolves with infants from six to fourteen months, Jerome Bruner noted that at around one year of age children begin to initiate as well as accept invitations to take part.[6] This important development could easily be missed by the casual observer. The striking thing is that the child is identifying with the adult by doing the kind of thing that she has observed the adult do in relation to herself. Previously, it had been the adult who invited, but now the child invites as well.

If this seems to over-interpret what is happening, then see how the twelve-month-old infant is doing many other things that seem to involve this special form of copying someone else.[7] The child begins to shake her head to express refusal, and to imitate other conventional gestures such as hugging or greeting someone with 'Hi!' or waving goodbye. Around twelve months of age, my own daughter Amy said 'Mm' in a tone of pleasurable anticipation every time I began to open a can of beer. Like other infants of this age, she was assuming the acts of another person for herself and incorporating these into her own repertoire. It was as if she had grasped that, if the adult could do it, so could she. She also started to copy adult activities such as putting the telephone to her ear. At the same time, she was relating in various ways to another person's wishes, attitudes and intentions – refusing and disobeying as well as obeying – just as her mother and father had been relating to hers.

Here we are going beyond *what* is happening at this stage of development, to describe *how* it is happening. The infant first takes the roles of other people by imitating them and assuming their attitudes. She does this automatically, in the sense that she is drawn into doing it – provided she is in the right mood, of course, and provided she is interested and engaged enough with other people. It is only because of this natural responsiveness towards others that she will eventually come to grasp what roles and perspectives are. These initial forms of perspective-taking are not intended as such by the infant – that is, they are not thoughtful attempts to put herself in the shoes of someone else. This happens later on, in the second year of life, when she begins

to choose to adopt the other person's perspective. For
is moved by others, and this happens because infants
equipped to be moved in this way.

At first, then, infants find themselves affected by the act.
attitudes of others. The reason why they have both the motive a.   the
ability to behave in these ways is that they observe and *participate in*
what they witness in other people's actions and attitudes. Their perception of others is not like their perception of cars or buildings. Being
affected by others is a design feature of human beings – a design
feature that transforms what a human being is.

The point is worth repeating, because it illustrates a theme that
runs through early development. Infants around the end of the first
year do intend to perform imitated actions, just as they do intend to
avoid a toy towards which mother has shown disgust. What they do
not intend – not yet – is to put themselves in the position of the other
person. The reason is simple: they 'know' the other person has a
psychological stance only in the sense that they can look to the other
and relate to her attitudes, or they can observe her behaviour and
register enough about her actions to copy them. They do not know
this in the sense that they can *think of* her as a person with her own
mental life. This ability emerges over the next six to nine months.

By the end of the first year, then, a baby is happily imitating the
adults around her, bringing things for her mother to see so that they
might share experiences, and learning what things mean and what they
are for by watching how her parents react to them and use them. The
adventure of exploring the world is one she can now enjoy with and
through others – a point also highlighted by the American developmen-
talist Michael Tomasello, who has been at the forefront of research in
this area.[8] Yet, for all this, the infant cannot think about events that
are distant from the present and immediate realities that confront her.
She cannot reflect upon the past or ponder what may lie in the future,
nor can she think about merely possible courses of action. She cannot
entertain thoughts.

So how could the subtle but pervasive toing and froing of feeling
and action between a baby and her parent constitute a cradle for the
development of thought? How might social engagement release human
mentality from the restrictions of the here and now and give access to

the boundless domain of the imagination? The frontispiece to this book, by William Blake, shows a mother (Enitharmon) cradling her son not only in her outstretched hand and flowing bodily gestures, but also in her gaze and in her mind. The setting is not one of restful peace, but of motion and dynamism. As Enitharmon watches her son's face intently, he looks to the distance. Blake's caption reads, 'Teach these Souls to Fly.' How does the interpersonal context of early development provide the impetus and support for flights of imagination?

When addressing these questions, it helps to have a picture of how thinking makes its appearance in the second year of life. It is always difficult to consider things in the abstract, and this is especially the case when what we are considering is something as elusive as the development of thought. It is one of the great benefits of studying very young children that one can see thinking taking place as it is lived out in a child's observable behaviour. Thinking is often hidden and internal in older children and adults, but it is nearer to the surface and in some ways more accessible in children who are only just beginning to talk.

Here I reach the last of the three developmental steps leading up to the ability to think. The first step involved the infant engaging with another person in one-to-one interactions. The second step involved the infant relating to another person's relations with the things and events in the world. Now I want to consider the final step in my account of the origins of thinking – this time, more a leap than a step – and move to the middle of the second year of an infant's life.

There are three areas of development that are especially relevant for our concerns. The first is the appearance of symbolic play as a new and exciting element in the child's repertoire of activities. The second is the growth of a new awareness of self and others. And the third is the most marvellous of all intellectual accomplishments – the emergence of language. Intertwined with these three achievements are changes in the child's interpersonal sensitivity and responsiveness. It will be a challenge to tease out just how developments in the personal sphere are related to the new-found advances in thinking that are expressed in play, self-awareness and language. What builds upon what in the construction of the mind?

I begin with symbolic play.[9] As far as I recall, it was somewhere around the middle of his second year that my firstborn, James, was sitting in his high chair at the corner of the kitchen table. He was playing with a spoon. He looked at the spoon, and his eyes twinkled. He looked at me, and his eyes twinkled some more. He looked back to the spoon. Then, with a somewhat mischievous and delighted expression (as if to say, 'So you think you know where I'm coming from!'), he gestured and vocalized that this was now ... a car. It was as if he had transformed our worlds – as indeed he had. He had created an alternative reality which I would (when I caught up) enter with him. And he knew what he was doing. He was pretending that a spoon was a car.

Pretending is a mental kind of doing, and one that entails a sophisticated form of self-reflective awareness. James knew he was making a this stand for a that. He was also aware (I think) that his newly invented meaning for the spoon would not be immediately transparent to me. He seemed aware that he and I were both looking at a spoon and not a car – yet, either separately or together, we could choose to relate to the spoon *as* a car for the purposes of pretend. The thought of a car could now be separated from an actual car, and the spoon could now be separated from what it was going to become for the purposes of play. The car-thought could be applied to the spoon-object, so that the spoon became a thought-car.

If James was mistaking the spoon for a car, or if he was simply making the spoon do things without actually seeing it as a car, then he would not have been pretending. On the evidence of this one vignette offered by a decidedly non-objective observer from a time long time ago, we cannot be sure of what was going on. And in fact there is a lot of disagreement among researchers about how soon genuine symbolic play appears in the activity of young children. It partly depends on the criteria one applies to decide whether the child is using one thing to stand for another. Last week, for example, I watched a fifteen-month-old girl fetching a nappy to put on her teddy. Some would say that the gentle endearments and occasional scoldings the teddy received may have meant nothing more or less than that the child had seen it receiving such attention from others. How far it stood for a person-like being, thought of as separate from the cuddly piece of cloth, we do not know (although I wonder whether this scepticism is misdirected, even if partly justified). In any case, it will be some weeks or even months before this little girl will start to have her teddy 'do' things, and to substitute one object for another in play.

Towards the end of the second year, however, many children reveal in what they say or in their searching for props that they are planning pretend scenes in advance. For example, a child might say 'Drink' just before she reaches for a cup to bring to her doll's lips, or she might be putting her doll to bed and seek paper for a blanket. The evidence suggests that, in the latter half of their second year, children not only begin to comprehend how one thing can stand for another in their own play, but can also respond to the pretend play of an adult.

I have pointed out that one cannot accidentally pretend. James could not make a spoon stand for a car without doing so on purpose. That is the point of pretending – one chooses to make this stand for that. If James did know that he was pretending, it implies that he was aware of something special in his own mental actions. Can it really be that a child less than two years old is already aware of himself and his own ability to alter the meanings of things by choice, to make a spoon stand for a car? Can it really be that he is also aware that someone else can be aware he is pretending this? Our scepticism may be lessened once we find other evidence that the infant's self-awareness has deepened.

Over sixty years ago, the pioneer developmental psychologist Charlotte Bühler made the following observations of infants' self-awareness:

The following experiment is very illustrative. The adult forbids the child to touch a toy that is within the child's reach. He then turns away or leaves the room for a moment. All the one- to two-year-olds understand the prohibition as cancelled at the moment that contact with the adult is broken, and play with the toy. If the adult returns suddenly, 60 per cent of the children of I;4 [I year; 4 months] and I00 per cent of those of I;6 show the greatest embarrassment, blush, and turn to the adult with a frightened expression. From I;9 on they attempt to make good what has happened by returning the toy quickly to its place. From two years on they attempt to motivate the disobedience, for example, by claiming the toy as their own. After the age of two the child expresses will, insistence on its own rights, and possessive impulses in its relations with adults.[10]

We all know that obstinacy attacks become especially prevalent with the terrible twos, but they will have been present for some while before this. They show us something important about the child's understanding of herself in relation to others. Other people are sources of opposition and competition as well as cooperation. They are seen to have their own motives to acquire, possess or persuade. They are recognized to have feelings of their own about the world as they experience it.

To recapitulate: in the earliest months of life, a baby begins by experiencing people as a special class of thing. Towards the end of the first year, she relates to them as beings with a subjective dimension. In showing them things, for example, she demonstrates an engagement with their attitudes. She has a new orientation to people, a new way of experiencing them. Now that we come to the middle of the second year, the infant seems to have a concept of people as selves. People have their own particular wishes, feelings and desires. As she emerges from infancy, the child comes to appreciate the force of the world-according-to-the-other with a new kind of sharpness and definition. She does not simply react to a person's perspective as shown in the person's bodily actions and expressions. She seems to *understand* what a perspective, and even what a particular individual's perspective, really amounts to.

There is plenty to indicate dramatic changes in an infant's self-awareness towards the middle of her second year. Consider the research reported by Jerome Kagan.[11] Children of this age were settled at play with toys, when the mother and an experimenter joined in. The experimenter modelled three acts that were appropriate for the child's level of maturity – for instance, demonstrating three brief scenarios with dolls for children just under two years old – and then said, 'Now it's your turn to play.' Although the children were not instructed to do anything, they seemed to feel that they should be copying the actions of the experimenter. From the middle of the second year, and especially around the second birthday, children reacted with distress and would cling to their mother, inhibit their playing, and sometimes cry. After some minutes the child would recover and leave her mother's side to play again. Then she would often display an exact or fragmented version of one of the demonstrated actions, and smile.

Kagan interprets these observations in terms of the child's new-found sense of obligation to follow the acts of the model, and awareness of her difficulty in meeting the standards required in doing so. He also has evidence that from the middle of the second year children display a concern for other kinds of standards – for example, in their responses to flawed objects and in their language ('broken', 'dirty', 'can't', 'hard to'). It seems that the child is acting in relation to an internal perspective – a set of demands or requirements that determine how she feels about what she is doing. The business of perspective-taking has been incorporated within the child's own mind, so that she is affected by the idea of what she is supposed to do or what is supposed to happen.

This is a change with many ramifications. As Bühler also noted, the young child who plans and holds fast to her goals is showing a capacity to evaluate herself. It is as if she takes a perspective on herself and her own actions. When the child achieves a goal through effort, such as by completing a puzzle, she shows smiles of mastery. Not only does she acquire standards that are linked with adult approval and disapproval, but she also has standards for her own goals and achievements.

These conclusions have been supported by studies of young children playing with their mothers at home. The focus here was the way in which children referred to themselves – for example, when they used personal pronouns or names tied to an object, such as 'my book', or when they referred to their own actions, such as saying 'climb' or 'up' when climbing, or 'Mary eat' when eating. In Kagan's research, self-descriptive utterances were absent at around eighteen months but increased dramatically between nineteen and twenty-four months, and by twenty-seven months they included sophisticated statements such as 'I do it myself' or 'I can't do it.' The fact that such comments have become frequent by the end of the second year reflects how the child has become motivated to comment on her own behaviour now that she has acquired a new level of awareness of what she is doing.

FIGURE 16

A further sign of the young child's self-evaluation is the way she relates to her own mirror image. Here the classic test (devised by Gordon Gallup) is to see how the child reacts to her own reflection in a mirror when a mark has been placed on her nose or forehead without her knowing it.[12] Even nine- to twelve-month-olds react with pleasure to their own mirror image, but it is only from around fifteen months (and especially after eighteen months) that they start to raise their hands to the mark itself. In addition, silly behaviour and signs of coyness or embarrassment are rarely seen in infants under fifteen months, but they become much more common around eighteen months. At this time children also start to make faces and stick their tongue out, or watch their face appear and disappear at the side of the mirror. One can see how the twenty-one-month-old shown above is quite taken with her own self-image.

Note how it matters to a very young child when her appearance is changed. The signs of coyness and embarrassment (and self-admiration, come to that) reveal that she has a sense of herself as embodied, and moreover a sense of herself as the potential object of other people's evaluations. The child sees and feels herself in relation to what might be seen and felt from another person's point of view. She cares about what others may think about her – where what others think has much to do with their attitude towards her. Once again we see that perspectives are more than something that other people have. Perspectives are also internal to the mind. The child is relating to the other person's attitudes towards herself, but also within herself.

I have said that the child is also becoming increasingly sensitive to other people as selves. Martin Hoffman provides some vivid examples from his research.[13] One description is of an eleven-month-old girl who saw another child fall and cry. At first she stared at the hurt child, looking as though she was about to cry herself. Then she put her thumb in her mouth and buried her head in her mother's lap, which is what she would do if she hurt herself. Another description is of a boy who at a similar age would respond to his own distress by sucking his thumb with one hand and pulling his ear with the other. He would also do this when he saw someone else in distress. At twelve months, however, something new happened. On seeing a sad look on his father's face, he himself looked sad and then sucked his own thumb while pulling on his father's ear.

Incidents involving somewhat older children show that they are sorting out what belongs to themselves and what belongs to someone else, in a psychological as well as physical sense. A fifteen-month-old boy called Michael was fighting with a friend over a toy, when the friend started to cry. Michael appeared disturbed and let go, but the friend continued to cry. Michael paused, then offered his teddy bear to the friend. When this did not work, Michael paused, went to fetch his friend's security blanket from the next room, and gave it to him. At this point, the friend stopped crying. Michael had worked out how his friend might be comforted by something that was important *for him*, just as he himself would be comforted by his own teddy bear.

Role-taking of this kind is not confined to sympathetic distress. Marcy, a girl of twenty months, wanted a toy that her sister was playing with. When she asked for it, her sister refused. Marcy paused, as if reflecting on what to do, and then went straight to her sister's rocking horse – a favourite toy that her sister never allowed anyone to touch – climbed on it, and began yelling, 'Nice horsey! Nice horsey!', keeping a watchful eye on her sister. Her sister put down the toy

Marcy wanted and came running angrily, whereupon Marcy immediately climbed down from the horse, ran directly to the toy, and grabbed it.

What can we conclude from these observations? It is not just that Michael and Marcy were aware of other people as that special class of thing with whom events can be shared, towards whom requests can be directed, and so on. They could also see other people as individuals who feel distress or desire, who can be comforted or provoked, and for whom objects have personal significance. The children had developed the ability to reflect on the characteristics and psychological states of individual selves, and to take appropriate action. Michael was sensitive to what mattered to his friend, and could act in relation to the friend's perspective; Marcy's Machiavellian manoeuvres depended on her working out what was special to her sister and what would prove insufferable from her sister's perspective. Here again we see that the children are understanding what perspectives are. They are shaping what they do in accordance with their thoughts about the people around them.

Which brings us to the flowering of language. I believe that these new forms of self- and other-awareness are tied in with the surge that takes place in a young child's expanding vocabulary in the middle of the second year. The reason is that role-taking is at the very core of language.

There is so much that unfolds in children's language at this time that it is difficult to know where to direct one's attention. Yet there do seem to be certain very fundamental aspects of language that develop in tandem with – and because of – the changes in social awareness we have been exploring. In part, this is bound up with the child coming to use symbols, and we shall consider language-as-symbols in the next chapter. For now I want to illustrate how early language development is built upon the child's new-found awareness of the relations between herself, other people and the non-personal world.

This is an approach that has been championed by Jerome Bruner.[14] Bruner has a long-standing interest in how language emerges in the context of joint action between an infant and her caregiver. He has argued that language in general, and grammar in particular, may be an outgrowth of joint action between child and caregiver. We have already noted that Bruner gives prominence to what he calls the formats of play between infant and adult. These are the repetitive and structured forms of game such as peekaboo, ride-a-cock-horse and give-and-take, in which there are subtle variations on a predictable theme. The theme is important in fixing the sequence of events so that the infant knows what is coming, and important too in allowing a gradual shift in the role of each participant. As the infant gets older, she can take a more active part in what becomes a reciprocal, to-and-fro, exchange.

In addition to this, and especially important for the development of language, the theme of these stylized games is a kind of topic for infant and caregiver, a given set of shared happenings. Any communication that is made by either party, whether this is simply establishing eye contact and vocalizing to indicate that the game is shared, or something more sophisticated like emphasizing a particular move in the game, already takes the form of a kind of comment on the matter in hand. In games, the infant has a greatly simplified task in referring to the common focus of activity. This orientating to a focus is a very basic characteristic of language – the use of words to comment on a topic. The topic is what the words are about. The comment expresses a particular perspective on that topic. It seems that topics and comments are implicit features of the games that precede language. And, of course, a caregiver is endlessly weaving language into the playful goings-on.

Moreover, when grammar appears in the more elaborate utterances of children in the middle of the second year, the structure of that grammar reflects those aspects of the communicative games that have been receiving emphasis over the previous months. Words pick out topics (they are no longer presumed), and words (no longer merely gestures) express some comment on those topics. Moreover, the kinds of words that appear – those that refer to agents, actions, objects of actions, recipients of action, where things are, and whose things they are – relate to the kinds of thing that were highlighted by the formats of the game. One final ingredient in this recipe for language comprehension and use is that the infant has been initiated into the way of using standardized means of expression, so she has learned that there are acceptable and effective devices to convey what she needs to convey. As with the child's growing awareness of standards in other areas of life, she appreciates that there are correct ways to do things – often like 'they' do. There are correct and incorrect words to use. All this means she is ready for something new – words – to take over the function of communicating.

We should note in passing that the wish to communicate may not be the only motive for acquiring language. If bodily expressions of feeling are such a vital part of our existence, then so too is human expressiveness in language and other symbols. Anyone who has witnessed the babbling of a child of fourteen months is likely to conclude that she is having a wonderful time expressing herself. Sometimes this seems to be just for herself, and sometimes it is directed to someone else. We can allow that one prime motive for using and comprehending language is to regulate someone else's attention and action, but there is also a need to express oneself. When the need is to express oneself to others, language can do the job of establishing as well as shaping the interpersonal contact.

Suppose we conclude that a major reason why a child develops language is in order to affect the minds and the actions of others, as well as to interpret what other speakers are trying to convey. This is a different way of making the claim that role-taking and self- and other-awareness are central to language. As well as finding that words can stand for things and events and qualities, children also grasp that words that have meanings for you have the same meanings for me. A word I hear *you* use to refer to something or to express something is a word that *I* can employ to mean the same thing for me, and to communicate that thought to you. Not only this, but words can convey an individual's own comments on topics that are established between speaker and listener. Each of these accomplishments is connected with and at least partly caused by a new awareness of the interchangeable roles of the child and others.

The crux of Bruner's message is that we should not be carried away in our wonder at the child's achievement in mastering language. Yes, language is remarkable, and the grammar of language is so subtle and complex that perhaps certain rules governing language are innate. On the other hand, there is much that happens in the earliest months of life that seems to prepare the way for language. In many respects, language slots into patterns of interaction and mutual adjustment between infant and caregiver that are already well practised before language. The patterning of an infant's social exchanges may do a lot to explain how language is acquired. Words can replace gestures and vocal expressions to achieve the communication the infant is seeking – provided, that is, there are already means to register and influence what someone else is attending to and expressing, and to recognize what someone else is doing in communicating. The infant 'simply' has to realize what words are for, and how they express meanings.

If it is true that children with autism lack intersubjective contact with other people, then autism may show us the ways in which personal relations are pivotal for the development of the mind. Up to now we have considered evidence that children with autism have abnormalities in person-to-person relatedness. We need to know whether the abnormalities also extend to interactions that link people and things, so that we can track the effects on the development of thinking.

This is an issue we can take up by returning to Dawn Wimpory's study of the early signs of autism.[15] Her semi-structured interviews with parents covered abnormalities that went beyond one-on-one person-to-person interactions: they also explored the infants' ways of relating to other people with reference to objects and events in the surroundings. Here, too, there were differences between autistic and non-autistic children. For example, *not one of the infants with autism* but at least half the infants in the control group were reported to offer or give objects to others in the first two years of life. The same was true of pointing at objects or following others' pointing. No children with autism were said to show objects to others, and not one was said to have looked between an object of interest and an adult – for example, when the infant wanted something out of reach. The evidence clearly suggests that their lack of interpersonal engagement extends to circumstances in which they might share experiences of the world with other people. They appear to be less connected with other people for their own sake, but also less connected with or concerned about others' attitudes to a shared world.

There is direct observational evidence to support this view. A team of British researchers led by Simon Baron-Cohen, Tony Charman and Tony Cox has involved family doctors and health visitors in screening for social abilities in 16,000 infants at their eighteen-month developmental check-up.[16] Ten out of the twelve infants who failed to point things out or to show things to the mother or to the person testing the child, and who also failed to engage in pretend play, were later diagnosed as having autism. Although it is common for any eighteen-month-old to be patchy in responding to social overtures, it is not at all common to show this combined lack of pointing, lack of showing things to others with checks on the eye gaze of the other, and lack of symbolic play. Indeed, it is a matter for serious concern.

As I mentioned in Chapter 2, the same research group gave a battery of tests to twenty-month-old children with autism, children with other developmental delays, and typically developing children.[17] What they found was that some of the social exchanges common among non-autistic children were rare among those with autism. Not only was there the failure to use social gaze in empathy, but also the children with autism did not make links between themselves, the investigator, and the events and objects in their surroundings. For example, a potentially anxiety-provoking toy was placed on the floor a short distance from the child. The toy might be a robot which flashed and beeped and moved around in circular sweeps, a car that followed a circular path around the room, or a pig that made noises and moved backwards and forwards. For each of the toys there was a control box with an electrical lead that ran from the box to the toy. Although there was relatively little to distinguish the autistic and non-autistic children in the amount they looked at the box that controlled the toys, those with autism very rarely switched their gaze between toy and adult. The great majority of children who did not have autism appeared to check out the toy with the adult; those who had autism did not. So, too, when tested for their ability to imitate another person in performing simple actions such as pulling toy dumb-bells apart, and when prompted to engage in symbolic play (in particular, to make one thing stand for another), the children with autism were relatively unresponsive. In every test, they seemed unconnected with the feelings and actions of others.

Similar abnormalities are also evident in older children with autism. Marian Sigman and her colleagues tested children around three years old with a small remote-controlled robot that moved towards the child and stopped about four feet away.[18] For thirty seconds the parent and the experimenter, who were both seated nearby, made fearful facial expressions, gestures and vocalizations. Almost all the non-autistic children looked at an adult at some point during this procedure, but fewer than half the children with autism did so, and then only briefly. The non-autistic children looked to an adult for between two and a half and six seconds. For those with autism, the average time was just over half a second. Moreover, the children with autism were not only less hesitant than the mentally retarded children in playing with the robot subsequently, they also played with it for substantially longer periods of time (approximately six seconds, compared with one and a half seconds for the non-autistic retarded children). It seemed that they were less influenced by the fearful attitudes of those around them.

If children with autism do not share the world with other people and do not relate to the world-according-to-the-other, then what of the other facets of development that caught our attention in normally developing infants: symbolic play, self-awareness and language?

Few children with autism show elaborate imaginative play. There is much controversy over the reasons for this, and no wonder: it is a tantalizing riddle why children who have such profound and characteristic abnormalities in their personal relations should also show such severe deficits in symbolic play.

I have already stated the gist of my own theory, that the failure in interpersonal relatedness *causes* the impoverishment in imaginative life. But there are competing theories about the relation between the social and symbolic deficits in autism. One theory suggests that there is something basic about the children's ability to generate new ideas, perhaps because of disease of the frontal lobes of the brain. It is suggested that the children get stuck on particular tracks of thinking and action, and a difficulty in producing creative play is one result. Another theory suggests that the problem is primarily an intellectual one – a failure in the computational powers of the brain. Here both the social deficits and the limitations in symbolic functioning are attributed to innate deficiences in the child's ability to operate on mental representations – rather in the way that a computer might be faulty in operating on the items contained in its memory store.

I shall not dwell on these alternative theories, but I do need to emphasize that the autistic child's deficit in symbolic play is striking and important to understand.[19] If the child is left to himself in a room full of toys, he is likely to pay little attention to the toys or perhaps spin the wheels of a car or perform some other non-symbolic and repetitive ritual, rather than weaving the toys into imaginative play. This behaviour is characteristic of autism, and not simply a feature of mental retardation. It is not that the play is absolutely lacking in any symbolic or creative content, for on occasion (and especially when prompted by an adult) the children may make one thing stand for something else. But both their symbolic play and their propensity to enact social scenarios appear to be severely limited.

When it comes to the children's self-awareness, it is interesting that young children with autism do remove a mark from their faces when they perceive this in a mirror.[20] It looks as if this should be evidence for self-awareness, but it seems to be a kind of body-awareness rather than personal self-consciousness. For what children with autism do not show are the signs of coyness so typical of non-autistic children. In everyday life, too, they are often startlingly unaware or unconcerned about their appearances or actions, so that they might be unabashed at being seen naked. Therefore, even though they perceive their own body in the mirror, and act towards that body as altered by a mark, they may not conceive of themselves as selves in the minds of others. In this sense, many children with autism are not self-conscious.

Connie Kasari and colleagues explored one aspect of this with autistic children who functioned at the level of normal two-year-olds.[21] The children were given a puzzle to complete, but on completion neither the tester nor a parent made any response. Then there was a second puzzle. This time both adults praised the child's success. The children with autism were like matched non-autistic children when it came to smiling at their own success. Yet those with autism were less likely to draw attention to what they had done or look up to an adult, and they rarely showed pleasure when they were praised. Indeed a number of the children looked away after the puzzle was finished. They did not seem to seek or enjoy the approval of others. They did not seem to experience themselves in the hearts and minds of others.

If this is the case, and if a major impetus to learning language is to affect the minds of others, then perhaps it should not come as a surprise that many children with autism never talk at all. One wonders whether they grasp the point of talking, which is to communicate with someone else. If one needs to *feel with* someone else to register that one is connected psychologically, and if such connection is a necessary part of understanding what it is to share and to communicate, then a lack in intersubjective contact might render the whole enterprise of language meaningless except perhaps in some shadow form to do with getting a desired action from someone else.

What of those autistic children who acquire quite sophisticated language? Still the impairment is greater than in other areas of intellectual functioning. For example, autistic children who are not severely mentally retarded are often good, and sometimes amazingly good, at solving jigsaw-type tasks that suggest their own solution. It is not unusual for a child with autism to be able to assemble jigsaws face down. By contrast, such children's language is almost always delayed and peculiar.[22] Their most striking abnormality is not how they understand or produce grammar, but how they use language and fail to adjust language to the context in which it is used. When individuals with autism say something, what they say often seems curiously stilted or off-beam. The same is true about their understanding of the speech of others, in that they can focus on the literal meaning of words instead of interpreting the words or utterances in context. The flexibility of mutual exchange and mutual adjustment is lacking.

So, when a young autistic man participating in a conference was asked from the audience, 'Do you have a hobby?' he replied, 'Yes.' That was all — just 'Yes.' A perfectly valid answer to the question, but not an adequate response to what lay behind the question, which was the questioner's interest in what that hobby might be. When another person with autism was asked, 'What did you have for dinner', the reply came back: 'Meat and cabbage and potatoes and gravy and salt and jam tart and custard and orange juice and cup of tea.' Again an accurate response, but not one that was sensitive to the questioner's intent in asking the question. Another child with autism always referred to the dog's dinner plate as a 'dish', and when asked to put some scraps in the dog's bowl, she gave food to the dog in the washing-up bowl.[23]

What these examples illustrate is that, although people with autism may understand and respond to the literal meanings of words and sentences, they are not so good at responding to what *the speaker* means in using those words and sentences. Nor are they able to adjust what they are saying in such a way that a listener naturally and easily picks up the drift. They find it difficult to sort out what is relevant or irrelevant for a listener. Most fundamentally, they do not adjust to another person's mental orientation, whether that person is a speaker or a listener.

Let me spend a moment on this idea of adjusting to another person's mental orientation. What I mean is this. At any moment, a person has a particular take on what is happening. The person notices this rather than that, and she has feelings and makes judgements about one rather than another aspect of events. If she is hungry, for example, she may notice that a shop is selling groceries; her friend may notice only that it sells newspapers. If she is short of money, she may resent that the fruit is overpriced; meanwhile her friend may feel tempted by some juicy peaches. In one sense the two friends are experiencing the same shop and its contents, but they are having quite different experiences of that shop. A more extreme case arises when one person construes things in an idiosyncratic way, for instance, in mistaking the shop for a cinema, or thinking and feeling that the shop is really a front for the secret services.

In each case, the person has what one might call a subjective perspective – how the world appears to that individual. Of course, this perspective may be more or less the same as the subjective perspective of someone else. If the perspective is the same as that of almost everyone else, so that the person is orientated to what we call objective reality, it is still the case that each individual has his or her own experiences of that reality. Therefore, if someone is able to adjust to the mental orientation of another person, it means that he or she is responsive to that person's particular interests, concerns, wishes, feelings, intentions and other subjective mental states. We have sometimes talked of this in terms of the ability to take someone else's role, or appreciate the other's perspective. We have also seen that there are different kinds or levels of role-taking, only some of which involve thinking about the other person's mind.

It is in this context that we are struck by the difficulties of the person with autism. In the dog-bowl incident, for example, the child was locked into one particular meaning of the word 'bowl' and could not focus instead on what the speaker was meaning him to do. He seemed to respond to the literal and unmodifiable force of the word itself, not what the person had in mind (and intended to communicate) in using that word. Sometimes it matters to distinguish a dish from a bowl — but whether this is so depends on what is happening between speaker and listener, or writer and reader, at a particular time. 'What is happening' is not essentially a linguistic matter: it has to do with what one person thinks and wishes to convey to another. It is here, in the understanding of what someone else may have in mind and mean to communicate, that the person with autism comes unstuck.

Once again, therefore, this time in the domain of language, we are faced with the possibility that the autistic person's principal handicap is in understanding *people* and what people think, feel or intend to convey. Many of the individual's other difficulties in using language are spin-offs from this basic limitation. For example, the words and sentences of our language are crafted to convey nuances of a speaker's orientation to things and events. The autistic child's idiosyncratic use of words often seems to reflect an obliviousness to such nuances. And this limitation in social understanding, a limitation in being aware of and adjusting to other people's minds, has its roots in even more basic abnormalities in interpersonal relatedness.

The central idea I have tried to convey is this: thought dawns through movements in mental orientation. The movements in mental orienta- tion are of a special kind: they occur through an infant's response to other people. They are movements that begin before thought, and they provide the foundations for thought. They do so in in two ways: they enable a one-year-old to grasp the perspectival nature of mind, in that different people can have different takes on objects and events; and they enable the child to understand how a person's meanings may be grounded in symbols.

The Copernican revolution at the end of the first year of life occurs because the infant starts to relate to someone else's relatedness to the world. The world is not just a world-for-the-infant, it is also a world-for-the-other. At the same time, the other person is not just a special kind of object that affords one-to-one interaction and sharing and gives the baby a special set of feelings and tendencies to act. The other person is also a source of attitudes towards the things and events that are happening in shared surroundings. Moreover, interactions are reciprocal: what the mother does in relation to the baby, the baby can do in relation to the mother. Both in action and in feeling, the baby can identify with others.

All this involves a baby's inbuilt capacity to be moved. Most important for the dawning of thought is the baby's capacity to be moved emotionally. The reason is that the baby's way of experiencing an object or event may be changed through her responses to the feelings of others. She is moved from one way to another way of construing things, as in our example of the visual cliff and its mother-altered meaning for an infant. In correspondence with this, the baby's ways of experiencing people are changed. A person can be related to through objects. The twelve-month-old will show toy after toy to those around her — and she watches their reactions. Just as she apprehends things as the potential targets for the attitudes of others, so too she apprehends others as the sources of attitudes to things.

Yet for this early point in life, we need to be cautious in what we deduce about the infant's understanding of people and things. What we see is that the infant relates to people and the world differently, and that she can be moved in mental orientation. As I have stressed before, this is not to say that the infant *understands* how objects can mean different things to different people. Nor should we conclude that she understands people as beings with subjective experiences or minds that differ from her own. All we observe is that the infant is no longer embedded in a one-track, for-me mode of experiencing reality. She is subject to mental pushes and pulls from other people, and as a result of this her attitudes to the world are changed. The meanings of things shift. Something can appear in such-and-such a way, then another person enters the picture and it comes to acquire new meanings. This is fertile ground for the infant to acquire new insight into the nature of minds — her own as well as those of others.

Why is the ground so fertile? It nourishes insight by allowing that the infant may *both* be moved to a new orientation towards the world *and* retain a sense of her own initial take on things. When this occurs, the infant is in a situation where simultaneously the world has a meaning-for-me and a meaning-for-the-other. And what is the insight? The insight is that people-with-minds have their own subjective experiences, and they can give things meanings. In turn, those meanings can be anchored in symbols. We have seen how, by the second half of the second year of life, this is expressed in new forms of self- and other-awareness, in symbolic play and in language. Here is the dawn of thought and the dawn of language.

Symbolizing in general, and language in particular, are poised at the interface between communication and thought. They arise out of communication that takes place before language, and they make new forms of communication and thought possible. But symbolizing, language and thought are possible only because of the nature of the emotional connections between one person and another, and because of each person's involvement with a shared world.

FOUR

The Cast of Thought

As I type this, I am sitting in the bay window of a cottage in the Lake District, about two hours' drive north from Manchester. I look out and immediately in front of me the land drops away to a quiet lane and the easy-flowing waters of the river Rothay, carrying rainfall from the fellsides of Helvellyn, Fairfield and other peaks to Lake Windermere and then out to the sea. On the other side of the river there is pastureland for sheep, and beyond that the land rises to the long ridge of Wansfell, now smudged by patches of mist. I think about the contrasts between this green landscape and the traffic-choked part of London where I work. I think about the hours of childhood when we threw sticks into the river and chased them downstream to the stepping stones. Two rooks fly overhead, and they remind me of a poem by Coleridge which expresses something of the wonder of this natural beauty. And then I realize that I am supposed to be writing a book.

What has been happening in my having all these thoughts about the scene before me? The first thing to notice is that the scene itself is more or less fixed, although those rooks appeared unexpectedly from stage left. Broadly speaking, it is the scene that all my thoughts are 'about'. Yet we can see how far I *move about* this anchor point, to times and places near and far, and to feelings and images that reflect experiences of quite different settings, each related in some way to this wonderful part of Cumbria. In one sense I am transported elsewhere, yet all the while I know I am sitting here on a day in February having thoughts that are different from my immediate experiences of present realities. And, as I write this, I am having thoughts about having thoughts, as intended. Obviously the objects of this process – what our thoughts are about – may be very abstract.

I think there is something telling about our use of language when we try to capture what is involved in thinking. I have written of being moved or transported to another time or place, yet remaining where I am; I have stressed that this movement takes place around a fixed anchor point, namely whatever is being thought about. Even when I become lost in thought, I never actually treat my thoughts as representing present reality. I am, as it were, entertaining thoughts, and I can always come out of my reverie and return to the here and now. In some sense, then, I must be aware that I am thinking about rather than perceiving something, or thinking about a state of affairs and not believing that it is actually happening or assuming it to be true. This is what distinguishes sanity from madness. When the madman hallucinates, he takes himself to be perceiving things, but he is only imagining; when he is deluded, he takes his distorted notions to be true, but he is only having ideas. When sane people think, they do not make such mistakes.

In the first place, then, a person is aware of the distinction between having thoughts and perceiving things. In addition, and perhaps more obviously, the person is aware not only that thoughts are connected with things — after all, they are about things — but also that they are separate from and distinct from the things they are about. Thoughts are mental, whereas things are physical. Thoughts and things have very different properties.

Now, when we have a thought about something, we take a particular perspective on it. For example, when we think about a hat, or look at something and say that it is a hat, we are attributing the property of hatness to this object of thought. We could have another thought about its nature — for example, we could think of it as a piece of cloth or whatever — or we could have another thought about its properties as a hat, for example about its colour or style. So when we hold something in mind and think about it, whether it be a scene before us or an object such as a hat or even another thought, we take up one set of attitudes towards it and then another. Even if we had only one thought about what was thought about, we could have other thoughts. This possibility of taking up different perspectives is essential to the very idea of having a thought about something.[1]

By now we have done almost enough to characterize human thinking, but not quite. I shall try to distil the essentials, and add one more thing. In the example of thinking I have given, I moved from thought to thought. With each thought, I myself was moved to distant times and places – but only *in* thought. I remained aware of myself as thinking, at least to the extent that I could come back down to earth. With each and every thought, I took a particular stance on the things I thought about; my thought of the cottage was a thought about this man-made structure *as a cottage*; my thought about the river Rothay was a thought about this water flowing before me *as a river*; and so on.

The one more thing to add is that, in writing about all this, I have used symbols such as 'cottage' and 'river' that have a remarkable effect on anyone who reads them. In so far as someone can interpret these words as standing for things, the words also transport the reader. The reader comes to have the thoughts that are encompassed by the words. The reader thinks of a cottage, a river, and so on. It is in this sense that the symbols stand for 'things'. They evoke just enough of the kinds of experience that are fitting for a cottage, a river, and so on. In other words, symbols do not really stand for the things themselves. Rather, the words evoke particular ways of conceptualizing or remembering or experiencing the things. To be more precise, they evoke how the writer and the reader have experienced the things in question. Symbols ground ways of construing the world.

The philosopher Mary Warnock has captured this well. She writes, 'If we are successfully imagining something, then, this is what we are doing: either by means of physical or non-physical analogues we are calling up the sense or significance of something which is not present to us in fact. It is for us affectively as if the absent object were present.'[2]

Perhaps it would help to anchor this rather abstract reasoning in something specific. This might show us how, while being what they are, symbols point to meanings beyond themselves. That is a quaint way of putting it – as if symbols do things like pointing – and it must not obscure what is at issue. The crux is that we assume a particular mental orientation to symbols so that we recognize them as things with their own physical properties (whether these are sounds, squiggles on a page, pictures, sculptures, or whatever) while at the same time apprehending their meanings.

To rescue us from the slipperiness of words and sharpen our focus

FIGURE 17

on symbol and meaning, consider how we appreciate works of art. Above is a famous painting by Turner: *Snowstorm – Steam-Boat off a Harbour's Mouth Making Signals in Shallow Water, and Going by the Lead.* Turner had had himself lashed to a mast to observe this scene. Do we see what one critic saw: soapsuds and whitewash? Or do we agree with Kenneth Clark's view, that 'the less defined, the more purely colouristic they [Turner's paintings] are, the more vividly do they convey a total sense of truth to nature'?[3] What sense is that, and what truth?

Whatever our answers to those rhetorical questions, the painting shows us something deeply significant about the nature of representation. One can see the picture as little more than soapsuds and whitewash. To do so is not wrong, merely Philistine. Or one can stand back, and find that the painting points towards a meaning beyond the paint on the canvas. Sure enough, there are some lines and patches of darkness in the middle of the picture that seem to depict a definite something, and the title of the painting tells us what that something is. But far more important is the meaning we apprehend through the swirls of paint and the tumult of colour.

Now take a more prosaic example, a painted portrait. Here one might think that the problem of interpretation does not exist. If the painting overleaf is very like the Duke of Wellington (as Goya's portrait assuredly is), then all one does is to recognize the said Duke. Not so: there is still the canvas, and still the pigment against it. Again Warnock is worth quoting:

> Thus, in looking at a picture and seeing it as a portrait, we are detaching ourselves from what might be described as the brute facts of vision ... we choose to see *in* the canvas the subject of the portrait, who is not present, but whom we feel to exist in the canvas ... Both artist and spectator have to detach themselves from the world in order to think of certain objects in the world in a new way, as signifying something else.[4]

In fact, of course, in looking at the picture you are tacitly doing something even more subtle. You are taking this to be a reproduction of a photograph of a painting of the Duke. At any given moment you can focus on the Duke himself, or on the marvels of Goya's style or technique, or on the quality of the representation of the painting on the page – or, as at this very moment, you can be thinking in a way that encompasses all these. As Oscar Wilde wrote, all art is at once surface and symbol.

Now to a final picture. I have stressed that we apprehend emotions in bodily expressions, and that we find meanings in symbolic works of art. In Picasso's *Woman Crying*, we do both at once. It is the sense or meaning of an expression that Picasso portrays in this picture, not the specifics of a human face.

So, symbolizing enables us to think of absent realities, but also to conjure imagined worlds; symbolizing allows us to fix objects and events as experienced, and then to think about them; symbolizing gives us mental space in which we can move to take up one and then another attitude to things; and, perhaps most important of all, symbolizing has a remarkable Janus-like quality in facing two ways at once, turned inwards to provide the mechanism for an individual's thinking and turned outwards to communicate thoughts between individuals. Not only words and symbolic gestures but also works of art communicate

FIGURE 18

as well as express – they would not be works of art if they were not intended to do so. From all this it would seem that if we can explain the developmental origins of symbolizing, we shall have uncovered the foundations of thought.

In explaining anything, it makes a big difference how you frame the starting point from which your explanation proceeds. Every explanation has a bedrock of givens – ideas that we start from. The givens may

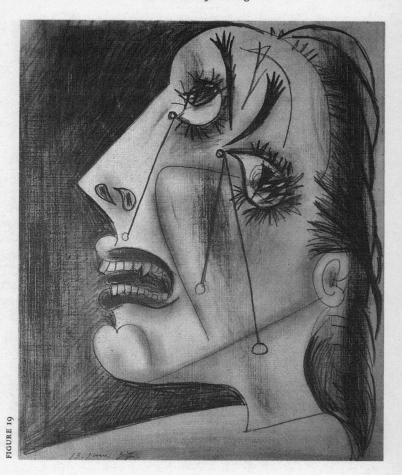

FIGURE 19

need their own explanation, but not immediately. For the present enterprise, therefore, it is going to be critical how we begin, and at what point we feel satisfied we have gone far enough.

Let me illustrate by citing another example from psychology. Where should we begin in explaining the behaviour of animals? It used to be thought that we needed to explain why an animal does anything at all, so that all kinds of drive were invented. Then someone realized that it would be much more of a problem to explain why an animal was *not* doing something. The most likely explanation would be that the animal was dead. This is because it is in the nature of live animals that they are active – this is the given from which we start – and what we need to explain is why at any time an animal is acting in this way rather than that, not why it is active at all. True, there are other levels of explanation. For example, one could give an account of how organisms down to single-cell amoebae are activated by their biochemical structure. But that is not a psychological explanation.

I do not think the right place to start our description of the mind is with an account of what is going on inside a baby's brain. Nor do I think we can focus merely on how the baby acts on the world, nor even on how she perceives the world. I think we need to begin with the different forms of relatedness between the infant and the things and people in the environment. As the philosopher-theologian Martin Buber stated, 'In the beginning is relation.'[5]

We need the concept of relatedness to capture how the connection between the baby and the world is there from the start. The baby perceives *and* feels *and* acts upon things in the world. Upon people and objects, that is. There is a fundamental distinction between what Buber called I–Thou and I–It relations. I want to say a little about how the infant's relation to objects makes its contribution to the development of thought, and then focus at greater length on the vital contribution of her relatedness to people.

In the beginning, the young infant experiences the world in terms of the ways it lends itself to her own actions and feelings. The only perspective she has on life is given by what grabs her through its attractiveness or its desirability, and what she grabs by looking, sucking, grasping – as well as what repels her and what she tries to get rid of, of course. As Jean Piaget stressed repeatedly, this is not really a perspective at all, because the baby does not entertain it *as* a perspective. For the infant, it is simply the way things are. In relating to things, then, the infant learns about things first-hand. She learns that a ball is something that can be held, sucked and squeezed, whereas an apple can be held and sucked but not squeezed. She is building up a picture of the nature of things, and is distinguishing different types of thing.

All this may seem rather obvious, but its importance for our purposes is that we can begin to see what it will mean to develop the capacity to think about things. It is all very well for an infant to be able to act on an object first by banging it and then by sucking it and then by throwing it to the floor, but this is not at all the same as being able to think about it. As Piaget took pains to emphasize, the object may be understood simply as something-to-be-banged, something-to-be-sucked, and so on. What needs to happen before the infant can think about objects or events is that the objects and events must have their own independent existence in the infant's mind. A ball has to be known as a such-and-such, an object with its own permanence and with the properties of being holdable, suckable, squeezable, and so on, even when the infant is not currently relating to it in any of these ways.

Not only this, but also the infant needs to be in a position to apply to objects or events one thought and then another thought, without mistaking that these are only thoughts. In thinking of banging an object, the thought is not going to make any noise; in thinking of sucking an object, the thought will not bring all the sensations of sucking the object itself, even though a child may salivate at the thought. To entertain a thought is to appreciate what it is to have a thought rather than to execute an action, otherwise these distinctions break down. If the distinctions do break down, then one is hallucinating rather than thinking. In hallucinating, a person thinks he is actually banging or sucking the object, not thinking about doing so.

So how does the infant escape from her unidimensional, sole-view apprehension of the world, to gain a vantage-point from which she can survey the scene from a number of perspectives?

Piaget thought that the infant does this all by herself.[6] Instead of experiencing a ball, say, as that-which-can-be-sucked-and-squeezed, she comes to conceive of the ball as having a separate existence by virtue of the fact that she can apply to it all kinds of actions. She can suck it, squeeze it, roll it, throw it and so on. Especially important here is the infant's discovery that actions are reversible – she can move the ball from this place to that and she can move it back again, just as a ball that is hidden can be found again – and so she becomes aware that the object's existence is not dependent on her acting upon it. Only when the infant has accorded permanence to things in the world so that they become distanced from her own immediate actions and reactions is she able to think about them.

But is this enough? Piaget brought in another consideration when he discussed the origins of symbolic thought. In a manner that many people have found bewildering, he suggested that the infant's capacity to show deferred imitation – that is, to imitate someone else when the person is no longer performing the act being imitated – is in some way critical for symbolizing. The problem is that Piaget was none too clear on what the role of deferred imitation might be.

In my view, Piaget was getting at something important, but he did not go far enough. By introducing imitation into his explanation, Piaget seems to have been trying to find a place for social factors in the genesis of thought, but there were two limitations to his theory that he could not transcend. The first was his preoccupation with action as the primary source of intelligent thought, to the relative neglect of feelings. Piaget has been quoted as saying, 'Freud chose emotions, I chose intelligence.' So, although he could characterize thinking as a kind of action-in-the-mind, and although he tried to import the deferred imitation of actions into his explanatory scheme, he was unable to find space for feelings. This was a serious omission. The second limitation was Piaget's preoccupation with the individual child's efforts to construct an understanding of the world, to the relative neglect of the part that might be played by the social construction of thought. He was unable to accept that the fabric of thinking may be woven as the warp and weft of transactions *between* people. The very means to thinking may be interpersonal relations.

Piaget understood that 'thinking about' requires the infant to achieve a certain kind of disengagement from her surroundings. She needs to coordinate perspectives around a topic, and this means she must have a kind of mental freedom to move from one take on reality to another. What Piaget failed to grasp is that this kind of mental disengagement comes about through specific forms of social experience. Following G. H. Mead in the field of sociology and Heinz Werner and Bernard Kaplan in developmental psychology,[7] I think it involves more than a disengagement of the child's self from her surroundings, and therefore of the child's thoughts from the things that those thoughts are about. It also involves a distancing of the child's self from other selves. Thinking becomes possible because the child separates out one person's perspective from another's.

More than this: thinking arises out of repeated experiences of *moving* from one psychological stance to another in relation to things and events. Critically important is the kind of mental movement involved. It is not enough that the baby shifts perspectives by herself. In order to grasp that she can move in her attitudes to the world, the movements need to happen *through someone else*. Especially significant are those occasions when a baby's attitude to something is changed because her reaction to the attitude of another person.

The mechanism by which all this occurs is the process of identification. As we have seen, normal infants are engaged with other people and with the actions and feelings that are expressed through people's bodies. Their subjective experiences are coordinated with those of their mothers or other caregivers. Then infants reach a stage in which they identify with the attitudes of others. To identify with someone is to assume the other person's stance or characteristics. Infants are now affected by another person's attitudes towards something, and at times towards themselves, in such a way that they assume the other's emotional stance towards the something, while still maintaining some awareness of their own starting state.

Although it might be stretching a point, this is not a million miles away from describing a special case of deferred imitation. To imitate someone after the person has ceased to act is also to assume something of the other's stance, at least in terms of action. For example, an infant watches her mother putting the telephone to her ear, and later that day the infant does the same. In a way, the infant is appropriating her mother's actions. The critical element in the kind of identifying I am describing is that it involves *feelings and attitudes*. This kind of identifying does more than change a person's actions – it changes the person's subjective experience of the world. The infant moves to occupy another stance in relation to the world. She is, as it were, lifted out of her own self-centred viewpoint. She comes to experience the world differently. From the outside, we might say that she takes another perspective.

However, to assume a perspective is not the same as understanding what it means to have a perspective. A cat has a perspective on the world, but that does not mean it knows it has one. What we need for our account is for the infant to grasp that she has moved to a new perspective. We need to explain how she becomes aware of herself and others as beings who have and who can adopt perspectives.[8]

It sounds baffling, but in order to do all this she first has to take a perspective on herself and her own attitudes. It is only by doing this, by taking a view on her own ways of construing the world, that she can begin to *think* in terms of her own and others' perspectives.

This happens through a particular species of identification: the child identifies with others' attitudes towards the child's own attitudes and actions. Once more, the child is lifted out of her own stance and is drawn into adopting another perspective – this time a perspective on herself and what she is feeling and doing. She becomes self-aware through others.

We are on the brink of seeing how communication leads to thought. We see that goings-on between people lead to new goings-on within the mind of the child. We have been thinking of this in terms of the infant's perspective-taking and have seen how it leads to the child becoming aware of herself and aware of what it means to have a perspective. Through others, she gains a vantage-point from which to relate to her own attitudes and actions. She has, as it were, taken the perspective of the other within her own mind. Now she can begin to sort out what it is to have one perspective among many.

All this means that the nature of her mind has radically changed. The change comes about through the child grasping something – or rather a number of things. First, that there are such things as perspectives, and perspectives are what people have. Second, that she herself is a person with a perspective. It is a perspective that may differ from someone else's. Third, that she can choose to adopt the perspective of someone else. She can even do this while retaining her own perspective. She can hold in mind not just one but two perspectives at once.

It is for this reason that she becomes able to adjust her actions to the perspective of someone else (recall how Michael comforted his friend, and how Marcy induced her sister to relinquish her toy). It is for this reason that she can adopt a perspective towards her own actions and attitudes (recall how children of under two years old apply standards to what they do). It is for this reason that, most wonderful

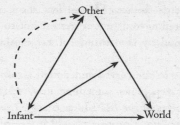

FIGURE 20

of all, she can choose to apply new perspectives to things. When she does this with the kind of non-serious intent of which she has been capable for months, she is engaging in symbolic play.

All this can be captured as a triangle of relations which works as follows. The infant is sitting there in the bottom left-hand corner, and the world is the object or event that she is engaged with. She might be looking at it, or acting upon it, or listening to it, or feeling things about it. It needs to be something that another person, labelled 'Other' in the triangle, can also perceive and engage with. In the triangle, the infant relates to three things: she relates to the world; she relates to the other, just as the other relates to herself (note the double-headed arrow between the infant and the other); and she relates to the other's relation to the world.

We can apply the triangle to the case of a twelve-month-old who is confronted with a disquieting object. A new toy suddenly pronounces, 'I am a robot!' The child is looking at the toy (the world), and now she feels both interested and afraid. She looks to her mother, who is standing nearby. The mother is looking at the robot with amused surprise. Noting her daughter's anxiety, she might also show faint pretend-anxiety. This would make it easier for the child to link in with her state, and at the same time to modify her own feelings. In the case we are considering, the infant perceives the mother's attitude to be directed towards the toy. The mother may look reassuringly at her baby, but by her alternating looks between her baby and the toy it is clear to any observer (including the baby) that she is giving her baby reassurance *about* the toy.

In this way the baby relates to her mother's way of relating to the toy – the arrow that bisects the triangle – and comes to modify her own feelings towards the toy. Her anxiety turns not to fear but to curiosity; her hesitation turns not to retreat but to timid exploration. She has been moved by the attitude of her mother to construe the world differently.

Now we come to the curved and dotted arrow on the outside of the triangle. This represents something new, which doesn't happen until the other aspects of the relatedness triangle have been in place for some time. It represents a process by which the infant is moved in a new way. The infant moves to the position of the other, in such a way that she assumes the attitude of the other *as* an attitude from outside herself. She can still make this attitude her own, just as she can imitate the actions of someone else and make them her own. The difference is that now she can maintain a sense of the separateness or distinctiveness of two alternative positions: her own and that of her mother.

There are two facets to the separateness between the attitudes of baby and mother. The first is that the attitudes of self and other are different. The baby feels anxiety, and the other feels amusement. The second is that the attitudes are held by people who occupy different spatial positions. The baby feels one thing from her position, and the other feels something else from hers. Yet there is something the two attitudes have in common: they are directed towards the very same object in the world. This is not only a fact, it is also a visible fact. The baby can see that it is so.

Before I follow the implications of all this, I should underline rather than skate over the most thorny problem: how does the infant suddenly become able to *think* that there are two perspectives here — one that is her own and one that belongs to the other? How does the infant leap over such a daunting developmental hurdle?

It is precisely this momentous leap that the relatedness triangle is supposed to explain. The triangle is meant to show that the leap may not be as momentous as it looks. For a start, the infant need not suddenly become aware. Awareness may dawn gradually. The infant has repeated experiences of the triangle. Each time, the process of identification exerts its pull *towards* the position of the other. And, each time, the child's experience of the world shifts as a result of the pull. It seems entirely plausible that these shifts are registered by the infant. What we need to explain is how the child comes to *know* that her movement into this position of the other amounts to her taking up a new perspective.

It is here that the notion of triangulation is critical. What triangulation gives is a fixed point, a kind of pivot, around which different things are brought together. The pivot is the world. The two attitudes bear upon the same thing in the world. A single thing is experienced as having two meanings. It is this that prompts the infant to separate out her own attitude from that of the other. It is not just that the mother reacts and the infant feels new things — it is also that the mother and the infant are reacting to the very same object. Through this experience of having both her own and her mother's attitudes to the same things, the infant learns something about things on the one hand and attitudes on the other. In reading her mother's reaction to a toy, the infant learns something about the toy; but at the same time, the toy tells her something about her mother. What it tells her is that her mother is different from herself, in a particular way. It tells her that her mother has an attitude to the toy that is separate from her own attitude to the same toy.

Events such as these are usually considered in terms of the infant finding out about the world through another person. Fair enough. But at the same time the child is learning about the nature of persons-with-minds through relating to a common world. Think how often and how repetitively a twelve-month-old shows things to people. Again and again the infant picks up something and waves it before her caregiver in a rather cavalier way. It is not really the toy that matters. The infant is intent on engaging and watching the caregiver. The object is a means to such engagement, and the infant is already exploring how a person may be engaged by something other than herself. She is discovering things about the human mind. People have their own attitudes to things. She discovers this by registering the fact in the context of relatedness triangles.

There is another kind of triangulation that maps on to the relatedness triangle, but in a special way. This is the triangle made up of the three-person relationship among infant, mother and father. Some psychoanalysts have considered that an infant's experiences within this three-way configuration of relationships are critical for the creation of mental space.[9] For example, the infant needs to have a position from which to view what goes on between others. She also needs a third party who introduces an extra dimension to the infant's relationship with her primary caregiver. Although I am unclear about the potential role of three-person relationships in the development of thinking, I think it is very likely that when an infant encounters serious problems in experiencing healthy links among herself, her mother and her father, impoverishment in thinking may result.

There is something else that the relatedness triangle is meant to explain. This is the origins of symbolizing. A child who symbolizes uses something to stand for something else. For example, she uses paper to stand for a doll's blanket. Or, to put this differently, she finds a blanket in the paper. As Werner and Kaplan pointed out, a child who symbolizes has to make a separation in her mind between what the symbol is really – in this case a piece of paper – and what the symbol is now taken to mean for the purposes of play. So, too, she has to achieve a mental separation between the meaning of something – in this case, the meaning of a doll's blanket – and the physical object used to carry that meaning. She has to transfer the meaning to something else, the symbol, without having to transfer an actual blanket.

All this involves a double dose of separating out attitudes. Just as treating like a blanket has to be separated out from relating to an actual blanket, so also the actual and real status of a piece of paper has to be set aside so that the paper can do its job of symbolizing something else. When this has been achieved, the child can transfer the meaning on to its new anchor, the symbol, and away we go.

The relatedness triangle shows how the separation of attitudes from objects of attitudes occurs through other people. Moreover, one can see that whatever serves as the symbol is itself a special kind of object in the world. It, too, is a target for attitudes. In the case of the symbol, however, the usual meaning of its attributes needs to be overridden so that it can come to mean something else (recall Warnock's point about detaching oneself from the brute facts of vision). Of course, this is much more straightforward when the symbol itself has little meaning to start with. It is much easier to make a boring piece of paper or a stick stand for something else than a meaningful thing such as a cup or a hat. This is indeed the case for early symbolizing, where a child of twenty months or so finds it possible to make relatively meaningless things stand for other things but is much less likely to make symbols out of things that have their own attention-grabbing meanings.

And, of course, the adults and older children around an eighteen-month-old have been introducing symbols into their play with the infant for some time. In communicating with the baby — not only in the realm of language, but also in the wider domain of gestural expression — caregivers have been adding and sometimes substituting symbols for more natural modes of communication. For her own part, the baby has been adopting these cultural expressions: 'Hi' and 'Bye', a shrug of the shoulders with raised eyebrows and outstretched hands to express 'Where's it gone?', 'Oh-oh' for accidents, words like 'Mama' and 'Dada', and so on. She has been learning to express meanings in signs. So, when she grasps the idea that attitudes can be transposed across situations and applied to new objects, and when she achieves the insight that the various symbols an adult uses are carrying meanings that reflect attitudes, all she needs to do is extend and amplify her use of these sounds (now words) and communicative gestures.

In a number of important respects, symbolizing in language is much more complicated and refined than symbolizing in play. Yet there are also important similarities. Foremost among these is the fact that words can stand for things. The sound 'hat' is merely a sound, and the squiggles h-a-t on a page are merely squiggles, until they are used to anchor meaning. When the word 'hat' does come to have meaning and thereby comes to carry with it the idea of hatness, it also becomes a vehicle of communication and thought. In standing for hatness or a particular hat, it acts as a symbol that can be spoken or written and understood by someone else. Or someone else can use it as a symbol, so that when we hear what the person says, or read what the person writes, we find that we come to entertain the very idea that the someone else has in mind. This is utterly remarkable as well as remarkably commonplace.

The arbitrariness of sounds is also a major advantage. Before it becomes a word, the sound 'hat' means nothing at all. It offers virgin territory for the attribution of meaning. Written squiggles on a page have similar properties. Not all words are arbitrary, of course. The most obvious examples are onomatopoeic words like 'splash' or 'quack-quack'. But language capitalizes on the fact that its symbols can be given whatever meanings we please, provided that such meanings become culturally fixed for the purposes of communication and thought.

For the very reason that a word is discrete and specific, it lends itself to being combined with other words, as in 'Please pass me my floppy hat.' This property might be loosely compared with a symbol in play, in so far as a block standing for a car can be pushed into a play-garage or crashed into a play-wall. We can see how a symbol anchors a thought, or acts as a vehicle of thought. As Samuel Johnson expressed it more elegantly, 'Language is the dress of thought.' Once a word acquires meaning, it keeps that meaning in place. It can be moved to a new place or brought into relations with other symbols. Its meaning is not cluttered up with all kinds of other bric-à-brac occupying the mind at the time the word is used.

> Language is a perpetual Orphic song,
> Which rules with Daedal harmony a throng
> Of thoughts and forms, which else senseless and shapeless were.

> Shelley, *Prometheus Unbound*, IV

Before we go on, recall that not all words stand for things in this way. As we have seen, language is also expressive. It is only in a special sense that an exclamation like 'Ouch, that hurts!' stands for anything. What it does is express something. There are other words that provide the glue to hold language together, rather than standing for anything. In addition there are the many delicate meanings that are captured and conveyed by the grammar of language, rather than by individual words. In all these respects language has its own special characteristics.

It is on two properties of words that I want to focus. I have already mentioned one of these, but I think it is worth repeating. This is that a word captures a particular way of experiencing what is being referred to. As Susanne Langer expressed it, a symbol is a vehicle for a conception of whatever is symbolized.[10] For example, if one happens to be thinking about a particular hat, one might think of it as a piece of material, as a fashionable article of clothing, as a grotesque monstrosity, or as something that weighs such-and-such. It is when one thinks of it as a hat, with all the specialness that goes with being a hat, that the word 'hat' comes into its own.

We can return to the idea of perspective here. A word anchors one among many potential ways of characterizing something. It embodies a particular perspective. The word 'hat' embodies the perspective of someone who is thinking of the kind of clothing one wears on one's head. If Martians do not have heads, or if they go around naked, they are unlikely to grasp the idea of what a hat is. This is a silly example, I know, but it may help us to see that to use a word is to operate within a web of meanings. The word and its meaning take their places against a background of much else that is experienced and understood. The word is used to crystallize a particular perspective on a particular something so that the meaning is lifted out from the background.

My second point is that in order to start using words for communication, the child has to grasp that the meaning for others is the same as the meaning for me. This is something that G. H. Mead emphasized: when an individual utters a word, she realizes that what the word means when she hears it from someone else is also what the someone else will understand when she herself uses it.[11] There is a kind of reversibility here, in that word-as-heard carries the same meaning as word-as-uttered. A child who understands symbols in language is a child who can understand that speaker and hearer can exchange roles. When a child is learning the meaning of a word (and the same applies to aspects of grammar), she has to apprehend or work out what perspective is being expressed by the speaker, so that she can use the word to express that perspective for herself.

This is a matter that concerns more than a given speaker and a given listener – it extends to the whole community of language-users. Words may be used correctly or incorrectly. If they are used correctly, then the meaning of the word for you, me or whomsoever else is the same. As the philosopher David Hamlyn has discussed, to learn language and to use words correctly, a child needs to receive correction as correction, and this depends upon her responsiveness to the attitudes of others.[12] The child must care about what she is told and shown.

If this were not the case, we would descend into the anarchy of life beyond the looking-glass:

> 'There's glory for you!'
>
> 'I don't know what you mean by "glory",' Alice said.
>
> Humpty Dumpty smiled contemptuously. 'Of course you don't – till I tell you. I meant "there's a nice knock-down argument for you!"'
>
> 'But "glory" doesn't mean "a nice knock-down argument",' Alice objected.
>
> 'When *I* use a word', Humpty Dumpty said in a rather scornful tone, 'it means just what I choose it to mean – neither more nor less.'
>
> 'The question is,' said Alice, 'whether you *can* make words mean different things.'
>
> Lewis Carroll, *Through the Looking-Glass*, Chapter VI

And, as the United Nations Secretary-General Dag Hammarskjöld insisted, our participation in a language that transcends the individual is what holds human culture in place:

> *Respect for the word* is the first commandment in the discipline by which a man can be educated to maturity – intellectual, emotional and moral ... To misuse the word ... undermines the bridges and poisons the wells. It causes Man to regress down the long path of his evolution.[13]

By now we can see how language takes up the possibilities that exist because of the eighteen-month-old's growing awareness of perspectives, and her experience of herself *as* a self who can switch roles with other people who are separate from herself. She can grasp how meanings are created by persons and therefore can be lifted out and anchored in symbols, whether in play or language. All this happens because of prelinguistic forms of interchange and communication between the child and the adults who care for her and speak to her. It is through interpersonal relations that are shaped by processes more primitive than language – in particular, through the child's propensity to identify with others – that language becomes possible.

Now that thinking is taking off through the medium of symbols, it has left the cradle which nurtured its growth. The means for thinking are in place. Language is going to preserve and amplify all that has been established during the first eighteen months of life. Yet it is important to appreciate how there are continuities in development from the time before language through to the early stages of language use – not least so that we can appreciate what language reveals about the interpersonal transactions that are its seedbed.

A good example of what language learning can show us is where we witness children acquiring new words simply by making sense of what other people are trying to do and what they are trying to communicate. In the settings Michael Tomasello and his colleagues have explored, one does not have to posit anything mysterious about how language is being learned: it is being learned on the basis of social understanding and social sensitivity.[14] Here are just three examples from a series of clever studies conducted with children between eighteen and twenty-four months old.

In a game of trying to find things, an adult said she was going to 'find the toma'. The word 'toma' was unfamiliar to the child (and to anyone else) and was being used for the first time. The adult proceeded to search in a row of buckets, all of which contained objects that were strange to the child. So any one of these objects might have been the toma. Sometimes the adult found it in the first bucket she searched, but sometimes she picked out objects, scowled at them, replaced them in the bucket, and continued with her search until she found what she wanted. At this point she stopped her search and smiled. Children learned the new word for the object the adult was seeking, regardless of how many objects were rejected during her search. They understood that the adult had used the word 'toma' for something she was looking for, and identified that object in accordance with tell-tale signs in her behaviour. The process of learning was bound up with appreciating what the adult was doing and intending and feeling, not just with witnessing an object labelled in isolation.

This interpretation of the study was bolstered by another version of the hiding game. This time the adult prompted the child to find four different objects in four different hiding places, one of which was a distinctive toy barn. Once the child had learned which objects went with which places, the adult said she was going to 'find the gazzer'. Then she went to the toy barn, but it turned out to be locked. She frowned at the barn and went to another hiding place, saying, 'Let's see what else we can find.' Next she took out an object with a smile. Later, children demonstrated that they had learned the word 'gazzer' for the object they knew the experimenter wanted to find in the barn. This was despite the fact that they had not seen the object after they had heard the new word, and even though the adult had frowned at the barn and smiled at the other object. Here we can see that the significance of a smile or a frown is interpreted according to what the person is intending to find. And it is in relation to those intentions that the adult's words are interpreted.

In a third study, an adult said that she was going to 'plunk Mickey Mouse' and then proceeded to perform one action seemingly by accident (spinning him clumsily, and saying 'Whoops!') and one action (tipping him off a slide) on purpose. Children learned the word for the action that was done on purpose and not the one that seemed to be accidental, regardless of which came first in the sequence. It was not that they associated the word with the action that came closest in time to the word being spoken. Rather, they interpreted what the adult had meant by the word in the context of what she was intending to do.

The take-home message is that important things in language can be learned and interpreted on the basis of a child's sensitivity to a person's non-linguistic behaviour and communication. Understanding language builds upon the child's understanding of how people relate to the world. Tomasello stresses the skill with which young children can read what an adult intends to *do*, as well as what the adult intends to communicate, and no doubt this is very important. As these studies illustrate, however, it is also true that children are sensitive to the attitudes of others, and these too provide an important part of the context within which language is learned. Words may be grounded in attitudes and feelings. One place where this becomes apparent is in verbal expressions of self-awareness.

❖

A problem with addressing the topic of self-awareness is that it is a complicated thing. There are different kinds of self-awareness. Any animal that finds its way about in the world must be sufficiently aware of its body and its own ways of picking up information about its surroundings to act effectively, and to avoid confusion between what changes in the environment and what appears to change because the animal is moving through the world or moving its eyes. Then one could list a host of ways an animal might be aware of itself – for instance, as the target of a predator or as dominant or submissive towards other members of its own species. It is obvious that the kinds of self-awareness one might grant to an insect will differ from those one would allow to a chimpanzee.

Our own concern is with a particular high-level form of self-awareness. It is the form of self-awareness to which the philosopher-psychologist William James drew attention when he distinguished between sciousness and consciousness.[15] The difference lies in the fact that we can say that any animal has some awareness of the world and therefore has sciousness. What we find in humans is something else that we call consciousness. Humans are aware that they are aware. They think of themselves as thinkers.

Once again, it is a matter not just of thinking, but also of feeling. We have seen that self-consciousness involves adopting a perspective on oneself through identifying with the attitudes of others. Given that others' attitudes can have different qualities, so can a child's attitudes to herself. For example, she may relate to herself with the kind of dis-approval we call guilt, as in Bühler's examples or the observations of Kagan; or she may adjust her own ways of relating to things and treating them in her mind, as when she chooses to make one thing represent another in play.

It is fascinating to witness a child's spontaneous expressions of self-awareness in language, not least because these illustrate how feelings are centre-stage. Personal pronouns such as 'I' and 'you', 'mine' and 'yours', and so on, are learned in personal exchanges that *involve* the child with the person speaking. At least implicitly, the child needs to understand the context of the relationship between a speaker and the person spoken to. 'I' am me to me – that seems simple enough; but 'I' when *you* say it refers to you, not to me. So how do I learn that 'I' refers *either* to you *or* to me? The same complexity attaches to the word 'you', of course. In order to understand 'I' and 'you', a child needs to have grasped how there are reciprocal roles in speech. It is the person who is speaking who anchors the meaning of the word 'I', and 'you' refers to the person being addressed, whoever the individual may be at any moment. Speakers and listeners can exchange roles, so there are shifts in whom 'I' and 'you' refer to. The critical thing to appreciate is that the person who utters the word 'I' is anchoring the meaning in *that* person's I-ness.

All this becomes a bit easier to grasp when we trace the details of how personal pronouns are first used by children, often towards the end of the second year. At first, these words refer to one person only – the child – but only so long as he or she occupies a particular place in the conversation. To begin with, one- and two-year-old children may comprehend 'your' when they are addressed, but this does not mean that they produce 'your' correctly to refer to others. So, too, their use of the word 'my' in the speaker role may begin with a more narrow meaning than usual. One study by Rosalind Charney reported that nearly all instances of the earliest uses of 'my' were produced while a child was acting on the object – searching for, grabbing, acting upon or claiming it ('My ball!', 'Gimme!'), usually when the object was *not* the child's – as opposed to indicating more permanent ownership, as in referring to a ball as 'my ball'.[16] 'I' and 'me' were used while searching for, requesting, affecting, claiming or noticing an object ('Iwanna'), but not while describing the child's own body or its movements. During this early period, children might employ their own *names* to refer to their body movements (e.g. Peter sit), their states (e.g. Peter sick), their possessions (e.g. Peter hat), and photographs of themselves, but they mainly reserved personal pronouns for settings in which they were participating agents, doing and sharing things. Only later were the pronouns used to single out self or others.

But how can children learn to use the word 'I' or 'mine', when it is only another person who is ever heard to use it about her own self? For example, the child witnesses someone else uttering an insistent 'Mine!' when grabbing an object. It must be that the child registers that the word expresses something of the other person's feelings ('I claim this belongs to *me!*'), and identifies with the feelings. In some sense she must know about the feelings from her own personal vantage-point and be able to recognize that at this moment they belong to the person who is expressing herself. Only in this way can she come to adopt for herself this same expression 'Mine!' when she herself has those same feelings at some future time. So children who learn these pronouns are aware not only of the distinction between self and other, but also that they have something in common with the other person. They understand that self and other can assume a similar orientation or action, and along with this the appropriate personal pronoun, on different occasions.

For some weeks my daughter Amy (now twenty-one months) has responded to the question 'Where's Amy?' by bringing her hand up against her chest. Yesterday her grandfather played a game with her in which he gestured to himself, saying 'I'm Grandpa', and then pointed to Amy and said, 'You are Amy.' He repeated this four times and then, gesturing as before, he asked, 'I'm Grandpa. Who are you?' The reply came back: 'I'm Amy.' Amy must have understood what he was communicating by identifying with his gesture and self-expression, and she adopted and then transformed his words to express the same thing for herself.

This brief foray into the domain of language learning will have to suffice to illustrate how it is grounded in role-taking and interpersonal understanding. Role-taking itself is not only a matter of appreciating different perspectives – perspectives that are exquisitely captured in language – but also a process of shifting between self and other as two sides of the same coin. From a complementary point of view, language reveals just how refined a child has become in adjusting to the mental orientations of other people. A twenty-month-old knows a great deal about the nature of people and their minds, a great deal about linguistic communication, and a great deal about the multifaceted meanings of reality as apprehended and interpreted by people.

We have now derived a view of what thinking is and where it comes from. Thinking of the kind we are interested in – creative, imaginative

thinking about things and ideas, but also logical thinking with concepts
– involves the use of symbols. Symbols anchor meanings. Meanings are
what *people* find in things or attribute to things.

It is through interpersonal relations that the infant is drawn into
adopting the meanings that another person ascribes to the world. She
moves towards the mental orientation of the other. And it is through
such unpremeditated engagement with others' ways of relating to the
world and through communication with other people that the child
discovers how meanings are detachable from objects and events and
then attachable to something new – symbols. One person may trans-
pose meanings and take a this to represent a that.

This account sounds (and is) too cut and dried. And too prosaic:
Emerson had a good point when he said that language is fossil poetry.
An infant who is beginning to apprehend symbolic meanings in another
person's sounds must be a bit like a spectator peering at Turner's
painting of the steam-boat in the storm. The meanings will eventually
become definite, but for now they are caught up in a maelstrom of
happenings. More specific meanings crystallize slowly, as figure and
ground separate. At the same time, the soapsuds and whitewash of
non-symbolic sounds and gestures are becoming transformed by the
attitude of the child/spectator into matter charged with symbolic
meaning. The infant becomes aware how symbols serve as a medium
for communication and thought.

Symbols play their part by anchoring meanings, so that meanings
can be kept separate from and combined with each other. They become
the coinage of thought. But they arise in the context of communication
between people. They come into existence, not privately and myster-
iously inside the head, but out there in the world through movements
in psychological stance that have their origins in the to and fro of
interpersonal relations.[17] The cradle of thought is one that swings back
and forth, giving the infant experiences of movement-through-others
about a shared and fixed world that has one meaning, then another.
Movements in feeling allow the infant to differentiate her own experiences and ways of construing the world from those of others. In so
doing, she recognizes the distinction between things and thoughts
about things.

Not all symbols are designed for precision or definiteness of meaning. They can also have openness of meaning, suggesting more than we can capture in the language of science. Yet still they render thinkable what would otherwise be lost to human contemplation.

> The poet's eye, in a fine frenzy rolling,
> Doth glance from heaven to earth, from earth to heaven;
> And as imagination bodies forth
> The forms of things unknown, the poet's pen
> Turns them to shapes, and gives to airy nothing
> A local habitation and a name.

Shakespeare, *A Midsummer Night's Dream*, V.i

Indeed, the meanings of symbols are rarely as discrete or particular as we suppose. They are suffused with the experiences that surrounded their acquisition. Few symbols are purely intellectual things, because they are anchored in a person's actions and feelings towards the world and the people in it. Indeed words would not be *about* anything at all if people were not connected with their surroundings emotionally. As the Russian developmental psychologist Lev Vygotsky wrote (probably less clumsily in his native tongue): 'every idea contains a transmuted affective attitude toward the bit of reality to which it refers'.[18] A word or an idea has a hidden glow of feeling.

> The firefly's flame
> Is something for which science has no name.
> I can think of nothing eerier
> Than flying around with an unidentified glow on
> a person's posterior.

Ogden Nash, 'The Firefly'

Perhaps now we can appreciate why computers cannot think – and why theories that treat thinking like the operations of a computer will never capture the essence of thought. Computers have something like symbols, in that they have items in 'memory' that can be said to stand for things and can be combined and recombined. The trouble is that their symbols do not glow. So the poor computers do not know what their symbols mean and only human beings can interpret them. And only human beings can apply them, so that they refer to anything. The fact is that one can use symbols only if one has the kind of emotional life that connects one with the world and with others. If only computers had feelings and the necessary kinds of interpersonal engagement...

We can also see a stark contrast between normally developing children and those with autism. Children with autism are human, not computers. Yet they, too, lack something that is essential to human development. This something is also essential for creative symbolic functioning. Children with autism get some way down the path to the goal of using symbols creatively, but they do not arrive. Through a cruel twist of nature, some of them have intellectual strengths in just the kinds of activity that typify computers. There are children with autism who can perform the most amazing calculations, but they cannot apply those mental processes to such simple everyday activities as working out how much change one should receive from a shopkeeper. Nor do their symbols transport them to a world of the imagination.

And there are other people for whom the development of thinking is compromised by interpersonal difficulties — as the next two chapters will show.

FIVE

The Fragile Growth of Mind

It would be reassuring to suppose that all is always well when it comes to the cradling of thought. Any mother or father wants to feel that they have done everything possible to foster the development of their infant's mind. But it would be foolish to imagine that one parent is just the same as another, or to convince oneself that the differences are merely matters of style. It is a painful fact that caregivers are not all the same when it comes to being sensitive and available to their young children. It is an even more painful fact that there are some things about parenting that come naturally to one caregiver, but not so naturally to another. So it is not just a matter of how motivated an adult may be to provide a baby with the right kind of intellectual stimulation or emotional support. Even with the best will in the world, a parent may struggle to engage with her infant in ways that are mutually rewarding and fulfilling.

In order to understand and perhaps help with difficulties in parenting a baby, we need to find out what creates and what militates against harmonious relationships. More specifically for the question of intellectual development, we want to know what facilitates and what hampers the chances that a baby will come to think flexibly and effectively. In order to discover these things, we cannot avoid making comparisons and contrasts between different parent–infant pairs.

I need to make it clear that I am not setting myself up as some kind of expert on early child-rearing. I am not even going to survey the different kinds of factor that influence child development. There is no doubt that there is an inherited component to intelligence, for example. There is also no doubt that children are disadvantaged if they are brought up in circumstances where few people talk to them or where there are limited opportunities to explore objects, play with toys, or look at picture books. Such things have a bearing on how soon or how successfully a child becomes able to think. It needs little more than common sense to tell us that they are important for early learning.

Much less widely recognized are the subtle ways in which the development of thinking is influenced by a caregiver's emotional relations with her infant. It is exclusively with this that I am going to deal. My aim is to retrace some of the ground we have already covered, from early caregiver–child interactions through to the emergence of thinking, only now with an eye to how disturbances in relating may lead to disturbances in thinking. Or, to look at it from a complementary perspective, I want to explore what troubled caregiver–infant relations reveal about the influence of personal relations on the emergence of thought.

Already we know that mothers and babies can be emotionally attuned to one another. The innate sociability of infants taps into the intuitive responsiveness of adults to forge a mental as well as physical linkage between infant and adult. This is a general feature of early social development. When now we concentrate on what distinguishes mother–infant pairs, we want to identify the qualities of mother–infant relations that make a difference to an infant's development. We also need details about the untoward effects when things do not go smoothly. It was uncomfortable enough when in an earlier chapter we witnessed the effects of experimental disruptions in the usual rhythm of mother–infant interaction. It will be even more uncomfortable if we find that something similar occurs in real-life relationships.

Yet it will be hardly surprising if some mother–infant pairs turn out to be more in tune than others. After all, there are many reasons why there could be a lack of fit between a caregiver and her baby. For example, a particular infant might have the kind of temperament that proves taxing for a particular mother. Some infants are floppy and hard to warm up, others seem supercharged and difficult to settle. One mother might find it difficult to manage a docile baby; another might be so stirred up by her energetic infant that she has to shut off. A mother might also have her own stresses to deal with – for instance, when distracted by her conflicts over managing life with a baby, or when troubled by psychiatric disorder. Just as one could make a long list of the ways in which infants affect adults — it often seems that babies get to emotional parts that other people cannot reach — so, too, the ways in which an adult may react to such delights and impingements are as various as humans are unique.

For the present purposes, I am going to oversimplify and stress a simple but important contrast between one mother–infant pair and another. It is a contrast that might also apply between a given mother–infant pair at one instant in time and that same pair only moments later.

Suppose an infant is in a particular state of mind and is needing an appropriate response from a caregiver. She might be excited and joyful, deeply upset, or screaming with rage. The contrast is between an adult who has the mental space to pick up and be sensitive to the infant's state, so that the infant feels responded-to and somehow encompassed within the adult's attentive care, and an adult who either cannot perceive or cannot take on board what the baby is feeling. Or the contrast is between an infant who can pick up and respond to the ministrations of her mother and one who seems inconsolable or unresponsive and for some reason unable to receive what is being offered.

In the former case, when things go well, the infant can feel her joy received and complemented, her upset soothed, her rage contained. Quite simply, the infant's connectedness with the caregiver enables her to experience and deal with feelings that might otherwise be unfulfilled or frankly overwhelming. In the latter case, where the adult is unresponsive or intrusive, or the infant is unable to register the adult's care, the infant's state is neither met nor managed. The situation is likely to spiral from bad to worse.

I have stressed the significance of intense feelings, but this is only part of the picture. There are also times of quietness and contemplation, or of pleasure and gentle affection, or of mild disquiet and restiveness. When the infant is in states like these, a caregiver may complement or disrupt her baby's feelings; or a mother who is in states like these may or may not find that her mood is reflected in the state of her infant.

Here is a short description of one mother with her two-month-old daughter, videotaped over just two minutes of face-to-face interaction.

A still from the videotape of this interaction has already appeared in Chapter 2, alongside a moment from the 'still-face' encounter.

The videotape began with the infant smiling in full face-to-face contact with her mother. The mother was returning the smile, and voiced a soft but emphatic 'Hel-lo'. The baby looked excited and made small movements of one arm and foot. The mother very briefly looked to the foot, touched it with another quiet but bright 'Hello', and immediately looked back to the baby's face – which was now creased up with delight. The baby murmured, as if contented and almost chuckling. The mother responded to this by saying a quiet 'Yes', and 'Are you talking? Are you talking?', followed by a pause in which she closely watched her baby's response. The baby was mouthing and moving her tongue during this period, and as she broke out into a smile the mother smiled too and said, 'Are you saying something?' The baby smiled more broadly and very briefly looked up above head of her mother, who at this moment tilted her head back and then re-established eye contact. The mother said, 'You're smiling ... you're smiling' with gentle but emphatic drops of her head towards her baby as she said 'smil-ing'.

What then happened was that the mother asked twice whether her baby could say something, and sure enough, in the second of the pauses she allowed, the baby made active tongue movements and a very clear two-syllable cooing sound. The mother responded by brightening her face and, with a rising tone to her voice, cooed back: 'Ooh. Are you talking too? What are you saying?' The baby seemed to light up, moving her tongue and making sweeping gestures of her hands and arms. Her mother responded with 'Yes, yes ... are you saying anything else?', and her baby vocalized, smiled, and gestured some more. When the baby opened her mouth, her mother widened her own mouth – an action that prompted the baby to open her mouth wider still. The exchange ended with the mother telling her baby how much Mummy loves her, and how beautiful she is.

It was a pleasure to observe these interactions. One needed to watch the videotape for only a few seconds to feel warmth and admiration for this mother and her baby. One also felt a deep respect for the qualities of human nature that gave life to the exchanges.

Now we can turn to another mother and her infant daughter,

videotaped under the same circumstances. In this instance, the mother has emotional difficulties of a kind we shall be considering in some depth later on.

At the start of the two-minute interaction, the baby was slumped back in the baby chair. Her mother was looking at her with a kindly face, half-smiling. The mother's first action was to lean forward, to try to adjust her baby's position so that her head was more upright. This did not really succeed in making them more comfortable together. As she was moving the baby, she said, 'Hello. Hello. Hello there', but this took the form of an insistent prompt for the baby to attend to her, rather than expressing intimate engagement. The baby was looking at her face seriously, while the mother herself smiled without pause. Almost immediately after the third 'Hello', and while her baby was still attending to her face, the mother looked down as if preoccupied with her own thoughts, and adjusted her dress.

The baby continued to look at her mother's face steadily and seriously. The mother's next move was to say, 'Have you got a tummy-full of wind?', and she repeated this. The baby began to make small movements of her mouth, and even vocalized fleetingly. The mother seemed to make a minor adjustment in response to this, as she inclined her head to one side. She had not interpreted the baby's actions as a communication, however, and she swiftly returned to saying, 'You look so full, don't you?' She then spent what seemed like a long period trying to elicit the baby's attention, for example by making clicking sounds and saying, 'Look at Mummy', even though the baby seemed to be doing so already. She continued to say 'Hello' brightly, though there was a forcefulness about this. Then she asked, 'What are you thinking of ... What are you thinking of now?' The baby responded by seeming to grow anxious, breathing more heavily, half turning away, and making indistinct sounds.

The interaction continued in this vein for the remainder of the brief session. There was an episode in which the mother correctly noted the seemingly uncomfortable posture of her baby. At this time the baby was making small grunts, looking at her mother's face. The mother said, 'What's wrong? Are you feeling uncomfortable?' but then 'talked over' her baby's continuing vocalizations with intrusive 'Chh-chh' sounds and further enquiries about her discomfort. These questions followed so quickly that there seemed no space for the baby's expressions to register. Mother pressed on with 'Are you feeling uncomfortable? Have you got wind? Bring it up', and it was only in this way that she could interpret the baby's looking, mouthing and vocalizing to her. At no point did the mother seem to mirror or take the lead from her baby's facial expressions or vocalizations.

Here was a mother trying her best to think about and engage with her infant, but this was only very partially successful. She maintained a monologue rather than a dialogue with her baby. She repeated her own thoughts about her infant's state in a rather insistent way, often cutting across what appeared to be the latter's attempts to vocalize and play some more active part in the interchange. What the mother actually said also seemed to reflect some of her own preoccupations, rather than elaborate her baby's current feelings and actions. It almost seemed as though she was talking 'at' her infant. She found it very difficult to pick up and respond to the baby's own expressions and seeming efforts to communicate.

It is not that the mother ignored her infant. It is not that she was uninterested in her or antagonistic towards her. Rather, she did not seem to be able to attune to her changes in emotional state and to follow her. She thought about the baby rather abstractly, and could not register how she actually *was* from moment to moment. If anything, she seemed to interpret and shape what happened in accordance with her own needs and feelings. She gave out more than she took in. There was little space in her mind within which the infant could move and develop.

It must be said that, compared with other babies, this little girl did seem rather flat. It is not possible to know how far this was already an effect of her social experience or something that shaped her mother's behaviour. On the basis of this one observation alone, we could not know whether she might be quite different at other times or in other situations. The only evidence we have is a short sequence of interaction between two individuals. The effect of watching these two minutes on videotape was to leave one strained and uneasy, with a kind of sympathy for both mother and baby. Nature seemed less bounteous than with the first mother and baby.

All these events took place in just two minutes of each infant's lifetime. The infants had had many, many periods of two minutes before the observations, and they have had many since.

We can pick up the story of these two mothers and their babies ten months later. On this occasion, we adopted Colwyn Trevarthen's technique of giving the mothers a plastic train set and two small human figures that could be slotted in the top of the two carriages.[1] The mother and her infant were seated across the corner of a table, and the mother was asked to spend two minutes teaching her infant how to play with the toys.

For the first mother–infant pair (pictured overleaf), the interaction began with the little girl seated in the high chair, sucking her thumb. Her mother engaged the baby's interest by drawing the train slowly away from her, giving her a glance as she did so, and then turning it back towards her. As she did this, the baby took her thumb out of her mouth and leaned forward. Her mother made a quiet comment to her, and allowed her to take hold of the front carriage and lift out a figure. 'Oh, yes,' she remarked encouragingly, and offered her the second figure, which she took in her other hand. Her mother adjusted the position of the train so that it was within easy reach, and held it there while the infant put the first figure on the train rather clumsily – at which point her mother delicately helped her to adjust it – and then positioned the second figure in the remaining carriage. The mother then leaned back and allowed her daughter to remove both figures. She again drew the train in a circle, returning it in front of the infant. This time, though, the infant had put her thumb in her mouth, so the mother took a figure and placed it in the train for her. When the infant took out a figure and laid it on the table, the mother placed both figures together, commenting that they were standing up, and drove the train around them. The little girl again took each figure and lifted them towards the train. The mother helped her by settling them in position. Once again, she drew back to give the infant space to make her next move. After a final round, the infant became a bit impatient and gently pushed the train away. The mother completed this movement by drawing the train in a circle, and making choof-choof sounds. This

FIGURE 21

captured the infant's attention, and when the mother shunted the train alongside her again the infant made a singing sound and carefully began to remove the figures.

Throughout, there seemed to be an almost rhythmical to and fro between mother and child. The mother linked in with her infant and gently coaxed her attention and actions towards the desired ends. She did not impose herself, but engaged her infant's interest and then enlisted her involvement to accomplish the task. She maintained an alert sensitivity to her child's state and orientation, and at the same time allowed her space to hold back or take the initiative.

With the second mother things were very different. The interchange began with the infant leaning across to take a carriage that was just within reach. The mother held on to the carriage so that the child could not take it, took up a figure herself, and said, 'Put the man in the train', while performing this action herself. The infant was not attending to what her mother was doing, and as she pulled the carriage towards herself the figure was left behind in her mother's hand. Mother repeated, 'Put the man in the train, put the man in the train', and once again inserted the figure in the carriage the child was holding, but without looking to check if she was attending. Then mother began to tug at the carriage, and the infant attempted to pull it in the other direction. The mother allowed the child to have her way, saying 'Choochoo' rather forcefully, and then quickly shifting her attention to the other carriage.

Although the first carriage was in her infant's hand, the mother devoted all her attention to the other carriage and said, 'Look – put the man in the train. Look', as she positioned the figure herself. This time the infant was watching, but her mother did not try to get her involved in what she was doing, and she ended by saying, 'Choo-choo. Look, man in the train.' The infant lifted up the carriage that her mother had been using, and the mother remarked, 'Oh, dear, it's gone out' as the figure fell out – but already her infant's attention had returned to her own carriage. The mother put a figure in this second carriage in the infant's hand, but the infant had turned away to the first and was shaking it.

There was a sense of impending chaos, as the mother leaned forward to control what was happening. Then she held back for a moment, and, as the infant began banging a carriage on the table, the mother said, 'Aargh!' She took hold of a figure again and held on to a carriage (with the infant already turned away, although holding on to it), and inserted the figure. The mother briefly removed the carriages, then allowed her infant to take hold of one – and this time the infant seemed to be exploring how the figure fitted into it. Despite this, the mother was now concentrating on the other carriage, saying, 'Look, look – choo, choo.' She then joined her carriage up to the infant's.

For a moment, the mother left her infant in charge of the train. The infant had managed to put her figure in her carriage, and for a brief instant she looked up to her mother, but they did not smile to each other. The infant moved her carriage so that the figure fell over; her mother tried to reach it, and the baby pulled the carriage away. Mother withdrew as if at a loss, whereupon the infant gave her a brief glance and for the first time looked round the room. When, in a rather desultory way, the mother tried again to join her baby in handling a figure, the infant seemed uninterested. Mother concluded by holding on to her child's arm, replacing a figure that she was holding in a carriage with a figure of her own, and more or less forcing the second figure into the train.

It was a relief for all concerned when the long two minutes came to an end. This mother found it very difficult to attune to her infant's current feelings and actions. Again and again she strove to impose her own focus of attention, or to intrude her own action, as the means to get her infant to behave in the way she wanted. She seemed always to be pulling the child towards her current activity, and often the child seemed to be pulling away. Even when the baby did things herself, her mother often supplanted what she had done with her own actions. So not only did she miss the opportunity to link in with her infant, but also she disrupted the infant's own efforts and interests and seemed to invade what space she might have had.

The question is whether a baby's experiences in the context of these close interpersonal interactions have an effect on the development of the child's thinking. If interpersonal relations are indeed the cradle of thought, then does it matter how the cradle is fashioned? What if the cradle seems to be designed more for the adult who provides it than for the infant? What if the cradle is not smooth and yielding, but hard or corrugated with sticking-out bits, or cratered with unsupportive gaps? In cases such as these, is the development of thinking compromised?

In order to answer these questions, we need to return to the story of early social development. Recall that an infant begins with a phase in which her engagement with her caregivers is more or less limited to face-to-face interactions, but that subsequently she relates to another person's relation to the world. She shares experiences of the things and events around her, showing and requesting things; she notes how others feel about the events taking place around her; she imitates others' actions on objects, finding new meanings in the objects that come to hand. If there are difficulties in the earliest phase of interpersonal relations, what effect might these difficulties have on subsequent interactions that connect the infant, her caregiver, and a world that they share?

We have seen already that there are certainly effects in the most extreme case: that of children with autism. In most cases of autism the difficulties arise because of innate impairments in the infants' ways of relating to others. Now we are interested in difficulties of a different kind. These occur when there is no reason to believe that the infant is handicapped, but where the quality of caregiver–infant relations affects the infant's development. Very little research has been conducted on the question, but recently I have joined with my colleagues Matthew Patrick, Lisa Crandell, Rosa García Pérez and Tony Lee in exploring the potentially revealing case of mothers who have serious problems in their interpersonal relationships.² These women have what psychiatrists call borderline personality disorder. The second of the two mothers I have just described falls into this category.

Women with borderline personality disorder have troubled intimate relationships and confused styles of thinking about their past and present relationships. To put it simply, conflicts rooted in childhood appear to crowd out their room to think. Emotional disturbance intrudes when they become deeply involved with other people. We decided to study mothers with this disorder because we wanted to see whether these difficulties had particular effects on their infants. Our reasoning was that, if one needs mental space in order to think, and if one needs freedom from turmoil in order to be sensitive and responsive to others, then individuals who lack mental space and who live with inner turmoil are at risk of having problematic relations with their infants. This in turn might compromise the infants' ability to manage their own feelings, and perhaps diminish their own space for thinking.

Our approach was to compare mothers with and without borderline personality disorder interacting with their two-month-old infants. We were particularly interested in how the infants responded to a still-face procedure. Having to deal with an unresponsive mother would challenge an infant's ability to manage an interpersonally stressful experience. Would infants as young as two months show any effects of having a troubled mother, for example in failing to maintain their emotional equilibrium when this was under threat?

Our findings are preliminary at this stage, but certainly suggestive. Our first discovery was that the women with borderline personality disorder were indeed less sensitive and more intrusive towards their infants than were the other mothers. Not only this, but there were also signs that this was affecting their infants, especially in their ability to recover from the stress of being confronted for ninety seconds with their still-faced mothers. Although most had started the interaction in a relatively happy state, by the post-still-face period the infants of the troubled mothers contrasted with the other infants in showing more dazed looks, and their engagement with their mothers was less satisfying and uneasy. They seemed to find it difficult to recover their equilibrium. Note that this was happening with infants who were receiving less than optimal emotional support from their mothers.

Already at two months, therefore, one could detect signs that these infants were less able to manage their emotions and re-establish harmonious contact after stress.

Then we followed up the mothers, with a specific issue in mind. In the background of our thinking were the abnormalities of children with autism, who may have relatively intact non-social abilities such as understanding the properties of objects, but impairments in sharing experiences with others and in relating to others' attitudes to the world. If the intersubjective impairments of autism have this specific effect in limiting a child's sharing things, pointing, gaze-following and the like, then perhaps other obstacles to achieving strong and satisfying interpersonal engagement between infant and caregiver might have similar though less drastic repercussions. We considered that the difficulties of mothers with borderline personality disorder could create just such obstacles. And, if this proved to be the case, there might be longer-term implications for their children's thinking.

Therefore we made a specific prediction. We predicted that the infants of borderline mothers would differ from other infants in showing less inclination or ability to share experiences with someone else, and less propensity to relate to another person in their interactions with the world. What made this a powerful prediction was the expectation that this group difference would be specific to interpersonal activities and not a feature of scores on tests of non-social understanding.

What we did was to compare the twelve-month-old infants of mothers with borderline personality disorder and a non-selected group of twelve-month-old infants on the set of prompts to interaction described in an earlier chapter.[3] To summarize, there was a set of non-social tests – pulling a string to get a key, pulling a towel and removing a cloth to find an object, finding a toy bunny hidden under a cup, exploring a box to find a marble – and a set of social tests – requesting the tester to blow bubbles, asking for a merry-go-round to be activated, following the tester's gaze, following the tester's pointing, passing a ball back and forth, reacting to a Chinese bell by looking at mother, and reacting to a remote-controlled car by checking mother's reaction.

The first thing to report is that as a group, the mothers with borderline personality disorder tended to be intrusive and insensitive towards their twelve-month-old infants, just as they had been with their two-month-olds. We have already seen the kinds of behaviour that justify such adjectives, in the account of the second mother described above. It was not that all the women in the borderline group were extremely intrusive or insensitive, nor were all the non-borderline mothers sensitive. What was striking was that none of the mothers with borderline personality disorder was very sensitive, and the majority were at least moderately insensitive; and none of them could desist from being somewhat intrusive some of the time. In other words, these mothers could manage to get only so far towards the sensitive and non-intrusive end of the spectrum.

Our second finding was that the infants of the two groups of mothers performed at very similar levels on the non-social tasks. This showed that we had not chanced upon less able infants in one or other group. Yet, when it came to the social tasks, infants of the mothers with borderline personality disorder tended to achieve relatively low scores. Although these infants were able to achieve success in non-social tasks that they could solve by themselves, in the social tasks they were less likely to refer to another person when needing things or noticing things, or when being encouraged to respond to another person's communicative gestures. At least in this situation of interacting with a relative stranger, they were less likely to engage with the other person's engagement with the world. On more detailed analysis of the results, we found that, even in the non-borderline group, the infants who most actively turned towards or responded to the stranger were those whose mothers were most sensitive and least intrusive.

These findings suggest that an infant's experiences in interaction with her mother affect her own propensity to link in with another person when either the infant or the other person is making reference to the things and events around them. Such behaviour appears to reflect how far the infant is inclined to coordinate her own experiences of objects and events with the experiences and actions of others. And this may also reflect the child's ability to learn through others.

Exceptional cases offer unusual insights into the development of thinking. This is developmental psychopathology in action. Our account has moved from studies of autism to research on borderline personality disorder. Another line of investigation has been followed by other researchers: the relations between depressed mothers and their babies. Importantly, this research has followed babies into their second year and beyond, and so has provided us with a bridge into the realm of thinking itself.

Lynne Murray and her colleagues found that, in face-to-face interactions with their two-month-old babies, depressed mothers contrasted with well mothers in being less well attuned to their infants.[4] They more rarely gave comments that seemed to acknowledge and support their infants' current experience, and they often made negative remarks. Not infrequently, depressed mothers were rated as hostile and intrusive, withdrawn, or showing negative feelings. As in the case when mothers have borderline personality disorder, even two-month-olds showed that they were affected by the interactions, at least in so far as infant distress and avoidance were common.

These qualities of mother–child relations appeared to have a significant impact on the early development of thinking. Murray has not focused on joint attention, requesting, and so on in the way that we have, but instead has tracked the children's abilities as they reached the ages of eighteen months and then five years. She found that maternal depression in the months after childbirth led to poor performance when eighteen-month-olds were required to search for hidden objects, and also resulted in boys (only) doing less well on a test of more general intelligence. Both at this stage and later at five years of age, what was most predictive of a child's intellectual skills was the mother's ability to focus on her two month-old's experience and to sustain the infant's attention in early mother–infant interactions. Murray speculates that sensitive parental responsiveness in the early months of life may directly influence brain growth and organization. She concludes, 'Thus the mother's success in sustaining the infant's attention and involvement in face-to-face interactions, repeated over a period of some months, may, by four to five months, have influenced the infant's capacity to attend and process information in the wider social and the nonsocial environment.'

A major problem in all this research is to disentangle the effects of mother–child interaction from the effects of circumstances that are often linked with depression and may also affect children's development. For example, it is difficult to determine how far the critical issue is the mother's depression itself, and how far associated factors such as low social class, marital discord, lack of a confiding relationship or other adverse circumstances are critical. Another thorough investigation by Dale Hay and her colleagues followed children of depressed mothers up to the age of four.[5] When tested on a standard IQ test that is suitable for children of this age, boys (but not girls) of mothers who had been depressed after childbirth performed less well than children of non-depressed mothers. The boys' performance was predicted by a number of factors that included the mother's IQ, the father's IQ, the mother's social class, the quality of the child's home environment, and the child's difficult behaviour during the test – and yet, when these factors were all taken into account, the mother's post-natal depression still had an effect in depressing the child's IQ. There do appear to be specific and lasting effects here.

It is impressive when one finds that something that appears to be important at one stage of development turns out to be important at another. This seems to be the case with a mother's ability to tune into the psychological orientation of her young child. In fact one can see the effects of this kind of sensitivity in several rather different areas of early child development.

A good example is the case of early language learning, where it makes a difference if a caregiver follows the child's lead when introducing words for things.[6] Children learn words more effectively if the caregiver homes in on what the child is attending to, and then speaks to that. In other words, if a parent can pick up what the child is involved with and attentive to, and amplify and embellish the child's experience – for example, by providing a word for an object that the child is examining, or by offering a comment on what the child is doing or seeing – then this is the best way to introduce language into the child's own intellectual repertoire. This description may not sound like an example of emotional sensitivity, but in a way it is. For, just as in the case of being attuned to an infant's state of mind, here again the issue is whether the adult can take the child's position and move to that, rather than ignoring the child's current experience or imposing a perspective of her own.

Here I am drifting from the 'abnormal' case to considerations that apply to all young children. And so it should be. Abnormality is often a matter of degree, and all along I have stressed that we are not restricting our interest to special cases. We are trying to learn more about the development of the mind in all human beings. Yet it might be thought that cases of autism or borderline personality disorder or depression are *so* exceptional that they tell us little about the situation where neither parent nor baby has a psychological impairment or a psychiatric condition. Therefore it is timely to turn to a study that is not about special groups of parents and children. This is a study of mother–infant pairs who were not selected for any exceptional characteristics, but who presented themselves as volunteers in response to advertisements in the local press.

The study was designed and conducted by my colleague Lisa Crandell and analysed and written up jointly with myself.[7] It involved the assessment of three-year-olds and their mothers. Three-year-olds are at an age when they can be given IQ tests, and the aim of the investigation was to see whether a child's measured IQ is affected by the qualities of the mother's thinking and relating.

The interpretation of IQ test results is controversial at any age, and this is so much more the case in children as young as three years old, where all kinds of factors such as inattentiveness and uncooperativeness may obscure abilities that become apparent at other times or in other settings. Yet still we can enquire whether young children's performance on IQ tests is affected by their experiences with caregivers. In the study I am about to describe, a standard IQ measure called the Stanford–Binet test was used to provide an objective measure of the ability of three-year-olds to accomplish such tasks as understanding words, using numbers, reproducing patterns, and remembering things.

Volunteer mothers of Crandell's filled out a questionnaire version of something called the Adult Attachment Interview. The mothers were asked to give descriptions of their important early relationships, and to give details of such events as separations and losses. The accounts could be used to divide adults into those who are able to think coherently about their own early relationships (who were said to be 'secure' in their attitudes, for reasons that will become apparent later) and those who find this difficult (who were called 'insecure').

The ones who find it difficult to think coherently either give very sparse and sometimes contradictory accounts of their childhoods – for example, everything was normal and there is not much to be said, and if father used to beat the child with a strap then that was simply the way things were done in those days – or provide lengthy and entangled accounts of what happened.

So there were two groups of mothers. One group was made up of twenty secure mothers who provided coherent accounts of their early relationships with their parents, even when these relationships were not especially happy. The other group was composed of sixteen insecure mothers who provided less realistic or balanced descriptions. The mothers were given an IQ test so that later one could assess whether their children's IQ was simply a reflection of their own intelligence.

Then there were two assessments of the children. The first assessment was that the children were given an IQ test. The second assessment was that, once the children had finished the test, they joined their mothers for a play session that was videotaped. The mother was asked to allow her child to lead the play for ten minutes, then she herself led the play for ten minutes, and finally there was a period in which she cooperated with her child in clearing up the toys. This meant that one could rate how well mother and child appeared to connect with each other, and how responsive they were to each other's communications and other cues. Each mother–infant pair ended up with what was called a 'synchrony score', a measure that captured how fluent and coordinated the interaction seemed to be.

Behind this study was the following line of reasoning (for which evidence will be presented later in the book). First, there is the idea that mothers who give incoherent responses to the questionnaire about their early relationships are those who have not been able to integrate their own childhood experiences in their minds. This is a controversial idea. Second, there is the hypothesis that mothers who have not been able to integrate these memories and feelings from the past tend to encounter problems in their current relationships. In close relationships they are likely to be troubled by emotional conflicts or feel things that they need to keep at bay. This is another claim that many people would dispute. Third, we are supposing that such emotional stresses influence their relations with their children and that this can be detected in the interactions between mother and child even in a brief play session. This, too, might be questioned – especially when one is taking only a single snapshot of what happens between a mother and her child: it is dangerous to assume that what one observes is typical of long-standing patterns of interaction. Finally, we expected that both the style of a mother's thinking about relationships and the pattern of her interactions with her child would influence that child's intellectual development. Needless to say, this is not an idea that would receive universal support. So, altogether, we have a chain of reasoning that is not only long, but also delicate. If *any* of the links in the chain were faulty, then our results would not turn out the way we expected.

As if this risk were not bad enough, we faced another problem. Suppose that we were correct in our ideas and that at least some of the results turned out the way we expected – how could we claim that the outcome was caused by the factors we had been emphasizing and not by something else? Suppose, for example, that the mothers who produced less coherent accounts of their childhoods and who were less fluent in their interactions with their children were those from a lower social class, or had had different educational backgrounds. These factors might account for any group differences, including differences in the children's IQ. In this case the story about emotional conflicts rooted in a mother's childhood would be irrelevant and perhaps downright misleading. In order to deal with this problem, Lisa Crandell evaluated the social class of the families and assessed the mothers' educational background. This meant that we could make appropriate allowances for such influences. Using a standard statistical method to sift out how much these factors contributed to the results, we could then see whether the things we were interested in still made a difference.

So to our predictions. The first prediction was that, even when a mother's social class and educational background and current IQ were taken into account, her ability to think coherently about her own childhood relationships would affect her child's IQ. The second prediction was that there would be at least suggestive evidence that the effects on the children's IQ might partly occur because the interactions between mother and baby were less synchronous in the cases of insecure mothers, in the sense of each party being less attuned and responsive to the other's cues. In other words, the prediction was that mothers who were not able to assimilate and deal with their own childhood memories would have greater difficulty in sustaining fluent and harmonious interactions with their children, and that this might influence the development of their children's thinking. Our third prediction looked at things from a different direction. We predicted that, if one separated out those children who had a much lower IQ than their mothers, then one would find that a higher than expected proportion of these mothers were insecure.

The findings were exactly as we had predicted. To begin with, even when the factors of each mother's social class and educational background and current IQ were taken into account, the children of mothers who were secure had IQ results that were 12 points higher than the children of mothers who were insecure. In fact, when we looked at the IQ values before the statistical adjustments were made, the results were that the children of secure mothers had an average IQ that was almost 118, and the children of the insecure mothers had an average IQ under 99 (where an IQ of 100 represents average intelligence). These are very substantial differences.

Second, the interactions were more synchronous in the case of secure than insecure mothers. It turned out that mothers who had an integrated and balanced way of thinking about their childhoods were indeed those who tended to have more fluent and sensitive ways of relating with their children. The evidence was also suggestive (but not decisive) that the degree of parent–child synchrony was related to the child's IQ. So gradually evidence was gathering to strengthen each of the links in our story.

Finally, what about our prediction about those cases where the children's IQ was much lower than the IQ of their mothers? Here what we did was to compare the six mother–child pairs in which the child's IQ was at least 10 points lower than that of the mother with the ten pairs in which the child's IQ was at least 10 points higher than the mother's. The results were that all six children in the first groups had mothers who were classified as insecure. By contrast, six of the ten children in the second group (where the child's IQ was at least 10 points higher than mother's IQ) were secure and only four were insecure.

We adopted one additional strategy to examine the results. This was to sift through the IQ results on the mothers without knowing which IQ went with each mother. This meant that we did not have information about the mother–child interactions and the child's IQ. All that appeared on the data sheets were two bits of information: the mother's IQ and whether the mother fell into the category of secure or insecure. We looked through the list to marry up secure and insecure mothers according to IQ, so that each secure mother was matched with an insecure mother of almost identical IQ. It was possible to do this for twelve pairs of secure and insecure mothers (with the remaining mothers having IQ scores that were either too high or too low to find matches). At this point, having established the two groups, we came to the critical moment of seeing what the children's IQ scores were like. The results were that in every single case, sometimes by a little and sometimes by a surprisingly large amount, the children of secure mothers achieved higher scores than the children of insecure mothers. The group difference was still significant when subsequently we took account of mother's social class and education.

The findings from this study reinforce the view that mother–infant relations can affect the developing child's thinking abilities. Let us go back to our ideas of why this might be the case. One reason we have been exploring is this: the quality of a mother's engagement with her child affects the child's ability or inclination to engage with other people's engagement with the world. There is so much that a young child acquires *through* others that there are real disadvantages for the infant or toddler who is unable or unwilling to engage with other people in their dealings with things. Through others, the child acquires new ways of seeing and acting on the world; through others, the child acquires mental space to take up this and then that attitude to objects and events; and through others, in due course, the child acquires the ability to use symbols, to transcend her own perspective and to think about things. It is through others that she gains a kind of outsider's viewpoint on herself, and becomes able to think and feel about herself.

These changes in an infant's relation to herself and her world depend upon something prior and more basic: the infant's engagement with another person, one on one. We are not simply talking about the infant interacting with someone else. An infant might interact with a person in the street, or with some other passing acquaintance, without this amounting to interpersonal engagement. We are not simply talking about smiling to someone else, or being shy of someone, or even requesting something of someone. In these cases, too, the interchange may be transient and have little lasting impact on either party. Truly interpersonal engagement is something more. It means that each person experiences a particular quality of emotional contact and exchange. It is almost as if each has a grip on the mind of the other. I could struggle to find better descriptions of what I mean, but I doubt that this is necessary. Most of us know what interpersonal engagement means, from our own personal experience. What has been overlooked until very recently (except among psychoanalysts), is what interpersonal engagement contributes to the development of the mind – and how disordered interpersonal relations affect the development of thinking.

There is a further implication to the story I have been telling. When an infant is engaged with someone else's mind, she is in a position to find out about minds. The child isn't just finding out about the world through the mind of the other, as she perceives the other acting on things and feeling about things; she is also finding out what it means for a person to have a mind. It should follow that a child who is not very much or not very deeply engaged with someone else's mind may be slow to come to understand how minds work. Is there evidence that this is the case?

Developmental psychologists have taken to calling a child's growing understanding of people's mental life a 'theory of mind'. In many ways this is a daft expression, because it suggests that a child theorizes about the nature of feelings, wishes, beliefs, intentions, and so on. This is not what happens at all. The child comes to know about such aspects of mental life, and the way the child comes to know is mostly very *unlike* theorizing. But never mind: the critical and interesting issue is just how this kind of knowledge is acquired over the early years of life. How does a child come to realize that a person is the kind of thing that has a mind? How does she come to understand that a mind is composed of thoughts, wishes, feelings and so on, and that thoughts, feelings and the like are very different to objects one can handle? The experiments that have charted the growth in a child's understanding of the mind are most revealing and important.

The study of the topic has a long history, but it gathered new momentum in the early 1980s with two experiments devised by Heinz Wimmer and Josef Perner.[8] These researchers tested three- and four-year-olds for their understanding of a person's beliefs. The significance of understanding beliefs is this. When a person acts in relation to the world, she acts on the basis of what she believes is the case, and not necessarily on the basis of what is actually the case. I look for my pen in my jacket pocket because I believe my pen is there, but this belief may be mistaken. I may have forgotten that I took it out to write a letter and left it on the bureau. So my actions are explained by my belief concerning the whereabouts of my pen, not by its whereabouts in reality.

Now suppose that you are trying to make sense of what I am doing. I am looking for my pen in my pocket, but you have just seen it on the bureau. Simple – you understand that I am acting on the basis of a mistaken belief about the location of my pen. In other words, you orientate to what I have in mind and realize that what I have in mind is a view of reality that is in error. So, to make sense of my actions, you need to understand what it is to have a belief – in this case a mistaken belief.

Wimmer and Perner tested young children's understanding of belief in the following ways. In the first experiment they used small dolls to represent a child and his mother, a cardboard stage to symbolize their living room, and three different-coloured boxes on the wall to act as cupboards. They enacted a story as follows:

Maxi is helping his mother to unpack the shopping bag. He puts the chocolate into the GREEN cupboard. Maxi remembers exactly where he put the chocolate so that he can come back later and get some. Then he leaves for the playground. In his absence his mother needs some chocolate. She takes the chocolate out of the GREEN cupboard and uses some of it for her cake. Then she puts it back not into the GREEN but into the BLUE cupboard. She leaves to get some eggs and Maxi returns from the playground, hungry.

The question for the children to answer was this: 'Where will Maxi look for the chocolate?' If they understand that Maxi has a mistaken belief about where the chocolate is, based on where he saw the chocolate, then they will say he will look in the green cupboard. If they fail to take into account that Maxi will go where he believes the chocolate to be, they are likely to say that Maxi will simply look where the chocolate really is. If they do respond like this, so the reasoning goes, they are not aware how the mind works according to beliefs.

Broadly speaking, the findings from this and similar tests have indicated that many four-year-olds but few three-year-olds answer correctly. Most children younger than four do not seem to grasp what it means to have, and act in accordance with, a belief; instead, they expect others to orientate to reality as they themselves see it. Their understanding of the mind is limited in this respect.

In another task, children were asked what they thought was in a tube of Smarties.[9] They were then shown that the tube contained a pencil. When three-year-olds were asked what someone else would think was in the tube, they said the person would think there was a pencil. And when asked what they themselves had thought was in the tube just moments before, again they responded that they had thought there was a pencil. In each case, they were unable to think in terms of a person's false beliefs — even their *own* false beliefs. Instead they spoke in terms of what was really in the tube. By contrast, four-year-olds could anticipate that others would have a false belief about the contents and also remember that they themselves were mistaken in thinking there would be Smarties.

There is another insight that children acquire at around the time they start to interpret behaviour in terms of a person's beliefs. They realize that an object can appear one way, but really be another.[10] A sponge may look like a rock, but really it is a sponge; a rod held in water may appear to be bent, but really it is straight. Appearance, or how the object may seem to you or me, is different from reality. Reality is how things really are, not merely how they appear.

Just as there has been heated controversy over the explanation for the emergence of symbolic play in the middle of the second year of life, so too there has been disagreement over what leads to the changes in the child's ability to think in terms of a person's beliefs. In particular, how important is social experience in leading to this new understanding at the end of the third year? One line of investigation has suggested that the ability emerges sooner in children who come from bigger families where siblings and parents argue and debate with each other. I do think social exchanges are critical here, and for a specific reason.

My bet is that the contrast between appearance and reality is critical. Earlier in development, the challenge was to grasp that one person's perspective may differ from another's. Now the conceptual hurdle is to understand that there is *one* perspective that transcends your perspective or my perspective or anyone else's perspective. This is the perspective we call reality. And reality is the perspective that any reasonable person would agree with, if they were in the right position to judge. That is why we spend so much time arguing and contesting what is the case, and why such discussions differ so markedly from disagreements over taste. In matters of taste, there is no reality to arbitrate. We can have different tastes, and that is the end of the debate. Not so about beliefs. If I am right and you are wrong about what is really true – that is, if I am right that you have a false belief about this or that – then, if I manage to get you to see things properly, you will come to agree with me. For example, if I get you to see that something is impossible, and therefore not even a candidate for being real, you will give up your belief. Unless you are the White Queen, of course:

'I can't believe *that!*' said Alice.

'Can't you?' the Queen said in a pitying tone. 'Try again: draw a long breath, and shut your eyes.'

Alice laughed. 'There's no use trying,' she said: 'one *can't* believe impossible things.'

'I daresay you haven't had much practice,' said the Queen. 'When I was your age, I always did it for half-an-hour a day. Why, sometimes I've believed as many as six impossible things before breakfast...'

Lewis Carroll, *Through the Looking-Glass*, Chapter V

If one learns what a belief is by coming to see that there is a gold standard for what is true (or possible), namely what everyone in their right mind would accept as being a correct statement about things, it seems to me entirely plausible that children are helped to acquire the concept of reality and of false beliefs through experience of agreement and disagreement with others.

This might lead us to wonder if children's understanding of mental things like beliefs depends on the quality of their relationships. As yet the evidence is only preliminary. Given that relationships may affect a child's general intellectual development, one has to be careful before concluding that differences in relationships have a *specific* effect on a child coming to understand the mind. Nevertheless, one suggestive study by Elizabeth Meins, Charles Fernyhough and colleagues reported that four-year-olds who had been securely attached in infancy performed better than insecure children of the same IQ on a version of the Wimmer and Perner Maxi task already described.[11] At the age of five they were also more able to judge whether or not a play figure would be able to use incomplete information to identify what was present in pictures.

The results suggested that the secure infants were more able to orientate to the 'mind' of Maxi and the toy figure in the tests. The investigators related this advantage to differences in the attitudes and behaviour of the children's mothers. In observations of mothers teaching their children to accomplish a difficult task, they found that mothers of secure children were more sensitive in adjusting their teaching to the abilities and needs of their children. And when asked 'Can you describe your child for me?', the mothers of secure children made a higher proportion of statements that referred to the child's own psychological characteristics such as imagination, interests, caring for others, and feelings.

We can draw the tentative conclusion that the security of attachment relationships influences a child's later ability to engage with another person on a mental level. Securely attached children seem better able to recognize and act upon the alternative perspectives of another person. This is a result of having the kind of mental space I referred to earlier, and it seems to be connected with a mother's ability to be sensitive towards her child's psychological attitudes.

The evidence, then, is growing. A child's ability to think about thought may depend on her caregivers' ways of relating to her. The child becomes able to relate to her own ways of relating to the world, and to understand and be sensitive to the mental lives of other people. Thinking is not merely an individual affair. At the same time, even when one does it by oneself, it is something one does knowing that one's thoughts belong to oneself. And this awareness of oneself and one's own mind, as well as other selves and other minds, is rooted in early relations with others.

In some ways the growth of mind is not so fragile as I imply. One is constantly amazed by the resilience of babies and how effectively they can find ways round potential disadvantage and get much of what they need from the people around them. But this is not always so. The quality of personal input a baby receives is very important, and it is only by recognizing this that we can take steps to help where help is needed. In addition, we shall only come to appreciate how the mind develops if we trace the factors that impede as well as foster that development.

At this stage of research the story is by no means complete. Take the example of borderline personality disorder in mothers. To date, we have only limited evidence that these mothers have troubled relations with their babies. True, the preliminary results from a systematic study suggested that a group of these mothers tended to be less sensitive and more intrusive towards their two-month-olds, and the infants seemed more affected by the stress of engaging with their still-faced mother. That evidence is not yet fully sifted, and the group of mothers studied was small. We also found that intrusive sensitivity in a mother can lead to her infant being less likely to follow points, make requests and the like at the end of the infant's first year. This does not yet establish that the young child's subsequent thinking will be affected. That bit of the puzzle is still missing. Despite the pointers, therefore, there is a long way to go before we can feel confident about the consequences of maternal disturbance of this kind.

Then there was the case of depression. If post-natal depression or associated insensitivity in a mother can influence the measured IQ of an eighteen-month-old or even a four-year-old, this does not mean that for ever the child will be behind in intellectual development. It is also important to recall that the depression was only one of many factors that seemed to be important for the development of early thinking.

Finally, we come to mothers without any psychiatric disorder. Here there was the striking evidence to suggest that an adult's inability to come to terms with her own early relationships might be reflected in her current behaviour towards her child, and that this could affect her three-year-old's performance on an IQ test. What this does not tell us is whether an affected child is merely less organized and successful in test situations, or whether she is more generally influenced in her thinking or behaviour. The effect of infant security on children's subsequent theory-of-mind reasoning also pointed to the potential impact of interpersonal relations on thinking about other people's minds. Still we need to determine whether this is a robust finding, and whether it is an index of the children's sensitivity in real-life situations.

Such caveats are important, but they must not detract from the potential significance of these recent studies. Insights into the interpersonal foundations of thinking can bring hope for the future. We need to know how thinking develops. This will help us to understand why it sometimes fails to develop, or develops in a more fragile condition than it might. At that point we can consider how best to identify cases where there is vulnerability, and offer support. In addition to this, understanding why thinking is sometimes slow or stunted in its development will help us to grasp why its growth is usually so impressive.

In all these respects, developmental psychopathology has much to show us. By focusing on instances where infant development may be compromised, whether because of difficulties in caregivers or infants or because of the broader social and physical environment, we can detect varieties of mother–infant interaction and relationship that illuminate the normal as well as the atypical case. We see things that would otherwise be obscured.

Is this also true when our focus is on adults? Might close study of the varieties of relationships and styles of thinking in adulthood – perhaps especially in adults with psychological disturbance at the very limits of what common sense deems normal – reward us with new insights into the functioning and development of the mind? Freud certainly thought so. In the next chapter we shall see if he was right.

SIX

The Inner and the Outer

There are adults who cannot think straight, those who cannot think flexibly, and others whose thinking is coloured by intense suspicion or frightful imaginings. It is often striking how such difficulties in thinking seem to mirror patterns in the individuals' personal relationships. Is this coincidence, or is there something more significant about this mapping of what is 'internal' on to what is externally lived out in relationships?

Although I shall address this question through the study of thinking in adults, I do so from a developmental perspective. With respect to 'normal' adults on the one hand and to those with depression or personality disorder on the other, we can set the workings of people's minds against the patterning of their relationships and see whether we are led to fresh ways of thinking about thinking itself. This approach is likely to influence our view of the development of thinking, perhaps especially by clarifying the influence of personal relations in shaping thought.

Although there are important insights to be gained from listening to people with psychiatric disorder, one is often tempted to sideline what troubled people say and how they say it.

> O the mind, mind has mountains; cliffs of fall
> Frightful, sheer, no-man-fathomed. Hold them cheap
> May who ne'er hung there. Nor does long our small
> Durance deal with that steep or deep . . .

Gerard Manley Hopkins, 'No worst, there is none . . .'

We may avoid disquiet if we hold cheap the heights and depths of the human mind. Even those whose job it is to study the mind are liable to banish signs of disturbance to works on abnormal psychology or suggest that, where we meet strange or morbid thoughts, this has more to do with problems of feeling than with those of thinking. As a result this territory is largely uncharted in psychology textbooks on thinking. Yet someone who thinks he is being victimized or disparaged does think this; if someone's thought is splintered by the force of emotional conflicts so that his thinking becomes confused or incoherent, it is his thinking that is deranged. So we may have to insist (even to ourselves) that, even when they seem disturbed or abnormal, the varieties of human thought may have something to show us about our more familiar modes of thinking. Disconcertingly, they may even suggest that what we think of as normal partly arises from the seeds of less rational mental processes.

Hopkins' poem conveys how we can face deep anxieties or conflicts for only so long. The mind has ways of evading such things. The defences we deploy to make our emotional life bearable may involve shutting things out of consciousness, and in so doing they narrow thinking. Moreover, human beings have one widespread but little known technique of maintaining equilibrium, which is to affect other people – often unpleasantly. We can alter how we feel by subjecting others to things that we ourselves find difficult to tolerate. This, too, can reconfigure our thinking.

The way to identify these processes is to examine them as they happen between one person and another. If we spend the present chapter analysing such interpersonal goings-on, this is not to be distracted from our mission of understanding thought. Not only are thinking and feeling integral to each other, but also disorders of thinking and disorders of feeling often go hand in hand. And each kind of disorder is somehow intrinsically social as well. The burning question is: how? The answer to that question may give us insight into the processes that shape human thinking, normal as well as abnormal.

The first approach to thinking-and-relationships I shall consider comes from a body of work known as attachment research. The attachments in question are those between one person and another, and especially the most basic and intimate relationships which have their prototype in the mother–infant or father–infant bond. Research into attachments

really took off at the end of the 1960s when Mary Ainsworth introduced a new procedure for assessing mother–infant relationships: the
Strange Situation.[1]

The Strange Situation involves a series of separations and reunions
in the strange setting of an unfamiliar testing room. The crux of the
assessment is how a baby of about twelve months reacts to her mother
when the mother returns after a brief separation. First, the mother
leaves her baby with a stranger for three minutes; on a second occasion,
the mother leaves the baby alone in an empty room, then the stranger
comes in and finally the mother herself returns. In each case the focus
is on how the infant reacts upon reuniting with her mother. What this
stressful procedure reveals is that the marked differences among mother–
infant pairs are relatively consistent in kind, so that it is possible to
classify attachments into three main categories: secure, avoidant and
ambivalent.

In secure attachment relationships, the mother's departure may or
may not cause the infant obvious distress. It is noticeable, however,
that even when she does not cry, the baby's play is often subdued and
she may look to the door where mother made her exit. She is clearly
affected by the separation. What matters most is that, when mother
returns, the infant who is less upset is likely to smile at her mother's
reappearance and may show her a toy or bounce up and down. She is
happy that mother is back. A more distressed infant goes directly to
her mother, actively seeking contact and clinging or moulding to her.
The storm soon passes as the infant settles smoothly in her mother's
arms, and she resumes her play.

Insecure attachment relationships look quite different. The avoidant infant may show very little reaction to separation from mother,
and will often go on playing, albeit rather superficially. She is upset
only when left quite alone in the second separation, and even then she
commonly settles when the stranger returns (whereas for the secure
infant, only the mother will do). Most importantly, her mother's return
prompts little more than a casual greeting. The infant may ignore her
mother or pointedly turn or move away from her. She does not even
respond if the mother makes a bid for contact. This pattern of
avoidance is even more marked in the second separation, so that, as the
stress of the separations increase, so does the avoidance. It *looks* as if

the infant is not distressed by what has happened, although there are tell-tale signs from her lack of exploration and from more subtle measures of arousal such as heart rate that she is more affected than she seems.

The second form of insecurity is where the infant shows marked ambivalence. Even before the separation, this kind of infant shows wariness to the stranger, and she is often inhibited in her exploration of the toys that are provided. She is very distressed by her mother's departure, but again the distinctive thing is how she responds when the mother returns. Like the secure infant, she seeks contact on reunion, but in this case she cannot find comfort. Instead of relaxing into her mother's arms, she stiffens her body and kicks or pushes her mother away. Even when she squirms to be put down, she cries to be picked up again. She both wants contact and resists it, or sometimes just cries in a passive way. She shows a mix of contradictory feelings, and is unable to return to her play.

These contrasting patterns of response to separations are not simply a reflection of babies' inborn temperamental characteristics. They are specific to relationships. For example, a given infant can show a secure pattern with one parent and an insecure pattern with the other. There is something particular to the relationship that has had a marked effect on the infant's own ways of relating to the parent and coping with distress. It is also very important to note that these patterns have long-term effects. Follow-up studies into middle childhood have shown that secure infants tend to become self-confident, resourceful and popular at school, avoidant infants often become children who are prone to aggression, and ambivalent infants are often clinging and attention-seeking. So a baby's early relationships do matter for subsequent relationships.

One way of describing what we observe in the Strange Situation is to say that there are marked differences between one infant and another in the way they *use another person* to regulate their own emotional states. The secure infant holds to mother and quickly settles; the avoidant infant stays at a distance; and the ambivalent infant is intensely involved with mother, but shows evidence of conflict. If we then consider the implications for later childhood, we find that the secure infant has become a child who seems able to turn to inner resources and to have a kind of mental space to think. Many insecure young children appear to be stuck in aggressive or attention-seeking patterns of relatedness, where they live out unsatisfying relationships and have less ability to reflect. So already we are seeing two things: a young child's relatedness to someone else appears to shape the child's relatedness to herself, and security in relationships seems to have a bearing on whether reflection and thought come to predominate over conflictual social interaction.

One of the important findings of attachment research is that the development of secure attachment relationships appears to be fostered by a mother's sensitivity towards her infant in the first year of life. This leads us to enquire why some mothers (or fathers) are more sensitive than others. Our obsession with thinking also leads us to ask whether something like sensitive or insensitive mothering is bound up with the mother's thinking processes.

Here I turn to a second and more recent empirical approach pioneered by attachment researchers: the Adult Attachment Interview.[2] In the mid-1980s an American developmental psychologist called Mary Main made contact with over forty parents (mainly mothers) who had been tested with their infants in the Strange Situation five years earlier. Then she did something rather clever. She interviewed the mothers about their early childhoods. Her aim was to see whether there was anything that distinguished mothers whose infants were secure from mothers whose infants had appeared insecure – either avoidant or ambivalent. She could now explore whether those earlier mother–infant relationships were in any way connected with the mothers' styles of thinking about their own childhoods.

What she discovered was that, yes, there were patterns of correspondence. The mothers with infants who had been rated as secure five years previously tended to be mothers who could think about their own early relationships in a balanced, integrated way. It was not that their childhoods had been especially rosy, although many had been relatively good. Whatever the mothers' early lives had been like, it seemed that they had come to terms with them. They could describe childhood in a manner that seemed free and coherent.

The mothers with infants who had been avoidant talked about

their pasts in a very different way, as if dismissing their childhood experiences. In their hesitant or terse responses, they themselves seemed avoidant towards the events of their own childhoods. They would be dismissive of what had happened, summing up their upbringing without vivid detail ('It was just what you would call normal') and sometimes giving a rather ideal picture that was out of keeping with unpleasant things which slipped out as they spoke. The picture that emerged seemed incomplete and sometimes incoherent.

A third (preoccupied or enmeshed) pattern was shown by mothers whose infants had been judged to be ambivalently attached. Here the mothers, rather like their own infants under the stress of separations, tended to show intense and often mixed feelings towards their parents and their childhoods. They got caught up with talking about their early relationships, often in a disorganized way. Sometimes this was so marked that they began to talk of the past as if it were the present, or they became muddled and lost the focus of what they were saying. They might also lurch from one viewpoint to a quite different one in the course of a single sentence.

There was one other distinguishing feature to some of the interviews. This occurred when the mothers were focused on the specific issue of trauma or loss in their childhoods. Some of the mothers became disorientated or in some way unbalanced when describing memories of such events. For example, they would cease to reason in a logical manner, or they would show unfounded fear or guilt, or they would start using the present tense for events that were in fact long past. This occurred in only some individuals, not all those who had experienced difficult circumstances. Such disorganization of thought betrayed that they were 'unresolved' with respect to the trauma or loss.

Estimates from a number of studies suggest that approximately 60 per cent of adults in Britain and the USA are rated as free to evaluate attachment, 25 per cent are dismissing and 15 per cent are enmeshed/preoccupied. The unresolved category is special in being considered alongside the others, and about 10 per cent of people would also meet the criteria for being unresolved with respect to trauma or loss.

Note that, so far, we have not been talking about what actually happened in these adults' early lives. We simply do not know what happened then. Nor are we focusing upon the good or bad things they reported from their childhoods. Rather, we are judging the manner in which they are talking about the early events. Do they keep to the point? Do they give an account that conveys a vivid picture? Is the story one that adds up, or does it seem inconsistent? This is what is meant by the coherence of their interview – the way in which the history is given. Without doubt these are qualities of thinking, albeit thinking about specific topics in response to a particular kind of interview.

Here, then, we have impressive evidence that mothers' styles of talking about their childhood relationships are related to the mothers' qualities of attachment with their infants. The startling conclusion is that an adult's ways of thinking about childhood are connected with her ways of relating to her infant. This was only implicit in the groundbreaking work of Main, but other studies have established it as a fact. We have already encountered one example of such research: mothers who produced coherent accounts of their childhoods on a questionnaire version of the Adult Attachment Interview were those with more synchronous and sensitive interactions with their three-year-old children. Another approach, pioneered by Peter Fonagy and Howard and Miriam Steele, was to give Adult Attachment Interviews to pregnant mothers, and then to evaluate their attachments when the babies had reached the age of twelve months.[3] What they found was that 75 per cent of the secure mothers had securely attached children, and 73 per cent of dismissing and enmeshed/preoccupied mothers had insecurely attached children. Especially striking was the much greater chance of an infant being avoidant (i.e. seemingly avoiding expressions of distress, and avoidant of contact with the mother) when the mother was herself dismissing in her attitudes to her past relationships.

These are remarkable findings. They make one wonder whether the qualities of a person's thinking about childhood might be important not only for parent–child interactions, but also for adult intimate relationships.

In order to address this question, I am going to turn to a study which my colleague Matthew Patrick, myself and other collaborators conducted with a particular group of adults who have a long history of stormy relationships.[4] These are individuals with what psychiatrists call 'borderline personality disorder'. We encountered mothers with this condition in a previous chapter. The people in question have a collection of emotional and interpersonal difficulties that take a certain shape. They have intense but often short-lasting relationships in which they are likely to feel that someone is ideal, but then suddenly change into being scornful and dismissive towards that same person. They are subject to intense swings of mood from depression to being over-optimistic, and they may have outbursts of anger, self-damaging behaviour such as wrist-cutting, and suicidal impulses. They may also suffer chronic feelings of emptiness and boredom. Some are very uncertain about their own identity, for example, whether they are homosexual or heterosexual, and others are prone to self-starving or binge eating. Frequently they are highly sensitive to any form of abandonment. So these are people with serious problems in their emotional and personal lives.

The issue that concerned us was whether adults with this psychiatric syndrome, largely defined according to the specific kinds of behaviour included in my list, might have particular ways of organizing their thoughts and feelings about their childhoods. If this were the case, then we would be a step nearer to seeing how a person's methods of dealing with emotional issues might determine the nature of that person's relationships – and how thinking is affected along the way. Our reasoning rested on the assumption that, when a person avoids talk of her past or gives an over-ideal account of her early life, she may be keeping difficult emotions at bay. Or when a person is confused and disorganized in what she says about her early relationships, this may reflect how she has been unable to manage and integrate emotional conflict or pain. Such undealt-with emotion, along with the defences used to keep feelings under control, may disrupt a person's ability to think.

What we did was to gather two groups of women of the same age (mostly in their late twenties and early thirties) such that the individuals in each group were similar in educational achievement, in the social class of their parents, and in their current occupational status. This was not really a typical sample, in that seven of the twelve women in each group had university degrees. The point in matching the groups was to make sure that the women were roughly similar in intelligence and cultural background. The women in one of the groups fitted the description of borderline personality disorder. The women in the other group had none of those clinical features, but instead suffered from chronic feelings of depression. People with borderline personality disorder also report feelings of depression, and we ascertained that the two groups were similar in the intensity of their depressive symptoms. This meant that, if the groups differed in their responses to an interview, this could not be because the women in one group were more depressed than those in the other.

All the women were interviewed with the Adult Attachment Interview. The interviews were transcribed and were sent away to be rated by someone who knew nothing at all about the aims of our study, or the kinds of women who were taking part. The rater simply received transcripts, and it was her task to allocate these into the various attachment categories. At this point all we could do was to wait with bated breath until the scored transcripts popped through the letter box.

When they did so, we were taken aback. All twelve of the twelve interviews from the group with borderline personality disorder showed that these women were enmeshed/preoccupied in their thinking about their early relationships. Only four of the interviews with depressed women had been classified in this way. In fact, ten of the twelve borderline women fell into a particular subcategory that did not occur at all in the depressed group, being confused, fearful and overwhelmed in relation to past experiences with significant figures. Therefore the women whose relationships were in turmoil, and who often showed very troubled relationships towards themselves (for example in cutting themselves or being self-destructive in other ways) were found to have *patterns of thinking* which were unusual and unlike the thinking of merely depressed patients. They were caught up in memories and feelings about their early relationships, and often overwhelmed by them. They could not see things straight or let things be. They seemed haunted by something they could not resolve. And even though their capacity for logical and intelligent thinking was intact in some areas — after all, the majority of the women we interviewed had university degrees — it seemed as if their minds became disjointed by unassimilated memories about relationships. When talking about early relationships, what they said was disorganized and sometimes frankly chaotic.

Here is an example of a woman with borderline personality disorder talking about her mother. She had used the word 'resentful' to describe her relationship with her, and when asked to elaborate on this with incidents or memories, she said:

> Well, I was just aware, I think, as a child the disparity between how she was with me and how she was with other people. Um ... she really disliked ... well, in relation to me she disliked my friends actually coming home. While my father said bring them in, my mother actually disliked that and she would rather I played with her, than with other children. I don't know if that was being withdrawn or what it was but ... (laughs).

When asked to which of her parents she was closest, she replied:

> Um, I felt closer to my mother, um, because she made me feel special, I think – that uh, that anything was possible and that I was going to do really well and uh, everything would be OK. Um, it was quite a nice feeling to have and it was quite different from my father's – the only thing that I got from my father which was like, you were going to be OK and things would ... there would always be blocks in my way and things would ... there would always be blocks in my way and one would always be infinitely disappointed by life ...

When another woman with the same diagnosis was asked to give an example of her description of her mother as 'overpowering', she explained:

> She used to make this food, they were horrible messes of food and like uh, scrambled egg and, uh, it was cold and she would make it for the dinner but my ... I remember sitting with this like plate of scrambled egg and I couldn't eat ... I wouldn't eat it, you know. I don't know if I ever ate it but this is an example of me doing things behind her back. There was a cupboard in the room and when my

mother gets fed up eventually, I think she went ... and I put the
scrambled egg in the room ... and the cupboard of the room, you
know, and my father would find all this scrambled egg in the room.

What these examples illustrate is that the women were able to
convey something important about their own experiences, but in the
process their trains of thought could become derailed. It was an effort
for the interviewer to keep up with the meaning of what they were
saying. There were oddities in the grammar of what they said, so that
one was left a little uncertain of what one had heard. The accounts did
not have the succinctness and focus that characterized descriptions
from mothers who were free to think and talk about the various
feelings and memories they had of their childhoods.

To return to the results of our study: there was an additional
finding that had to do with how the women dealt with trauma and
loss. This result was the more striking because the overall rates of
trauma and loss were not appreciably different in the two groups. Nine
out of the twelve borderline women and ten out of the twelve depressed
women reported such episodes. Of the ten depressed women, only two
were unresolved with respect to these difficult early experiences, and
the remaining eight were able to talk about them in a balanced way.
The findings were very different for the borderline group: here all nine
of the women who reported trauma or loss showed the signs of disturbed thinking that were a feature of the 'unresolved' interviews.

When we focused more specifically on early trauma, we found that
six borderline patients reported such experiences – ranging from
frightening beatings from parental figures to childhood sexual abuse.
Five patients from the depressed group reported horrifying events of
similar severity. However, all six of the borderline patients were
classified as unresolved with respect to these traumatic experiences,
while none of the five depressed women was classified in this way.
Once again, the depressed but not the borderline women seemed to
have come to terms with what had happened.

So here we have evidence for a strong relationship between an
inability to *think about* relationships and traumatic events from the past
and difficulties in sustaining reasonably stable and non-conflictual
relationships in the present. Although one might imagine that troubled

people have an inborn tendency to impulsiveness that affects their relationships and their capacity to think in a balanced way, there is no evidence to suggest that this is the case. There is also no reason why the difficulty in thinking should be especially severe when it comes to talking about relationships. To find a more satisfactory explanation of what is happening, we need to look elsewhere. One place to look is in psychoanalysis.

Psychoanalysis is a method for studying the mind, not simply an approach to treating people. One of Freud's important insights was that, if a person cannot recall emotionally laden events in a way that can be thought about, then the person has to repeat those events as a kind of substitute for remembering. Experiences that are too painful or conflict-ridden to be managed may be banished from consciousness, yet they continue to exert effects. The effects may be of various kinds, and often there seems to be a kind of compromise between expressing what has been buried and continuing to keep it concealed. Sometimes the memories find their way into troubling dreams, often in partly disguised form. Sometimes they find expression in neurotic symptoms. And sometimes they are lived out in patterns of relationship that seem self-defeating or strangely repetitive and driven in quality. In each case, 'thinking about' is replaced by some other form of mental and behavioural expression.

When I refer to events that cannot be managed, I do not mean single traumatic happenings, although these too may lead to trouble. More usually the background difficulties seem to be integral to the person's experience over time, and in particular the person's experiences in close relationships. For a number of reasons, not least the limitations in young children's ability to reflect on what is happening to them, early experiences may be especially formative in shaping patterns of relationship later in life. Recall those two-minute videotaped episodes described in the last chapter, and the powerful impact of the two mothers' interactions with their babies. Recall, too, the findings of attachment research, where sensitive and responsive mothers tend to have babies who are secure in their expectation of finding reassurance and comfort after the stress of separation. Mothers who have been relatively distant and unresponsive over the first year of life tend to have avoidant infants, and those who have been inconsistent in attending to their baby's distress often have unsettled ambivalent infants.

It may seem odd that, at the very moment I begin to consider psychoanalytic perspectives on mental development, I cite research that is not really psychoanalytic. I do so in order to show that a number of psychoanalytic ideas are far more plausible than many people suppose. First, infants of only twelve months already show distinctive ways of relating to their mothers and of dealing with their own feelings of distress or conflict. Second, these ways of relating correspond with what the babies have experienced with their mothers over the first year of their lives. So patterns of relationship are already becoming established.

Now back to Freud. Freud's theory of mental functioning changed substantially as his researches deepened. An especially important turning point came with the publication of a paper entitled 'Mourning and Melancholia' in 1917.[5] Freud exhorted psychiatrists to listen, really to listen, to patients who are severely depressed. He noted how such melancholic patients portray themselves to us as worthless, incapable of any achievement and morally despicable. They reproach themselves, and expect to be cast out and vilified. How can this have come to be?

One response to this question is to suppose that, because the patient's ideas are mad, that is the end of that from a psychological point of view. If there is no sense in what the patient says, then there is no point in trying to find it. Better to explain the clinical picture in terms of deranged thinking arising from malfunction in the nerve cells of the brain. Freud's response was different. He wrote, 'It would be equally fruitless from a scientific and a therapeutic point of view to contradict a patient who brings these accusations against his ego [his self]. He must surely be right in some way and be describing something that is as it seems to him to be . . .' But in what way is he right, and what might this tell us about the cause of his condition?

Freud concluded that, although one seems to be listening to a single, individual patient expressing his woes, in effect one is witnessing a relationship. An *internal* relationship. And an unpleasant relationship at that. There is one part of the patient who cruelly accuses and torments another part of the patient. The person we hear about is the downtrodden and beaten underdog, but if we listen carefully, we can hear how the patient has a sadistic relish in unleashing the fearsome attacks on himself. The patient is the perpetrator as well as the victim of the horrible onslaught.

Freud went further than this: he also suggested how this relationship becomes installed in the personality. It has been internalized from outside. The person with melancholia begins by hating someone in the world, often someone who is hated because he or she has abandoned the patient or has been lost through separation or death. The patient *identifies with* this lost-and-hated someone. He goes on attacking, but now he himself (or rather a part of him) is felt to be the figure who is hated, and as a result, the patient's hateful attacks become redirected towards himself. In this way an external relationship becomes an internal relationship. According to Freud, there is a developmental process at work.

I want to give a brief clinical example of the kind of thing that Freud was trying to explain. I shall describe the very beginning of an interview I conducted many years ago with an adult patient whom I have disguised for the present purposes. The patient, a middle-aged woman who had undergone several unsuccessful attempts at treatment with antidepressants, presented with chronic depression. She gave permission for the interview to be recorded, which is why I am able to provide brief verbatim excerpts. They allow us to follow how this person's thinking processes take a form that reflects her relationship to herself *and* that affects someone else with whom she engages. The patient's thinking has very specific effects on the therapist's own thinking and feeling. Remarkably, what is internal to the patient becomes external in the relationship with the therapist, and then, as a further part of this process, internal to the therapist himself. This is a powerful way in which feelings and thoughts are transferred – and, as this patient comes to suggest, a mechanism that may explain how a caregiver can profoundly affect a child's thinking about herself.

The patient (Mrs A) arrived on time for this first assessment interview. I greeted her with a handshake, and she began by recounting in a monotone how she didn't know why she got depressed, there didn't seem to be any reason for it, '. . . and if I'm feeling OK, when I do anything, I'm the type of person that always likes to have everything perfect. When I feel OK and I do what I have to in the office, no matter what it is ... well, when I try to tackle anything, if I do, I just feel that it is not the way I want it to be. Do you know what I mean, no?'

During this account, which was substantially longer than I have conveyed here, I found that my heart was sinking. I felt sympathy for Mrs A, but the way she spoke sounded almost like a soliloquy, addressed to no one in particular. She spoke with her eyes averted, so I was a bit startled when at the end of this initial statement about herself she suddenly looked up at me and then away again. In her words she seemed to be asking if I understood, but there was little to suggest she was interested in what I might have to say.

Struggling for words, I began, 'You convey...' But before I got any further, Mrs A interrupted: 'When, say I have got this filing to do, well, when I feel OK I will do it and, although I'm never really satisfied with it, I mean, it's the best I can do. And say my aunt came to see me, I would say to her I feel everything is a mess, and she would say to me I'm too fussy. Well, I am, I know myself that when I do something I do it better than most people, I'm more fussy than most people, but I never feel satisfied, and when I get depressed I won't even attempt to do it because I will never get it really in order. That's just the way I feel about everything really.'

At this point there was a pause. By now I felt hopeless and at a loss. I felt I wanted to say something to help, but didn't know what that something might be. I felt Mrs A herself was hopeless about the possibility of receiving help, and I wondered if she felt there was little point in trying to communicate with me. I said: 'And even trying to describe it to me you get quite worried that you will be able to get it across.'

Mrs A gave a sighing and distinctly unenthusiastic 'Yeah'.

Like a man losing his balance running down a hill and unable to stop, I added, 'And give enough reasons and give a description that is good enough.'

Mrs A's response was to ignore what I had said, and to continue as if I had not spoken: 'I suppose in a way I hate myself for being like this, but I can't control it. I don't know what else to say, really. It's just that, you know, no matter what I do I'm never satisfied.'

There was a long pause. There was little to suggest that Mrs A was expecting me to say anything, and I tried to gather my thoughts. My attempt to offer an understanding remark had fallen flat, to put it mildly. It seemed a clumsy and useless thing to have said. But then something struck me. Sure enough, what I had said did not ring true for Mrs A at the moment I said it. But it did ring true for what *I* was feeling. *I* was worried whether I would be able to get anything useful across, and I felt *I* would be unable to give enough reasons or give a description that was good enough. So someone in this relationship was feeling both anxious and intimidated by the pressure to come up with something worthwhile.

After one or two more stuttering exchanges in which Mrs A said she did not know what else to say, I remarked, 'What you convey is that there is something in you that requires nothing less than perfection'.

The point of this remark was to take up an issue that Mrs A had emphasized and that seemed important for her own self-criticism, but also something that was relevant to what was happening in relation to myself at that very moment. With a sigh, Mrs A resumed her monotone: 'I don't know, really. Since I was a child I used to ... even the likes of getting my things ready for school and that, although my grandmother did them for me I preferred to do it myself because I felt that nobody could do it the way I did it and I think, I don't know whether it started from (*pause*) when I was (*pause*) it used to be just ... when I was at school I remember that I used to just like everything to be perfect and no one could do it the way I did it. I preferred to do it myself: I think it's just escalated from there.'

I said, 'So there's something additional. It's not just that you can't do things well enough, but even before that, at school, there was a feeling that nobody else could do things well enough – that only you could approach perfection with your getting ready for school and other things.'

My comment was hardly the most arresting intervention. I was simply trying to distil what Mrs A had been saying. Mrs A's reaction was to sigh again, and to convey that what I had said was really not worth my breath. Yet at the same time, when *she* resumed her account – that is, when she was doing something rather than I was doing it – she seemed to express very similar ideas: 'Yeah, it was just ... It wasn't really at school, it was just ... I was just giving you an example of it – when I was getting something ready, or if I was going somewhere. Even when I was small I elected to do it myself because I thought no one could do it the way I did it.'

By now I realized that I had to be very careful not to take the lead in anything I said about Mrs A. Any suggestions or even insights that I might have would be dismissed rather than thought about. Therefore, when Mrs A returned to the idea that all this might have started when she was small, I steadfastly avoided following her lead, and instead questioned whether she herself really believed this. After considerable hesitation, she said in a convincing and moving way, 'Oh, I supp ... I think that it's ... Well, when I was small, my grandmother used ... No matter what I did, it was never right, she used to always ... Well, that's just it in a nutshell. No matter what I did it was never right, or never good enough or, I don't know ... Well, it's just that no matter what I did it was never right. I couldn't do anything right. I suppose it was because I was the oldest – she used to take things out on me. Maybe she didn't even mean ... She was just dissatisfied with her own life.'

Perhaps I should add that it is very unlikely that Mrs A had ever had previous contact with a psychotherapist or had read psychoanalytic literature. Anyway, this last description had the ring of truth about it, and I felt genuine sympathy for Mrs A's continuing struggles with herself and her relationships.

Although I do not know what actually happened in Mrs A's childhood, I believe that what she described was probably accurate. What I knew first-hand, and therefore with confidence, was the kind of unsatisfied and unsatisfying relationship she was liable to establish with someone else. I realized why previous physicians had become exasperated with their failed attempts to help. The relationship she was living out with me had the very same pattern as the relationship towards herself that she had described right at the start of the interview.

I hope this brief vignette conveys what it means for a person to have an internal relationship, and how this is translated into an external relationship. The relationship comes alive in relation to the analyst, here and now. The relationship evolves as the roles shift, but certain patterns of attitude and interchange persist between the patient and the analyst on the one hand, and between the patient and herself on the other. Mrs A also offered a theory about the mechanism by which her internal relationship became established in the first place. She suggested that it arose from an external relationship with someone important in her early life.

The vignette also serves to illustrate how a person's thinking may be shaped by patterns of relationship. Mrs A thought and felt that everything was a mess, but during the early part of the interview her thinking itself also was jumbled and repetitive (a feature I have edited out from my excerpt). This had a specific effect on my own thinking, in that I felt bewildered, I found myself thinking of prescribing the latest antidepressant to cut through the patient's tangle of complaints, and I had thoughts of being useless myself. In addition, of course, when I offered something her thoughts became critical and negative; when she offered something her thoughts were that she would never get it right. So both the form and the content of her thinking seemed to be bound up with the pattern of her past relationships, and at the same time to shape her current relationships. Yet, when I *did* find some mental space to think rather than to react, Mrs A too became more reflective and thoughtful. This shows how personal exchanges can enable as well as disable thought.

Unfortunately, there is a further lesson to be drawn from the vignette. This is that, even with insight and the remembering that goes with it, a person is not guaranteed freedom from the compulsion to repeat unhappy patterns of relationship. Mrs A was very impressed with what emerged in our meeting, and over the coming weeks she was much more positive and energetic than she had been hitherto. Within the next year, however, she had dropped out of psychotherapy and had presented herself to physicians with her usual complaints. But, before I get waylaid into a discussion of why change is so difficult, I want to pick up where we left off our previous discussion about the developmental relation between what is internal and what is external.

*

There is more than a passing resemblance between the theory of the developmental psychologist Lev Vygotsky and that of Freud. Vygotsky suggested that the more sophisticated forms of thought develop through the interiorization of interpersonal processes.[6] In simpler language, what begins as a happening between people becomes an intellectual process that takes place within an individual's mind. Freud pictured that something very similar may take place in the sphere of interpersonal relations, so that feelings, judgements and attitudes that happen between people become internal relations within a single individual's mind. They are qualities of relatedness that determine how the person feels about and towards herself, as well as qualities of relatedness that can be 'transferred' on to new figures who enter the person's life. Hence the pivotal importance of the transference in psychoanalysis. It is in the relationship with the analyst that a person's enduring patterns of intimate personal relations are transferred on to the analyst. It is here that internal relationships are relived, recognized and, if all goes well, modified.

What has happened in psychoanalytic practice and thinking since Freud is that much attention has been paid to the nature of a person's internal relationships. Through the analysis of very young children who express themselves in play, as well as through the analysis of disturbed and not so disturbed adult patients, Melanie Klein and those inspired by her have found that there are sometimes internal relationships of a black-and-white, malevolent or idealized kind.[7] Indeed, it is possible to distinguish between two principal stances that a person may occupy at any given moment. The most nightmarish pattern is where a person experiences others as persecutors, and where there is a background threat of annihilation; the more integrated pattern is one where other people are experienced as separate and valued individuals, and here the principal anxiety is not of being invaded or destroyed but of losing or harming someone who is loved. Although in most people these ways of relating to others are not conscious, they may nevertheless colour a person's experiences and shape his or her relationships. In addition, they may distort a person's ways of thinking about others.

This account provides a new vantage-point from which to examine how people come to differ from one another in their thinking about themselves and others. For example, if the emotional stances that Klein described originate in early childhood, as psychoanalytic investigations of young children's play seem to suggest, then we might wonder how they change over time and how they affect an individual's capacity to deal with feelings and to think about emotionally charged events. We might also begin to recognize features of disturbed thinking in 'normal' people, including ourselves. Before we come to consider such issues, however, we need some evidence that Klein's account does capture something important about human experience. What is the evidence that the two patterns of relatedness described by Klein, and which are after all unconscious, exist at all? Do they happen in all of us, even though we are not aware of them? And why is any of this relevant for the development of thinking?

One thing at a time. I have said that the nightmarish and more integrated patterns of relatedness were first discerned in young children and disturbed and not so disturbed adults. It is often in adults who have psychiatric conditions that they surface in more overt forms. So my colleague Matthew Patrick and I decided to study them in adults with borderline personality disorder.[8] Through our own clinical work we had become convinced that these are indeed pervasive and important forms of relating that amount to different states of mind. We came across them again and again in our analytic practice. At the same time, we acknowledged that people who had not shared our clinical experiences would find it difficult to accept this idea. We could also understand how some people feel that all this is imagined by psychoanalysts, rather than something that really goes on in people's minds. So, in order to pin down the ideas, we decided to conduct a scientific study.

For some years I had been asking NHS patients whether they would allow me to videotape my assessment interviews. These are interviews that last ninety minutes, during which I attempt to understand something of the difficulties the person is bringing, and assess whether psychotherapy will be helpful and whether it is really what the patient wants. By the time we had decided to embark on our study, I had collected seven videotapes of interviews with women who had the kinds of problems I listed earlier under the description of borderline personality disorder, and seven videotapes of interviews with women who had none of those problems but instead presented with chronic depression.

What we did was to edit out the first thirty minutes of these fourteen videotapes, so that the amount of material to be rated was not overwhelming. We mixed the edited tapes in a random order and presented them to trained psychotherapists who did not know the nature of the patients I was interviewing or the purpose of the study. Their task was to observe what happened between the patient and myself, and then evaluate how each patient described her relationships with others, and/or how she was experiencing me and the relationship between us. The judges had a list of thirty items to score, half of which were designed to capture the qualities of the more nightmarish and half the more benign patterns of relatedness. For example, there was a rating of whether the patient seemed to experience others as vengeful and retaliatory, operating by the law of an eye for an eye, a tooth for a tooth; another item concerned the patient's experience of herself and others as able to benefit from the capacities and contributions of other people; another item was about the expectation that relationships involve people who treat each other as things, without mutual concern; another rated the extent to which interpersonal exchanges seemed black or white, perhaps wonderful or awful; and another rated clear or subtle indications of hostility, abuse or victimization.

Here is a brief excerpt from an interview that illustrates someone whose description corresponds with the more nightmarish end of the spectrum. The interview began in a strained way, with the patient saying that she supposed she was expected to say things, but finding it very difficult to do so without being told exactly what to say. 'Can you tell me what to talk about, please. I don't know what you want to know.' She was intensely preoccupied by my assessment of her, and this made her so defensive that she was loath to expose herself by saying what she herself felt was important. Despite my attempts to address this difficulty, it seemed that only if I asked her specific questions or otherwise forced the issue was she going to talk about herself. She commented, 'I could do what I do sometimes, which is to go all hostile on you and just sit there and say there's nothing wrong with me and I'm not going to talk to you. I do that sometimes'.

She then reported that a doctor had said he didn't think there was anything wrong with her, but 'He sends me to mental hospital, and then I get defensive and get thrown out.' I tried to take up how she had said that she might go hostile on me, as she felt I was subjecting her to an unhelpful and even cruel interview and forcing her to talk. I said I thought she had been tempted to walk out (which she confirmed). I added that she also felt I might attempt to fob her off, and she replied, 'That's what people at home say: there's nothing wrong.' She told of a counsellor who had stopped seeing her abruptly: 'She didn't tell me. She just refuses to give me an appointment, she refuses to speak to me ... It makes me feel that nobody cares — nobody at all ... I get really scared, but at work they are really rude to you, they just brush you aside, and someone told me I should go and kill myself...' When I took up the hostility she felt, she said she got hostile when people offered her sympathy; but she could also say how angry she felt at the prospect of coming to see me and being left in silence. She went on to describe how she thought that everyone at work was talking about her. She added, 'I just react, and then think; and I don't think until I've reacted ... it's not healthy'.

In this brief vignette, we can see how attacked the patient feels, and how the people she encounters (including myself as a psychotherapist) seem untrustworthy, neglectful and often downright hostile or abusive. Clearly this affects both the content of her thoughts, which are preoccupied with the unpleasant ways she is treated, and also her ability to think at all. As she herself expressed it, 'I just react, and then think; and I don't think until I've reacted ... it's not healthy.'

Our study was intended to highlight rather than to downplay these qualities of thinking, and to see whether they were characteristic of people with the kinds of behavioural difficulty shown by adults with borderline personality disorder. The first result was that raters who separately judged the videotapes were in good agreement in their ratings. Such nightmarish forms of thinking and feeling and relating can be identified reliably by different people who make their judgements independently. The second result was that for any particular patient, the items that captured the more disturbed style of relating tended to be given similar scores, and so did items reflecting the more integrated style of relating. This indicated that there was indeed a *pattern* to the clinical picture that corresponded with what Klein and other analysts had proposed. The third result was that the patients with borderline personality disorder scored higher on the nightmarish items, and lower on the remaining items, than did the patients with depression.

Recall that borderline patients have a psychiatrically defined syndrome that includes self-harm and impulsive behaviour as well as turbulent relationships. There is no common-sense reason to think that individuals who fit this description should experience others as vengeful, lacking in concern, and so on. The conclusion from our study (and from psychoanalytic practice) is that, as a matter of fact, they do. For this group of troubled adults, what I have called the nightmarish pattern of relatedness seem to be more or less explicit in their relations with others.

Many psychoanalysts believe that most individuals are prone to experience these states from time to time, albeit not so floridly as described in the case of borderline personality disorder. Here one needs to appreciate that the different patterns of relatedness are not set or fixed in nature. An individual can move from one state to another. There are those who spend more time in one or the other state, but under conditions of stress almost anyone might enter the world of nightmare where everything seems untrustworthy and threatening. This very fact suggests that, instead of being the exclusive province of psychiatry, there might be something more basic about this way of experiencing people. Our nightmares seem to reveal a stratum of our minds where persecution, malevolence and betrayal hold sway. The atmosphere may be filled with threat or suffused with beauty; the forces at work are part human, part demonic, part angelic; the characters depicted range from the monstrous to the beatific. Then a world containing love, concern, loyalty and commitment may return. These contrasting emotional worlds are often evident in the play of young children, and it is no coincidence that they are also depicted in myths and fairy tales. The evil witch is pitted against the beautiful princess; the granny is eaten by the wolf. There is paradise and there is hell.

What all this suggests is the possibility that such states of mind are in some way basic to mental functioning. This is just what some psychoanalysts propose: the states of mind I have described take the forms that they do because they are rooted in experiences to which infants are prone. The mind is innately structured in such a way that the infant experiences other people or aspects of people as beings with emotional qualities.[9] It is very difficult to describe quite what that means because, however infants experience others, this will be much less coherent and definite than can be captured by our adult language.

What we need to remember is that infants do not have a grasp of a stable reality, and it is very likely that their experiences will be intensely affected by their own emotional states. To express it as best we can in words: when under the sway of powerful feelings, the infant reads her own unintegrated and primitive kinds of wishes, motives and intentions in the appearances and actions of others. When the infant is overwhelmed with hunger, for example, she feels gnawed at by something or someone (or more precisely, by an 'object' that has certain human-like qualities); when she feels angry and attacking, she can easily feel that the figures around her or within her mind are attacking her. These pre-human figures can assume fairy-tale forms and be felt to occupy a kind of internal world. It is a world that affects us at all stages of life.

> Such tricks hath strong imagination,
> That, if it would but apprehend some joy,
> It comprehends some bringer of that joy;
> Or in the night, imagining some fear,
> How easy is a bush suppos'd a bear!

Shakespeare, *A Midsummer Night's Dream*, V.i

One especially important element in all of this is that other people become implicated in the infant's fantasies. This is true for older children and adults as well, and the case of Mrs A illustrates how it happens. Mrs A involved me in her mental life by seeing me in a certain way, treating me in a certain way, even inducing me to respond to her in a certain way – and getting me to carry some difficult feelings that really belonged to her. Her internal world threatened to re-create itself in the exchanges between us. In the event, what transpired was affected by the way I dealt with the feelings she stirred up in me, and together we achieved some space to think. If we now imagine similar things to be happening between an infant and her caregiver, we can appreciate how the quality of care an infant receives may be critical in enabling her to manage and integrate intense and potentially over-whelming emotions. The infant's emotions are already in the interpersonal domain, because the infant is experiencing them *in relation to others*. If the caregiver can register and manage the feelings of distress or aggression or whatever – and these may be feelings that she experiences as *her* feelings, albeit induced by her baby – then the baby comes to assimilate and contain the feelings herself. If the infant has repeated experiences of being cared for and sensitively responded to, then her internal world softens and she comes to feel less threatened and more able to integrate her positive and negative feelings. One result of this is that she gains a much more secure and integrated sense of herself and others, and comes to feel concern for other individuals as people in their own right.

If the infant has more negative experiences, on the other hand, or suffers deprivation of the kinds of responsiveness and emotional containment that she needs, then the more persecuting and nightmarish forms of social experience may persist or worsen. An incapacity to weather mental storms arises in the interpersonal sphere as an attribute of infant and caregiver together, but becomes a characteristic of the individual infant and infant-grown-up.

Essentially, this yields the psychoanalytic explanation for the development of borderline personality disorder. Women with this pervasive pattern of difficulties in relationships (and most are female) are also individuals who have particular styles of dealing with emotional conflict within themselves. They relate to others in ways that are characteristic, and these very patterns of relating are mirrored in how they relate to themselves. In each domain there is mistrust and aggression, so that their stormy social lives have a counterpart in self-destructive behaviour such as self-cutting and addiction, in violent lurches from idealization to self-denigration, and so on.

The integration or unintegration of the internal world also has an impact on the ability to think. Thinking requires that a person tolerate the frustration of the moment, so that intemperate action can be supplanted by the sometimes painful and often ungratifying business of thinking about things rather than having them or doing them. If a person has not been helped with integrating strong feelings, then action may take the place of thinking. Moreover, when someone projects aspects of the self into someone else, the person is in danger of losing part of the capacity to think. It is as if some of the individual's own mental faculties are lost along with the feelings that are disowned. Again, these impediments to thinking often characterize women with borderline personality disorder, whose social entanglements and impulsive actions seem to have a counterpart in their incoherence of thought about emotionally charged relationships.

This is an instance of a more general rule, which is that a price has to be paid by anyone who (unconsciously) tries to defend against mental pain or conflict by projecting their feelings or otherwise blotting out memories or experiences. The price is often a restriction in the capacity to think, and a corresponding loss of insight into the sources of one's behaviour and one's misperceptions of others. I shall illustrate how this happens by a final clinical vignette, which I hope will crystallize much of what has gone before: how there is an internal world of relationships (here given detailed expression in a dream), how this becomes lived out in relation to others, and how a current relationship can (but may not) modify the patterning of what is experienced and what can be thought about. It is because what is internal becomes external, and what is external may be internalized, that relationships can promote the development of a capacity to think even in adulthood.

I shall describe a part of a session that was reported to me by a trainee psychotherapist.[10] The patient, Mr B, was a young man who had suffered a succession of bereavements within his family. The patient was nearing the end of a year's once-weekly individual psychotherapy. The session to be described was the last but one before the psychotherapy ended. The therapist had already recognized her own reluctance to stir up Mr B's feelings, so that her attempts to address what the ending meant for Mr B had been half-hearted. The therapist reported this particular session in a matter-of-fact way, as if the events she related were of no particular importance. The following are extracts from the therapist's account of the session:

As always, Mr B arrived on time saying that he was about the same as last week. He spent the first half of the session reassuring me repeatedly that he was all right ... He proceeded to list a number of changes that proved to himself that he was recovering ... He then described a terrible dream he had had about a friend a few nights previously: 'I dreamed that someone had cut his head off and the blood just squirted everywhere, and over everyone. Then I remember my partner and his partner putting his body in the back of a coach and covering it with a sheet. It was horrible.'

The topic changed to a difficulty with this friend, and Mr B said, 'I just try not to think too much about it.' He then talked with some regret about how his family was breaking up ... 'Since my relatives have died none of them seems to care – nobody keeps in touch. Everyone is leaving. I cannot understand why.'

Following this I [the therapist] referred to the fact that we had only one more session left and remarked that it must be difficult for him knowing that someone else was leaving. I was surprised that it had not been mentioned. He immediately reassured me that he did think about it but that he was sure it would be all right ... 'Well, I hope it will be all right ... I am sure it will be.'

This, then, was the therapist's report of what had happened. What was most striking was that Mr B had recounted his dream in a deadpan fashion, even though he had described it as terrible. Within the session, as within the supervision hour, the therapist seemed to be unmoved.

Time and again within his psychotherapy sessions, Mr B had indicated how deeply he was affected by separations. But, although both he and the therapist recognized this, they seemed to 'try not to think too much' about the feelings stirred by the forthcoming ending of psychotherapy. In these circumstances, the dream seems to provide a graphic picture of what was occuring in the session itself. For the dream represented something awful that had happened or was happening, and depicted how this event was being subject to a cover-up by two conspirators. If the dream was horrible, there was no sense of this in the session. The dream was severed from its felt meaning, just as the head had been severed from the body in the dream itself. Mr B appeared to be enlisting the therapist's help in carrying an emotional carcass — the remains of Mr B's emotional state after thoughts about the meaning of his dream had been cut away — on towards the final session and in covering over his true state of mind. Mr B and the therapist maintained a relative peace of mind, but only on the surface, by communicating and then banishing thoughts about the emotional implications of what was happening.

As with scientific experiments, so with accounts of psychotherapy sessions: one cannot allow oneself to be convinced by one or two examples, because there are always other equally plausible ways to construe and explain what is observed. All I can say is that, from my own experience of many other sessions with many other patients, it seems to me that the kinds of happening recorded here are typical. So often, the shape of events in the mind mirrors the shape of events that occur between patient and therapist in psychotherapy. And, again quite characteristically, a dream provides a picture of what is happening. What it displays is an internal relationship — one that for the purposes of the dream is clothed in the guise of particular individuals in a particular setting, but one that has much more general significance. It has significance for revealing what a patient is doing with and to her own mind, which in Mr B's case involved cutting off the means to think. It also has significance for what a patient is likely to be doing within his relationships, as in Mr B's attempts to involve the therapist in covering over what was too painful to bear.

It is a pity that in this example we do not see what happens when a therapist can identify and think about what a patient is recreating, rather than fitting in with the patient's habitual ways of involving others in propping up his defences. If the therapist had both registered what the patient was needing her to carry and been able to tolerate the discomfort and anxiety caused, then the situation might have been transformed. Both the patient and the therapist might have established an ability to think about what was happening and to manage together those feelings that seemed intolerable for the patient in isolation. As it transpired, the developmental potential to change not-thinking into thinking was only partly realized.

It is time to come full circle, and to relate the findings of attachment research to these insights from psychoanalysis. Studies of mother–

infant attachments have shown that babies are deeply affected by the emotional care they receive. The quality of such care is an important factor in determining an infant's strategies to manage both her own feelings and her relations with people. These strategies fit with the ways in which infants have been related to in the past, and they predict important aspects of social behaviour and self-esteem later in child-hood. More than this – they partly determine a person's ability to reflect on herself and to think.

In research with the Adult Attachment Interview, the way in which a person organizes her thoughts and feelings about childhood has been found to correspond with the way that person relates to others. These others may include the person's own baby. The mother's relations with her baby then have an impact on the baby's social and intellectual development. Our work with adult psychiatric disturbance in the form of borderline personality disorder shows that adults with this disorder have enmeshed styles of thinking and a failure to achieve balanced reflection about past trauma and loss. Again, this time in people with marked relationship difficulties, patterns of relating and patterns of thinking map on to one another. As we saw earlier in one of the videotaped mother–infant interactions, and as is beginning to emerge in our research on mothers with borderline personality disorder, a mother's intrusive and insensitive forms of relatedness do affect her infant's own style of managing feelings.

It is worth spending just a little more time on what the different categories of response to the Adult Attachment Interview really mean. The person who is free to evaluate attachments is able to assimilate and *think about* her own past experiences in relationships, even when these have been unsatisfactory. She has mental space to relate to her own relations with others. She can reflect on her own feelings and impulses and can forgive and tolerate her own shortcomings. So, too, she has space to relate to her own baby as an independent and separate person and to be sensitive to her baby's states of mind in such a way that the baby is likely to become securely attached.

The person who is dismissing towards attachment-related experi-ences, the stiff-upper-lip type of individual, seems to have a constrained and in some ways impoverished relation to her own past. Much emotion seems to have been repressed or dealt with in other ways that make it unavailable for thought. A dismissing mother is often restricted in her sensitivity towards her infant, often finding it difficult to be emotionally flexible and responsive. Her infant is likely to respond by becoming avoidant and in some ways tightly controlled in turn.

The person who is enmeshed appears to have been unable to accomplish a full separation from her early caregivers. Once again, but for different reasons, she has little room for emotional flexibility. In her case the lack of space to think seems to result from overwhelming and highly ambivalent feelings crowding in and taking charge of thought. The enmeshed mother is likely to have an ambivalent baby, tangled up and conflicted with her mother.

I recapitulate this condensed account in order to bring home just how intimately attachment research accords with psychoanalytic research in drawing together patterns of *thinking and feeling* and patterns of *relating to others*. Where attachment researchers highlight an individual's styles of 'mental representation', such as having dismissing or enmeshed attitudes towards emotional issues in relationships, psychoanalysts give parallel descriptions in terms of an individual's defence mechanisms like repression or projection of unpleasant conflicts and feelings. Where attachment researchers think in terms of maternal sensitivity or warmth towards a baby, psychoanalysts speak of a mother's ability to contain her infant's feelings. In each case there is the movement from the individual to the interpersonal, and from the interpersonal to the individual. There is a constant interplay in development between what social interactions and relationships create in the individual and what the individual creates in his or her social relationships.

The strength and the limitation of attachment theory is its focus on what can be observed in behaviour or in discourse; the strength and limitation of psychoanalysis is its focus on intersubjective experience. We can see how the two perspectives are complementary in understanding the different types of response to the Adult Attachment Interview. The person who is free to evaluate her past is also someone who makes it easy for the interviewer to have a coherent emotional response to her account; the terse responses of the person who is dismissing is likely to induce frustration or disaffection in the interviewer, who may struggle to get more feelings from the story; the enmeshed/preoccupied person is likely to stir up very mixed emotions

in the interviewer — not only confusion, but also dismay and disturbance. Even here, what is inner and what is outer, what is a pattern of
thinking and what is a pattern of relating, even what is past and what
is present, reflect one another.

The same thing can be seen in the research that my colleagues and
I have been conducting on borderline personality disorder. The
outcomes of our two studies on the very same kind of patient were
both different and related. There is no reason why women with
borderline personality disorder should not be enmeshed in their
attitudes towards attachment-related experiences (as shown by our first
study) *and* prone to experience other people as persecuting, untrustworthy, and so on (as shown by our second). In fact, this is just what
they are. The descriptions of these patients' thinking about significant
other people were very different but complementary in the two studies.
The first study highlighted the incoherence of the patients' thinking
and how they seemed confused and overwhelmed by their early
attachment relationships; the second showed how they are prone to
think of others as insensitive, malevolent, and so on. When one views
thinking and relationships in developmental perspective, it becomes
possible to see why these aspects of mental functioning are so closely
intertwined.

Clinical work has also given us a sharper picture of one of the
most important mechanisms that link the inner and outer worlds of
the mind, and that bind the individual and the social: identification.
An individual's own mental processes, both emotional and intellectual,
are imbued with the qualities of feeling and thought which the
individual has experienced and witnessed in others. The process of
identification means that what starts outside as a feature of another
person moves inside the mind as a quality of the individual's own
mental functioning. For good or ill, one's experiences of relations with
others become a feature of one's relations with oneself. At the same
time, a related process is at work whereby projected feelings lead other
people to carry and become identified with parts of the self. Not only
does outer become inner, but also inner becomes outer.

Attachment research and psychoanalysis are demonstrating what
many people have long wanted to deny: that people have internal
relationships that affect thinking. Moreover, these relationships are

rooted in the early months and years of a person's life. What happens between an infant and her caregivers is vitally important. It is important not only for the way the infant will come to relate to herself and to other people, but also for her developing capacity to think.

SEVEN

Fettered Minds

The theme that has thread its way through every chapter of this book is that thought emerges not merely in the context of, but rather *through*, personal relations. From the Blake frontispiece of a mother monitoring her infant's focus of attention through to discussion of interpersonal sources of incoherent thinking in adults, we have traced a variety of means by which interactions between people promote or distort thinking processes. It is time to consider the most extreme cases, where a profound lack of social engagement fetters the development of creative flights of thought. It is here that we find stark indication of just how vital human contact is for the growth of the imagination.

The point of reference is early childhood autism. When we try to understand autism, we do so against the backdrop of what we take to be normal human mental life. We find that, in order to identify what is missing or what has gone wrong in the exceptional case, we need to characterize the processes that make human mentality possible. What makes this undertaking so challenging is that autism forces us to think more deeply about what human perception, or human relations, or human intelligence, or human language, or human creativity, actually are.

When someone asks me what causes autism, the person posing the question is usually looking for an answer that decides between one of two options. Either autism is caused by something wrong in the brain, perhaps the result of genetic factors, or else it is caused by bad parenting. Often one senses that the questioner has a strong investment in one of the two options, and a strong antagonism to the other. In my response to the question, I begin by stressing that I do not think autism is caused by bad parenting. I also say that, yes, genetic influences are often a factor, and in the vast majority of cases the children's brains are not working properly. And then I begin to suggest that, unfortunately, these statements do not really address the question adequately. I might even offer the idea that the clinical features develop because of a disruption in the system of child-in-relation-to-others. At this point, almost invariably, my questioner's face goes blank.

What I would like to explain, but often do not, is that my experience of autism has convinced me that such a system not only exists, but also takes charge of the intellectual growth of the infant. Central to mental development is a psychological system that is greater and more powerful than the sum of its parts. The parts are the caregiver and her infant; the system is what happens when they act and feel in concert. The combined operation of infant-in-relation-to-caregiver is a motive force in development, and it achieves wonderful things. When it does not exist, and the motive force is lacking, the whole of mental development is terribly compromised. At the extreme, autism results.

This is a way of restating what I proposed earlier in the book, about there being a common pathway to autism. There may be different things 'in the child' and different things 'in the environment' that sufficiently disrupt interpersonally coordinated feelings to cause autism. It is time to flesh out what I mean by this suggestion. A question about the causes of autism is relevant not because it prompts us to review the medical conditions that can underlie autism (a matter I am deliberately leaving to books on child psychiatry), but because it leads us to examine what kinds of psychological deficit might derail a child's mental development in this strange and serious way. If we are interested in uncovering the foundations of interpersonal relations and creative, flexible symbolic thinking, autism is a good place to start – precisely because it is in autism that we find a unique combination of abnormalities in these two domains of mental functioning. Autism promises to disclose the conditions that make symbolic thinking possible for those of us who are not autistic.

For the present purposes, I am going to begin with the issue of thinking. Is there something to be learned from the profile of abilities and disabilities in autism – for example, as revealed by IQ tests and in language? I want to see whether the findings from tests of thinking draw us to the other side of the equation, the interpersonal deficits in autism. Are the patterns of thinking and the patterns of relating mirror images of one another? If they are, might there be other circumstances in which these two kinds of abnormality are associated?

Children with autism show a specific pattern to their intellectual strengths and weaknesses. It is not that they are delayed or impaired in all the tasks and all the everyday challenges that require intelligence, only in some of them. In my view, autism presents a kind of negative image of what social experiences contribute to intellectual life. What the person with autism lacks in the capacity for thinking, is what interpersonal relations provide for the rest of us.

There is one complication to this claim. I really mean that what is *characteristic* of thinking in people with autism is linked with their social disability. Autism is often associated with general mental retardation, which probably arises on the basis of whatever brain disorder usually gives rise to the autism itself. In these cases, the part of the individual's mental handicap attributable to brain disorder is like the impairment of other mentally retarded people, and neither more nor less tied up with social disability. We have to look to what is specifically impaired in people with autism, what makes them unique compared with individuals of similar general intelligence, if we are to target the kinds of thinking that are affected by their lack of social experience. And once again I need to stress that this lack of social experience might itself be caused by brain disorder.

There are two ways to illustrate the special qualities of thinking in individuals with autism. One way is to give case histories, and the other is to report the results from formal testing. I have already given some examples of the impoverishment and oddness of thinking typical of individuals with autism, and I shall describe a further case in a later chapter. Here I want to illustrate the kinds of abnormality revealed by tests of thinking.

Standard IQ tests tend to focus on two rather separate areas of ability. The first is sometimes called non-verbal ability, because it does not seem to depend on a person's skills in understanding and using language or in acquiring knowledge that is expressed in language. For example, completing jigsaws and recognizing the regularities in meaningless patterns do not require much in the way of language skills. The second area of ability does depend on language.

The impressive thing is how children with autism do relatively well on the first, non-verbal, parts of IQ tests. They can recognize visual patterns, and they can sometimes complete jigsaws very rapidly even when these are presented with the pictures facing down so that only the shapes are available to guide what goes where. In addition, those children with autism who can speak also do well on the more matter-of-fact or mechanical kinds of language comprehension, such as remembering lists of numbers or meaningless words, or giving bits of information such as how many days there are in a week. As Leo Kanner observed in the very first description of the syndrome of autism in 1943, 'The astounding vocabulary of the speaking children, the excellent memory for events of several years before, the phenomenal rote memory for poems and names, and the precise recollection of complex patterns and sequences, bespeak good intelligence in the sense in which this word is commonly used.'[1]

Yet, when we think of an intelligent person, we also expect the person will be able to apply that intelligence, at least to the most straighforward situations. The person will be able to tell what is relevant or irrelevant in what people say, or pick out the most important facts in order to accomplish an intellectual task. It is here that people with autism come unstuck. One standard IQ test includes questions like: 'What is the thing to do when you cut your finger?', 'What is the thing to do if a boy much smaller than yourself starts to fight with you?', 'What does fur mean?' and 'In what way are a cat and a mouse alike?' These are said to test general comprehension, although it will be apparent from the examples that they also test social understanding and an ability to explain things to someone else. The person with autism is often at a loss how to respond.

Why should this be? Whatever the explanation, it should also account for the fact that children with autism are limited in creative and imaginative symbolic play. And we need to explain why they get stuck on particular ways of seeing things and seem to lack the flexibility of thought and attitude that is a cardinal feature of the human mind. I tried to summarize my own explanation in a book on autism published in 1993, as follows:

... the greater part of autistic children's *characteristic* cognitive and language disabilities arise as sequelae to the children's relative failure to engage in I-Thou relatedness with others. What results from this failure are difficulties in understanding and identifying with the subjective orientations and mental states of other people, in recognising the nature and varieties of interpersonal sharing and communication, and in appreciating and adapting to the range of co-referential attitudes that people may adopt towards a shared and objective world. This account is one that applies not merely to autistic individuals' problems with pragmatic aspects of language [i.e. adjustments in language according to context] or to their inflexible, one-track lines of thinking, but also to their impoverishment in the very sources of higher cognitive functioning – the capacities for creative symbolisation, for 'as-if' thinking and for self-reflective thought.[2]

Can we really bridge the gap between autistic children's basic impairments in interpersonal relatedness and their difficulties in thinking? I think we can. It is a challenge that needs to be tackled on two fronts. We need a developmental theory that does the job of explaining how the one set of impairments leads to the other; and we need enough evidence to suggest that the story is not just plausible, but is also correct. With regard to the evidence, let me throw two studies into the pot.

In the first study, my colleague Tony Lee and I looked *within* an IQ test for evidence that a given IQ score might mean something different for children with autism.[3] The test is one in which children are presented with a series of pages in which drawings are arranged in sets of four. The instructions are to 'Point to ... dentist', or 'Show me ... surprise', and the child responds by pointing to the appropriate picture. What we did was to ask colleagues to look at this test and to judge which items were related to emotional life. They selected word–picture combinations in which the words to be judged were 'delighted', 'disagreement', 'greeting' and 'snarling', as well as more obvious emotion words that happened to be part of this test, such as 'horror' and 'surprise'. What we could now do was to compare children with and without autism who had exactly the same scores on this very same

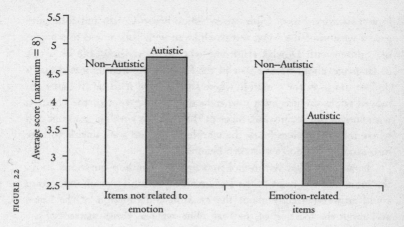

FIGURE 22

test, to see if the ways they achieved these scores were different. It turned out that they were.

The figure above shows that the non-autistic retarded children achieved similar scores on emotional and non-emotional items that are equally difficult for typically developing children. The children with autism who had almost identical overall scores proved to have relatively greater success with the non-emotional items, but were more often incorrect on the emotional items. Therefore, even if one takes a standard IQ test, one can find indications that the language and thought of children with autism are especially weak in aspects that have to do with emotion.

The second set of studies moves us to a different level of understanding people and minds. This concerns the child's grasp of such mental states as intending or believing, as discussed in Chapter 5. Do children with autism understand such concepts – do they have a 'theory of mind'? This may seem a rather selective and even idiosyncratic area to investigate, when our topic is thinking in general. On the contrary, it is one aspect of a subject I have been stressing repeatedly: how a person's ability to understand and adjust to the mental orientations of others is integral to the fabric of thought and language.

Theory of mind in autism has been a major topic of research over the last ten years. The take-home message is that children with autism have a weak or incomplete idea of what people's minds are like, and how they work. For example, when Simon Baron-Cohen and colleagues gave a version of the Maxi test to children with autism and to a group of children with Down's syndrome who were even less able on a test of language, about 85 per cent of the Down's children indicated that a doll would look for a marble where she believed it to be (it had been moved while she was away), whereas only 20 per cent of the children with autism did so. Instead, most of the children with autism indicated where they themselves knew the marble to be, and were unable to take into account the doll's mistaken belief.[4]

In another task, Baron-Cohen asked the children questions about the brain and the heart.[5] The large majority of children in each group could answer correctly about the location and function of the heart, and about the location of the brain; but, whereas three-quarters of the non-autistic children spontaneously referred to mental functions of the brain such as 'thinking', only one-quarter of the children with autism did so. Most of the remainder referred to the brain's role in causing behaviour – for example, 'It makes you move', or 'Running and walking'.

A third task involved items that required the children to distinguish between appearance and reality. For example, they were given a realistic plastic chocolate. When asked, 'What is it?', all the children said it was a chocolate. They were invited to handle it, and when then asked, 'What is it made of?' the children replied that it was made of plastic. The question about appearances was 'What does it look like?', and the question about reality was 'What is it really?' The results were similar to those already reported, with two-thirds of the non-autistic group but one-third of the autistic children responding correctly. The majority of the errors made by the autistic children involved the claim that the object was really the way it appeared to be – and a number of the autistic children persisted in trying to eat the plastic chocolate. In contrast, the normal and non-autistic mentally retarded subjects tended to laugh at the fake food and make comments like 'It's pretend chocolate!' As Baron-Cohen discusses, such a finding might indicate that the autistic children were dominated by perceptual information, rather than being able to draw upon knowledge that set appearances to one side.

The evidence suggests that children with autism fail to grasp how minds function. This is one way of putting it, anyway. I think a better way of putting it is that children with autism fail to grasp how *people* function as beings with subjective experiences. Minds do not exist in some ethereal world, separate from bodies. Nor do living human bodies exist in a realm that is partitioned off from the mind. Most important of all, young human beings do not come to understand the mind in some way that is independent of their relations with persons who have both bodies and minds. No — most young children come to understand the nature of persons with bodies and minds through their own very special kinds of experience in relating to other persons. Young children with autism miss out on such interpersonal experience, and their limited understanding of minds is one result.

As I said earlier on, the ability to think and know about minds is an ability that has implications for more than social understanding, because it provides the basis for certain forms of adjustment to others' thinking, and this in turn is very important for context-sensitive thought and language. However, for my money at least, the kinds of theory-of-mind concepts tested in these experiments are developed out of something earlier and deeper in the realm of interpersonal relations and understanding. From early in life, children with autism have failed to connect with people mentally. It is this that has limited their understanding of minds. Has it also given rise to their other intellectual impairments?

I have stated my view that the pattern of intellectual abilities and disabilities in autism is the result of selective impairment in those areas of thinking for which social experience is essential. But there are rival theories. One theory that also posits early deficits has it that children with autism lack a cognitive mechanism that normally switches on around the middle of the second year of life.[6] This mechanism allows a child to think about her own and others' ways of construing the world. The theory has no place for all the social-developmental background I have described, it gives short shrift to talk of interpersonal engagement or identification or other forms of early role-taking, and it rejects the idea that feelings between people have a pivotal position in the developmental picture. All is explained by a computational mechanism, that is, some bit of neuronal functioning that works like a program in a computer: if this is innately given, the ability to think in the new ways is turned on; if it is innately lacking, autism results. The theory makes the strong claim that a lack of this mechanism is specific to autism.

What evidence might decide in favour of one or other of the two theories? One approach is to see whether children with autism have social impairments before the time when the computational mechanism is supposed to come on line which, in the normally developing child, is around the middle of the second year. We have seen that there is strong evidence for such early impairments, and the computational theory has had to be modified as a result. A second approach is to see whether the range and quality of impairments in people with autism are consistent with a purely cognitive—computational account — one that posits a specific and limited disorder in operating on mental representations (more or less, thoughts) in the brain. I find it totally unconvincing that the deficits in very basic aspects of interpersonal relatedness, which as we have seen are characteristic of people with autism, could arise as the consequence of difficulties in processing certain kinds of thought. A third approach is to study the patterns of abnormality in less severe variants of autism and in relatives of people with autism for whom genetic predisposition might lead to partial expressions of the disorder. Here the jury is out. Then there is a final approach, which is to explore whether there are special conditions closely resembling autism in which the developmental picture helps us to decide whether primary social deficits or computational mechanisms are responsible for the clinical picture.

It was in the context of this debate that our research team decided to study congenitally blind children.

Consider the case of Kathie, described some years ago by the American psychoanalyst Selma Fraiberg.[7]

When Kathie was two years old, her language competence compared favourably with that of a normal child of the same age. On the other hand, Kathie's confusions in personal-pronoun use were unusually marked: 'Want me carry you?' she said to her mother when she herself wanted to be carried. Then, between the ages of two and a half and three years, it became clear that Kathie could not represent herself through a toy or doll. She could not re-create or invent a situation in play. When tested at the age of just over three years, Kathie could neither pretend that playdough was a cookie nor understand personal pronouns: when someone asked, 'Can I have a bite of the cookie, Kathie?', Kathie put the playdough in her own mouth and said, 'This cookie different.' It was not until after she reached the age of four that Kathie began to represent herself in doll play and, in parallel with this, to master the use of personal pronouns.

What is most interesting about this case is that, although Kathie showed several of the features one associates with autism, it was clear from her sociable and engaging behaviour with others that she was *not* autistic. In fact Kathie was congenitally blind.

Now, it is fascinating and important that complete lack of vision should so delay the development of symbolic play and correct understanding of the pronouns 'I' and 'you'. This is exactly what one would expect from the theory I am presenting. The critical thing is that, when blind children relate to objects and events, often they are not aware that these objects and events may also be at someone else's focus of attention. They cannot see how other people's emotional attitudes are directed to a world that the children themselves encounter. Nor can they see when those attitudes are directed towards themselves. Therefore they are more or less deprived of the experience of shifting perspectives on objects, events and themselves through identifying with the attitudes of others. The peculiarities in their language, thinking and play begin to make sense.

It was an exciting moment when, in the late 1980s, I came across this description of Kathie. I was embroiled in controversy about the origins of autism, and now it suddenly struck me that in blind children we might find evidence that social-developmental factors and *not* innately missing computational mechanisms give rise to autism-like difficulties in thinking. When I went to the literature on blind children, I found a smattering of case descriptions and occasional more systematic studies suggesting that individual signs and also the full house of clinical features of autism are relatively common in congenitally blind children. What these accounts left unclear was *how* common autism or autism-like features are in such children. More uncertain still was whether the quality of the psychological impairments is really so like that in sighted autistic children.

So, together with colleagues, I decided to embark on a programme of studies of congenitally blind children. Armed with our theory, we needed to come up with some predictions on what we would find. On the one hand, we expected that, if we studied a group of congenitally blind children in special schools for the visually impaired, we would find that the signs of autism as well as the full syndrome are much more common than one would normally find in pupils. On the other hand, the theory suggests that, in cases where blindness is a factor leading to autism, the underlying cause of the syndrome is both similar to and different from that in sighted autistic children.

The similarity is this: in each case there is something that makes it very difficult for the young child to relate to someone else's orientation towards the world and towards himself. This is critical if the child is to be lifted out from his own viewpoint, if he is to recognize how perspectives differ according to a person's take on the world, and if he is to grasp how one can make one thing stand for another in symbolizing. The difference is this: in the case of blindness, the child cannot *see* how other people relate to the world; in the case of the sighted child with autism, the child cannot see how other people *relate* to the world. The blind child lacks vision, and so cannot see how the world is something that is also at the focus of others' minds; nor can he see that other human beings are creatures that construe his world this way and that. Although some blind children may have additional handicaps that arise from the conditions that cause blindness (some of which affect the nervous system more widely), the inability to see other people's relations with themselves and the world plays a critical role. For the sighted child with autism, the difficulty is also with 'seeing', but in a sense that extends beyond vision.[8] Here the child seems unable to perceive other people as having feelings; he does not respond with feelings to the feelings of others, and he does not identify with the attitudes of others when these attitudes are directed to objects and events in the world. In this case it is not vision itself that is missing, but rather the ability to see and hear people and the expressions of people with appropriate feeling.

So what should we predict from this theory? Certainly that blind children are predisposed to autism. Yet, if we found that some blind children had autism and others did not, this might simply indicate that blindness is sometimes associated with the neurological disorder which causes autism. In other words, the neurological disorder and not the child's lack of social experience might cause the autism. Those blind children who were autistic might have had autism from this alone, even if they had not been blind. What we needed in order to make our case was to find a range of autistic-like clinical features in congenitally blind children, with some children having the full syndrome and others having fewer features of the disorder. The occurrence of autistic-like phenomena in the absence of the more severe forms of affective impairment would make it more likely that blindness itself – the actual lack of visual experience – had caused this or that feature of autism. It would also make it less likely that the typical full house of features had arisen as a completely independent phenomenon, on the basis of brain pathology. In addition, we should also be able to test blind children who do not have autism, to see if they have partial but less severe forms of the difficulties in thinking that characterize sighted autistic children. Finally, we might expect that there would be tell-tale signs that even the full syndrome of autism in blind children is not exactly like autism in sighted children. Some of the impairments in social responsiveness may not be present when blindness is the source of psychological difficulty.

There was a delicate balance in which we predicted similarities and differences between blind children and sighted children with autism. So, what did we do and what did we find?

Perhaps the first thing to record is what struck me when I first visited a school for blind children. I was both shocked and moved by what I saw. The shocking thing was to discover just how difficult it is for many young blind children to sustain contact with other people, especially their fellow pupils. It was common to see children sitting quietly by themselves, fiddling with their fingers or rubbing their eyes, rocking silently. Of course this was not the case for all the children, and it was moving to witness how courageous and resourceful blind children can be in negotiating a physical and social environment they cannot see. It was also moving to see teachers working very hard to establish both bodily and verbal contact with the children. Yet it *was* very hard work to do this, and frequently a child would lapse back into self-stimulating and repetitive behaviour once the adult had left her side. In addition, there seemed to be a lack of creative play in the children's activity, either when alone or when encouraged to use play materials. It was not that such play was completely lacking, but it rarely seemed to get anywhere or to have the life and colour of sighted children's play.

The next thing to say is that, if one makes careful, systematic observations of congenitally blind children who do not have the syndrome of autism, one finds confirmation that their engagement with other people is severely affected. In one study, a colleague, Martin Bishop, recorded the interactions of five- to nine-year-old congenitally blind children in the playground.[9] Together we decided that he should watch a group of blind children who were relatively successful in engaging with others, and another group who, although not autistic, had clear difficulties in their social relations. The observations confirmed that the latter children spent much of the time socially isolated, they were unlikely to be involved in reciprocal play, and they rarely engaged in to-and-fro conversations with other children. This was despite the two groups being equal in IQ. What this established was that even children who were not autistic had the *kinds* of difficulty in social engagement that are typical of autism.

In our principal study, another colleague, Rachel Brown, visited six schools for visually impaired children in England.[10] We decided to concentrate upon children who had been totally or near-totally blind from birth, because it seems to be the case that even a small amount of visual experience can make a substantial difference to a child's development (which is also interesting). We selected children who were between three and nine years of age and had no identifiable disorder of the nervous system. We tested the children for IQ, and observed each child for at least three periods of twenty minutes at free play, in the classroom during a lesson, and in a session of language testing. On the basis of these observations, we completed a standardized rating scale for the clinical features of autism and another checklist that covered areas such as relatedness to people (for example, responses to active attempts at engagement by other people, the nature of physical contact sought and interactive play), relatedness to the physical surroundings, motor disturbances and language impairment. We also interviewed teachers about the children's behaviour.

It turned out that no fewer than ten of the twenty-four children we studied satisfied the clinical criteria for autism — a proportion that is about 400 times as great as one would expect in sighted children. Then we made close comparisons between nine of the blind children who met the criteria for autism and nine sighted children with autism who were of similar age and IQ. The two groups were similar in many respects, but there were also tell-tale signs that the picture was not identical. In particular, there were indications that the blind children were not so impaired in their emotional expressions and that their relations with people were better. The majority gave the impression of being less severely autistic. In addition, seven of the nine blind children but only two of the sighted children with autism were observed to show some pretend play, although the pretending was almost always of a simple kind and did not involve the use of one object to represent another. Finally, in the clinical judgement of our child-psychiatrist investigator, Rachel Brown, only two of the nine blind children displayed the *quality* of social impairment that was characteristic of the sighted but autistic children, a quality that involves the special feel one has of a lack in emotional contact.

These findings from studies of the most severely affected blind children were in keeping with our expectation that the full syndrome of autism would be common among this group. It seems that, when children are blind from birth, they are predisposed to autism even if their social impairment is somewhat less profound than in sighted children with autism. Their lack of vision plays a role in causing the picture of autism, even when their intrinsic social disability is not so severe. On the other hand, one can see that blindness per se is not sufficient to cause autism. This, too, we expected, on the grounds that there are alternative ways to help a constitutionally social child to coordinate her own attitudes towards the world with those of someone else.

If blindness is a causative factor for autism in blind children, then one might expect that the course of such children's autism should be different from that of autistic children who have sight. In the realm of interpersonal relations, there are ways to circumvent the handicap of blindness. It is not easy to help a blind child to recognize that other people are relating in different ways to a shared world, but it is not impossible to do so. In a way this is obvious, because many blind children are remarkably like sighted children in their development. One needs to use touch, emotional expressions and active guidance. Once language develops, it is a powerful ally in this process. These kinds of social intervention might help even the more autistic-like blind children, who seem to have difficulties in their social relations that extend beyond the effects of blindness. At least in some cases, they could gradually lose their autism.

To find out whether this is the case, we are now studying how the nine autistic blind children have got on in the five years since we first observed them. So far, it looks as if some may have become less autistic-like than the sighted children with whom they were compared, as they find ways to link in with other people on a personal level. If these preliminary observations are borne out, they may point to the value of intensive social input to the children. They also remind us that there may be several routes to the same syndrome. For all the evidence that autism may be very difficult to treat, some children with the disorder may change substantially.

I have been focusing on blind children with the full syndrome of autism. We also predicted that there would be some indication of autistic-like problems even in those whose social relations were less affected by blindness. In order to test this prediction, we compared the children who were *not* autistic with sighted children from mainstream schools who were similar in age and IQ. Not one of the mainstream children showed any autistic-like behaviour, whereas every one of the blind children did so. The two groups differed in several respects, including relating to people, responses to objects, communication of all kinds, motor coordination and interactive play. Only the blind children had a tendency to echo back what other people said.

This last comparison, the tendency to echo back what others say, is especially interesting. Why should children with congenital blindness tend to echo the speech of others? Both in blind children and in sighted children with autism, such echoed speech is often associated with confusions in the use of the personal pronouns 'I' and 'you'. We saw an example in Kathie's 'Want me carry you?' It seems that the children hear a sentence or a phrase and, with little or no modification to the utterance, echo back what they have heard, word for word. The phrasing is adopted wholesale, as it were, as if the utterance were disembodied from the person who first made it. It is attached to the event as experienced by the child listening, not attached to the experience of the person who is speaking. This is not what happens in typical development, where the child interprets what is said as coming from someone else, and then adjusts the form of words for the child's own viewpoint. To return to our earlier example, what is heard as 'Mine!' expressing the other person's claim to ownership is adopted as 'Mine!' expressing the child's claim to ownership. Here in the blind is a single but telling instance of the kind of difficulty in identifying with the stance of someone else that I have been stressing all along.[11]

The evidence thus far has strengthened our claim that there is an important overlap between the development of blind children and the development of sighted children with autism. It has not established what that overlap amounts to. We took one further approach to testing whether congenitally blind children may have autistic-like problems. Here the focus was on whether they can work out that people have differing but coordinated mental perspectives. We tested whether blind children who do not have autism nevertheless encounter difficulty in understanding or focusing upon other people's beliefs, a critical aspect of theory-of-mind understanding.

The two tasks my colleague Maggie Minter administered were modelled on the experiments of Josef Perner and his colleagues, and involved twenty-one blind children and twenty-one sighted children between five and nine years of age who were similar in verbal ability.[12] In the first task she gave the children a lukewarm teapot, and confirmed that they could identify it. Then she asked, 'What do you think is inside here?' In order to ground this question, she either tapped the teapot or, in the case of some visually impaired children, felt it with the child's hands. Then she helped the child to pour out the contents into a cup and to feel what the cup contained. This revealed that the pot contained not tea, but sand! She asked, 'So what *is* inside the teapot?' The children were able to answer appropriately.

Then came the critical part of the experiment, in the form of two questions. The first question was as follows: 'When you first felt this [taking the child's hand to the teapot, or tapping it], before I poured it in the cup, what did you think was in here?' This was to test whether the children could think back to what they believed was the case before they changed their view to what was actually the case. In order to respond appropriately, they would have to be able to hold in mind the difference between a mistaken belief about a situation and the reality of that situation. The second question was this: 'Now Sue is coming in next. What will she think is in here when she feels this?' The point of this question was to explore whether the children could correctly ascribe a mistaken belief to someone else, even though the children themselves knew what was really in the teapot.

The results were that nearly all the sighted children answered the questions correctly, but approximately half the blind children answered one or both of the questions incorrectly, basing their replies on their current awareness of the teapot's contents. In other words, half the blind children gave answers that seemed to reflect their focus upon current reality and not upon the way that reality might have been construed by themselves at an earlier time or construed by another person who was misled by appearances.

In a subsequent task we used three large matchboxes and a small pencil. Each matchbox was covered with a different material, so that it could easily be distinguished from the others by touch. One box was covered in sandpaper, and was referred to as the rough box. A second box was covered in cotton wool, and was called the soft box. The third box was covered in foil, and was called the smooth box. Rachel sat next to the child and Maggie opposite. Rachel enlisted the child's help in putting her pencil away in the box with the rough top, and then made an excuse to leave the room. Maggie asked the child to help her move the pencil to the soft box. She checked that the child was aware (a) that Rachel had not witnessed what had happened, (b) that Rachel had put the pencil in the rough box and (c) that it was now in the soft box. Then she asked, 'Does Rachel know it is in the soft box?' and 'When Rachel comes back in, where will she look for her pencil?' In this case, all the sighted children made a correct prediction, but a significant minority (20 per cent) of the blind children failed to do so.

What impressed us when conducting these tasks was how careful we had to be in communicating to the blind children, through language and touch, what we were talking about. At times it was also difficult to interpret what they meant, and we had to set a number of responses aside from the main results because they were ambiguous. Therefore we have to be cautious about concluding that some blind children lack concepts of belief and so on. On the other hand, this study has revealed just the kinds of difficulty in coordinating attention between the blind child and another person, and just the kinds of difficulty for the child in homing in on the mental perspective of someone else, that seem to be vital for the development of thinking. We administered these theory-of-mind tasks to blind children who were more able and less socially impaired than many, and these children's errors may represent little more than shadows of the far more serious impairments in thinking of blind children who show the full syndrome of autism. If this is so, it illustrates how far growth in social as well as non-social understanding draws on what children perceive to happen between themselves and others and what they perceive to happen between others and the world.

The message from these studies of blind children is that there may be more than one way to develop autism, because there may be more than one kind of serious barrier to experiencing personal relations with other people who are seen to have attitudes towards a shared world.

Until three years or so ago, I took the view that only something abnormal in a child's constitution – in exceptional cases compounded by sensory handicaps (and specifically blindness) – could create barriers to social engagement that are serious enough to result in autism. To be sure, severe deprivation or maltreatment of young children might lead to psychological disturbance and slowness in intellectual development, but such disturbance or slowness would not conform to the pattern of autism. My reasoning was that the inbuilt propensity to react with feelings to other people, and to read and identify with the attitudes of others towards their surroundings, is a robust feature of a human being's innate endowment. It is what makes us human. What I had not reckoned with is that infants may face a degree of social deprivation that means they can just about survive, but survive with a terribly blunted capacity to respond to other people. I had not reckoned with the kinds of living conditions to which babies were exposed in the orphanages of Ceauşescu's Romania.

*

One of the most appalling discoveries that came with the end of the Ceauşescu regime in Romania was the plight of young children who had been left in orphanages, often because of the extreme poverty of their parents. Many babies were confined to their cots, without toys or other playthings, and they were fed by bottles that were sometimes left propped up for use. There was very little sustained interpersonal exchange, and there were no opportunities to establish relationships with caregivers. The physical environment was also extremely harsh, and it was not uncommon for children to be washed by being hosed down with cold water.

There have been several studies of the effects of these conditions on the children's development. There were often remarkable improvements when the children were subsequently adopted into caring homes. In what follows, I shall be summarizing the findings from an especially revealing study by Michael Rutter and his colleagues.[13] It was revealing because it uncovered something that had been entirely unexpected, but which dovetails in a most interesting way with our own findings from the blind: that a small but much higher than expected proportion of the children who had suffered severe and prolonged early privation developed the picture of early childhood autism.

The study concerned a group of 111 children who before the age of twenty-four months were adopted into families in the United Kingdom from Romania. The children were assessed at the ages of four and six years. These were mostly children who had been placed in orphanages early in the first year of life and who were moved to the UK in their first or second years. In a nutshell, what emerged was that about 1 in 16 of the children showed a picture that closely resembled that of autism, and a further 1 in 16 presented with milder autistic features.

The investigators made an in-depth clinical evaluation of those children who had been picked out by professionals or adoptive parents as having possible autistic features. The features were of different kinds in different children, but in all instances there were severe problems with social relationships and communication. Concerns were expressed about the children's difficulties in forming friendships, their impoverished reciprocal communication with others, their lack of empathy towards others, their poverty of eye-to-eye gaze and gestures in social exchanges, and their limited language and to-and-fro conversation. A majority of these children had preoccupations with sensations and intense interests of unusual kinds, for example, being fascinated by watches or vacuum cleaners or plumbing systems or new (and only new) £10 notes. Nearly all had been admitted to institutions during the first months of life, usually from the time of birth.

The aim of the research was to document the abnormalities through systematic interviews with parents, questionnaires to parents and teachers, and observations of the children themselves. The most comprehensive results concerned three children whose IQ results were in the severely retarded range and six children who were less intellectually disabled.

The three severely retarded children all came to the UK at a relatively late stage (after twenty months of age), and each had previously experienced very poor institutional conditions. One was reported to have been very premature, one had some hearing loss, and one had been kept isolated in a single room. The picture of autism seemed characteristic, and the investigators took the serious retardation to indicate probable brain damage of some sort. Yet even in these very handicapped children there was something atypical about their autism. Each of the children made spontaneous efforts to communicate with sign language, and two made social approaches of a kind that would have been unusual in typically autistic children. One of the children also improved considerably between four and six years with correction of a hearing impairment – suggesting that, even in this case, something about the child's *experiences* (and not just brain damage) was a factor in causing the clinical picture.

The six children who were not severely retarded and who were tested at four and six years were compared with children from a separate study who had classical autism. What this revealed was that the Romanian adoptees became progressively less autistic in their behaviour over the two years, whereas the comparison group became more autistic. The Romanian children also showed striking gains in IQ, from an average of 57 to 77 (where 100 is average for most of us). In addition, there were again atypical features to the autism. One child used sign language spontaneously, and another adjusted her language when she was not at first understood. Several made social approaches, or were emotionally animated. By six years, one child had friendships involving shared play and talk, and several brought things they had done to show off to their parents, something that is very unusual in autism. Yet still they tended to lack the reciprocal to and fro of social exchange, they showed limited social awareness and empathy, they found it difficult to maintain social interaction, and they would rarely turn to their parents for security and comfort. Most also showed repetitive behaviour and had unusual circumscribed interests. Once again, these children with what the investigators called 'quasi-autistic patterns' had all received an institutional upbringing, in most cases from around birth. All had entered the UK relatively late, after they were twelve months old. There was little to suggest that they were specially malnourished or otherwise physically at a disadvantage compared with orphans who did not show autistic features.

Then there were an additional small subgroup of children who showed some milder autistic-like features, often repetitive rituals and a lack of social boundaries. This group had entered the UK at an earlier age, and they were not low in IQ. When these children were combined with those who had more marked features of autism, just over half were female – again atypical for autism, where males usually outnumber females in the ratio of 3 or 4 to 1. This suggested that the factors leading to their autism might not be typical for other children with the disorder.

In the formal scientific paper in which the research group presented these findings, Rutter and his colleagues wrestled with the problem of whether the children's early adverse experiences might have caused the quasi-autistic patterns. They drew the tentative conclusion that those children with severe mental retardation had brain damage, but considered that prolonged experience of terrible social and non-social privation was almost certainly responsible for the symptoms in the remainder. I say that the researchers wrestled with this conclusion, because they are a group who have been (rightly) impressed by the evidence that brain disorder may cause autism but (wrongly, in my view) unimpressed by the suggestion that primary impairments in a child's capacity for normal social-affective experiences might give rise to the syndrome. As they wrote in their introduction to their report, 'Indeed, in terms of what is known about the organic basis of autism and the very strong genetic component that is involved ... autism would not be expected to arise as a result of severe privation.'[14] Yet Rutter and his team are fine scientists, and scientists allow evidence to contradict their erstwhile beliefs. It appears that autism, or something very like it, *can* arise as a result of severe privation.

Whatever our point of departure, whatever the gifts and handicaps with which we come into the world, we all need to proceed along a certain path if we are to acquire the ability to think. This is a path that involves us with other people. In order to follow this path, we need enough by way of mental equipment to perceive and experience other people *as* people, and we need enough of the right kinds of experience of other people to do the developmental job.

Children with autism have not found that path. The reasons may be various, and almost always they include a constitutional abnormality in the child. Whatever the reason, the syndrome of autism arises because there is disruption in the child's experience of patterned interpersonal relations with other people.

The challenge is to be clear just what this means. It means that autism is the result of a disorder of the system of child-in-relation-to-other. Certain kinds of brain damage can disrupt a young child's ability to experience other people *as* other people. I have already suggested that one way it can do so is by affecting a child's emotional responsiveness to others. I do not claim that this is the root of every single case of autism, as must be clear from my account of blindness. For example, even blind children who present with the full syndrome of autism often appear to have some (perhaps limited) emotional responsiveness to others. Rather, what we shall find in any particular case is a combination of factors that together cause a severe limitation in the child's experience of other people in the interplay of emotionally patterned interpersonal relatedness. Such relatedness reaches beyond people to the things and events that people experience together.

I do not share the optimism of many researchers that we shall locate a particular area or pathway of neurones in the brain that we can blame for autism. Not for autism in general, anyway. In a given case, yes, at least in principle, we might one day locate an area of malfunction. There are some parts of the brain, such as the limbic system — a widely spaced but closely interconnected network in the brain that is ancient in evolution and important for the organization and communication of feelings — that may often be implicated. In other cases of autism, however, a part of the abnormality may be located beyond the brain. I say 'a part of the abnormality', because we do not need to insist on a black-or-white, either/or, choice here. The crux is that, whatever the mix of innate deficits in the child and deficiencies in the child's environment, the child's experience of other people is compromised.

I still believe that nature has so prepared infants for those special qualities of experience that come with relating to other people that they can make a lot out of a little social input. The study of Romanian orphans shows that infants may develop the syndrome of autism if they are deprived of virtually all human care. There must be a reason why this discovery has not been made before. The reason is probably that *only* in the most awful circumstances does autism develop in this way, and then only in a small minority of cases. In almost all other instances of autism, something in the child is contributing to the developmental breakdown.

Let us presume that there was no initial brain disorder in at least some of the blind children and Romanian orphans I have described. This is not to claim that brain development is undisturbed by the lack of experience that comes with blindness and severe psychological deprivation. Brains feed on experience, and without food the nervous system withers. Having said this, the fact that the clinical features of autism can arise in these circumstances — a fact that has only come to light from very recent studies — represents a severe challenge to traditional accounts of autism. There must be serious doubts about explanations of autism that locate the sole source of a unique and characteristic psychological deficit in the affected individual's brain.

The intersubjectivity theory that I espouse is one that locates the unique and characteristic deficit in autism *between* the affected individual and others. I can at least claim to have predicted the findings from the studies of the blind, and I wish I had predicted those from the studies of the orphans. The evidence seems to fit. What is so striking in each of these cases is that the children display almost the whole syndrome of autism, even the peculiar preoccupations that I have not accounted for in my own writings on autism. When elaborated further, the intersubjective approach may explain more about autism than even I imagined.

One thing that I had imagined, however, was that autism might help us to define how intersubjective experience is vital for developing a self, and enable us to see how self-awareness and thinking share common origins. These are topics for the next chapter.

EIGHT

Self and Others

Self-awareness is something we need if we are to think. We are aware of ourselves as entertaining thoughts, or trying out this idea and then another, or struggling to reason correctly. It is a component of having the mental space to think that I can separate myself as thinker from my mental activities of thinking. For example, I can ~oose to think of this rather than that, or I can follow a particular ~h of reasoning but know that I am doing so only to see where the ~ment takes me. Therefore the ability to think in these ways is ~ bound up with the ability to think of oneself as a mentally ~ing.

~is is easy enough to say. It is not so easy to understand.

> I am hands
> And face
> And feet
> And things inside of me
> That I can't see.
>
> What knows in me?
> 's it only something inside
> ~at I can't see?
>
> ~aura Riding, 'Laddery Street Herself'

~d thinks, and it is somehow connected ~ and feet. The something is oneself. A ~nk. At the same time, a person needs to think if she is to acquire a developed sense of self. And if one cannot think straight, then this is likely to affect one's self-awareness. If one's thinking becomes muddled or one's mind seizes up altogether, then one becomes disorientated and lost. It seems that we can maintain a clear sense of ourselves only when we can think properly. For example, people with borderline personality disorder not only have difficulties in thinking about relationships, but they also struggle with conflicting feelings about their sexuality, their professional identity and their self-worth. Their problems with thinking are associated with problems in finding and defining themselves.

These reflections take us some way to seeing that thinking and awareness of self are bound up with each other, but they leave us with many unanswered questions about the self of which we are aware. If we are asked to describe ourselves, we do not usually talk about how we are able to think. Instead we might begin by saying a bit about our appearance and then go on to talk of our history or the kind of person we are or our likes and dislikes. These things are what are particular about ourselves, what distinguish each of us from one another. At least implicitly and often explicitly, they involve comparisons between oneself and others. I am not so good-looking as she, he is cleverer than I, and so on. The conceptual distinction between self and other that is made in the second year of life paves the way for children and adults to spend a great deal of their lives thinking and feeling about their standing and their qualities vis-à-vis the standing and qualities of others.

For all this, it is a notoriously difficult thing to get hold of the self, as philosophical texts on the topic testify. When we feel we have clarified at least something about it – and no book on thinking and the self would be complete without quoting Descartes' triumphant 'I think, therefore I am' – even this seems to slip away into doubts as to whether the self is a part bodily and part mental fiction rather than something that really exists. Perhaps we should be grateful that we have our Ariadne's thread to lead us through the maze of philosophical speculation: we can turn to the case of autism and follow real-life observations and experiments that show us what happens when the self is *not* properly formed. This may not solve all the problems of philosopy, but it will help us to specify how and why the self really matters as a dimension of human existence.

The first and most impressive thing we discover is that, when a child does not experience the forms of social engagement that are typically human, then both self-awareness and thinking are seriously affected. Even more illuminating is what we learn about the *qualities* of self-awareness and thinking that are defective. It is not that everything goes, but only some aspects of self-consciousness and only some kinds of thinking.

We can see this in the following description of a man who seems unable to follow the normal pathways of thought, but only in specific respects. The selectiveness of his deficits tells us that we are not encountering someone with general mental retardation. This is not a person who, for some genetic or environmental reason, lacks adequate hardware in the brain to support thinking processes. On the contrary, he seems to have the potential for quite extraordinary feats of memory and deduction. Yet he is so obviously handicapped when it comes to common-sense thinking. It would also be an exaggeration to say that this person does not have a self. He can conduct himself through his physical surroundings, and has even learned to use the word 'I' in certain contexts. Yet he does not seem to have the kind of self-consciousness that is characteristic of most human beings. His limitations in thinking about things go along with lack of thought about himself.

This person was one of the first people with autism to be described in detail, in a paper written by Martin Scheerer, Eva Rothmann and Kurt Goldstein in 1945.[1] There he was referred to as 'L'. L was first seen at the age of eleven with a history of severe learning difficulties. In fact he had an IQ of only 50 on a standardized test of intelligence. Clearly, he found it a struggle to understand and to think about things. Yet, despite serious and disabling intellectual difficulties, he was capable of telling the day of the week for any given date between about 1880 and 1950. He could also recount the day and date of his first visit to a place, and could usually give the names and birthdays of all the people he met there. He could spell forwards and backwards. He could play melodies by ear.

At the same time, L was unable to understand or create an imaginary situation. He did not play with toys, nor did he show any sign that he understood make-believe. It is really extraordinary to see that a person who seems so clever cannot understand what it means to pretend and is utterly unmoved to play out the goings-on of life through dolls or miniature postmen, policemen, mothers and fathers. For L, this dramatic stage for the interplay of selves had no meaning.

In fact L had never shown interest in his social surroundings. In his early years he barely noticed the presence of people and appeared emotionally indifferent to other children, even when they cried. He was eerily unconnected with others. Even when he learned to speak, he was unable to converse in give-and-take language. The to-and-fro exchange of talk between self and other was missing. And, when L did converse, he rarely commented on the reasons for actions or events — it was as if their meanings escaped him or were not worth communicating to someone else.

These social and intellectual deficits were accompanied by another striking abnormality: L appeared to be unaware of himself. He was apparently oblivious to what others might think of him and his behaviour, and was remarkably unselfconscious. For example, he showed no shame in parading naked through the house. He would run up and down in a way that was strange and troubling, as he slapped his sides and rubbed the four fingers of each hand in a drumbeat against his thumbs. He seemed distracted and inattentive to those around him, and inattentive to their attentiveness to him. It was as if, in his own mind, people hardly figured at all. The lack of linkage between himself and other people was also apparent in his failure to imitate others' actions. He would not even react if other children took away his possessions. This is *so* unlike most children.

If we look closely, we can trace some of the connections between L's peculiarities of thinking and his lack of self/other-consciousness. Up to fifteen years of age, L could not define the properties of objects except with reference to their use in particular situations or with reference to what he did with them — what the authors of the paper called self-centred usage. For example, he defined an orange as 'that I squeeze with', and an envelope was 'something I put in with'. He could not grasp the meaning of metaphors, so that he would have been utterly stumped by any meaning of 'cradle' that did not make reference to a literal cradle in a real-life setting. In other words, he was unable to lift the meaning of a word out of its standard usage and adjust to what others might mean by the word in other settings. He could not understand similarities, differences or absurdities. Even at the age of fifteen, L defined the difference between an egg and a stone as 'I eat an egg and I throw a stone.' Once, when the doctor said, 'Good-bye, my son', L replied, 'I am not your son.' When asked, 'What would happen if you shot a person?', L replied, 'He goes to the hospital.' Note how in this last example L's response 'He goes to hospital' is *not wrong* – but it is definitely weird. L's reply betrays a completely different framework of experience. He understands every single word, and makes sense of the sequence of words as these are put together in the question; what is lost on him is the emotional meaning of what would happen if he shot someone.

It is an emotional meaning that bears on himself as a self. If *he* shot someone ... And yet there is a kind of paradox in the quotations I have been giving. In his teens at least, L had come to use the pronoun 'I', and he defined things in apparently self-centred terms. So in some sense he had a notion of self. What the quotations indicate is the thinness of this notion. It seems that his self-centredness was not the kind that arises from putting oneself before others or pitting oneself against others, nor was it a self that moved flexibly to follow the orientation of others (as one needs to do in order to understand metaphor). Rather, the world had only one centre, only one place from which it was experienced. This was not a self in relation to other selves. It was a self that floated unanchored.

In the person of L we see a vivid example of someone with autism whose marked difficulties in thinking were associated with very restricted self-awareness. How could someone achieve these remarkable feats of memory, calculation and even musical production, yet have an IQ on the level of a person only half his age? In the face of what appear to be highly efficient intellectual computations and impressive feats of memory, how can we account for the autistic person's very patchy ability to think? For some time we have been working on an answer to these questions: that thinking cannot become a flexible and creative medium for human intelligence without passing through the minds of others. Without the right kinds of involvement with other people – and, come to that, without the right kind of self in relation to others – a person lacks both the grounding and the mental flexibility for intelligent thought.

It is difficult to appreciate just how shocking it can be to encounter someone who seems so limited and narrow in his imaginative life yet so sharp in computing or remembering things that seem unimportant. L's story reminds me of a visit I made to a school for children with autism, where I first met a boy about ten years old. He approached me with what seemed a well-rehearsed list of questions, which he delivered in a monotone. 'What is your name?' 'Where do you live?' 'Where were you born?' 'What date were you born?' I answered each question dutifully, although I felt that he had little interest in my replies – he merely swept on to the next question. Finally I broke off what seemed like an endless process, and he left for his classroom. Then, six months later, I had reason to visit the school once again. As I came through the front door, I was confronted with this same boy for the second time in my life. It was as if the list of questions repeated itself. 'What is your name?' I gave my name. 'Where do you live?' I told him. 'Where were you born?' 'In London.' 'What date were you born?' I said, 'You tell me.' He did so – the exact date and year. Not the most extraordinary feat of memory, but shocking nonetheless.

Some have argued that the self is a kind of fiction, something that exists only because we think it does. If it is real, then how come we think of it as something mental at one moment, but then treat it as something physical the next? The argument has some force, but this does not make it correct. If thinking requires a self, then it is possible to think up this supposed fiction only if one has a self in the first place – in which case it turns out not to be a fiction at all. And we can parry and follow-up the question by posing a question of our own: people, too, are both mental and physical, but does one want to say that people are not real?

In fact my concept of myself is a concept of myself as a person. It is difficult to imagine that I could have a concept of myself otherwise.

To experience oneself as a person among others is an essential part of being a self at all. Behind the question of the body-and-mind self, therefore, lurks the deeper question of how we come to know that persons have bodies and minds.

As a start to addressing that question, we can turn from abstract reflection to some facts about human person-perception, and more specifically to the perspective on those facts afforded by the study of autism. We can ask whether children with autism have what it takes to experience other people *as* people and therefore whether they have a basis for deriving a fully textured concept of self.[2]

You may be convinced already that, no, they do not. We have encountered descriptions of how it feels to relate to a child with autism, where it is precisely in the area of experiencing personal contact that something seems badly wrong. It can feel as if the child is a changeling, someone from a different world. We have seen how as infants, autistic children do not engage with parents in the ways that are typical of other infants, how as toddlers they are often unmoved by the distress of others, and how as adolescents they do not greet or depart from others with looks, smiles and other gestures of engagement and disengagement. And we have evidence from a range of experimental studies that they seem not to notice or understand feelings in the bodily expressions of others.

Yet, for all this, there are many scientists who are unconvinced. It is certainly important to entertain the possibility that the autistic child's inattentiveness and unresponsiveness to others are the secondary effect of some other disorder in psychological functioning, however basic it may seem. For example, some psychologists have suggested that it may be the children's impaired language that affects their ability to categorize emotions, not a difficulty in perceiving and responding to people's expressions. They point out that the deficit is not absolute, and that children with autism do arrive at some limited understanding of others' feelings. So let us look again at whether children with autism are arrested by the feelings of other people.

In the following experiment by Jane Weeks and myself, there were no right or wrong answers.[3] It was merely a question of whether children with autism would notice the same things as non-autistic children. Two photographs of the head and shoulders of different

FIGURE 23

adults were stuck to the front of a box. These two individuals differed in sex, facial expression (one was mildly happy, the other glum) and the type of hat they were wearing (woollen in one case, floppy in the other). The children were told that they should notice *one* way in which the two pictures were different.

Then the children were presented with sixteen other photographs of faces, one by one. Each showed a new person, and the task was to judge which of the two target faces they should 'go with'. The children were shown that there were two slots in the top of the box, one above each target photograph, so that they could post each of the sixteen photos into the slot directly above the target photograph which they thought was similar. The sixteen photographs to be sorted showed a mixture of people with all combinations of male or female, happy or glum faces, and woollen or floppy hats. This meant that, when a child had posted the photographs, we could tell which feature the child had used to sort by. Happily, nearly all the children sorted consistently, so there was no difficulty in seeing what feature they had selected to guide their sorting.

Then the task went into its second stage. Suppose that a child had initially sorted by hat, so that, regardless of the sex and expression of the people, all the photos of people with floppy hats were posted into the slot above the target photo which showed a floppy hat, and all the photos of people with a woollen hat were posted in the slot above the target photo which showed a woollen hat. This strategy was perfectly correct, and it simply showed that this child had noticed and chosen hats rather than features of sex and emotional expression as the basis for sorting. The target photos were now replaced with two new targets, showing two individuals wearing the same hat but still different in sex and facial expression. The same sixteen cards were shuffled, the child was asked to notice *another* way in which the targets differed, and the procedure was repeated. If the child sorted by sex, then the target photos would be changed once again, so that the people depicted now wore the same hat and were of the same sex. The child was asked to notice another different feature, and to sort again. At this stage only a single feature remained as a basis for sorting.

Our prediction was that, even in judging immobile and therefore relatively unexpressive faces in photographs, the children with autism would differ from the non-autistic children in being less likely to notice and sort by the facial expressions. (Before you know the results, how much would you bet on such an unlikely result?) On the other hand we expected that they would notice and sort by other features of the photographs, so this functioned as our control task.

The first result was that two-thirds of the children in each group began by sorting the photographs according to sex (although this might have amounted to hair length in the photos we employed). There was therefore no doubt that *both* groups of children could notice something that distinguished one target photograph from the other and then sort their pile of photographs in a consistent way. The next result was that the number of autistic children who sorted by hat in preference to facial expression was three times greater than the number who sorted the other way round; among the non-autistic children, by contrast, twice as many participants sorted by expression before hat.

This was not all. Equal numbers of autistic and non-autistic children spontaneously sorted by sex at some point during the task, and equal numbers sorted by hat; but, whereas all fifteen of the non-autistic children sorted by facial expression sooner or later, only six out of fifteen autistic children *ever* did so. For the remaining nine children with autism, the contrast in facial expressions did not seem to register, even when it was the only feature of the target photographs left as a basis for sorting the remaining photographs. And, even when given explicit instructions to sort by facial expression at the very end of the task, there were five out of fifteen children with autism who were still unable to do this consistently.

One is tempted to say that children with autism are almost blind to the feelings of others. This is largely true, but the problem goes deeper than this. They are not *moved* by people's feelings. As I have stressed before, the business of being moved by others is vitally important for thinking as well as for refinement of feeling with our fellow humans. In the course of our social interactions, each of us is pushed or pulled or nudged or drawn or wrenched towards the psychological position of the other. So emotional responsiveness proves to be one facet of something even deeper and more pervasive. It is this something that is so important for the development of the self. Might we find less explicitly emotional events where movements that occur in contexts of self-in-relation-to-other-selves transform an individual's mind?

Imitation may be exactly the kind of event we are looking for. In imitation, one takes in or takes over something from someone else. One only has to sit and observe a one-year-old at play to see that what she does and how she does it are profoundly imbued with what she has picked up from others. It is not just that young children often copy what their parents do, and the style with which their parents do it. There are even more subtle forces at play, as the characteristics of an adult become characteristics of the child. There is something about our propensity to imitate others that is as basic as our intellectual prowess, something that makes us *Homo imitans* as well as *Homo sapiens*. What is the something? It is the capacity to identify with others – a capacity that autism reveals to be a thinly disguised emotional process.

There is something of a mystery surrounding imitation in children with autism. There are clinical reports like that describing L which indicate how people with autism lack the kind of pull towards imitation that is so prominent in typically developing infants and young children. There are also formal studies that point to abnormalities when autistic children have been prompted to imitate other people's gestures – for example, wrinkling the nose or forming shapes with one's hands. Yet, for all this, individuals with autism sometimes do remarkably well when they are tested for their ability to copy novel actions demonstrated by others, even when a time interval separates the demonstration and the imitative response.

It was against this rather disconcerting background that my colleague

Tony Lee and myself decided to adopt a new tack in exploring the imitative abilities and disabilities of people with autism.[4] We had three ideas to guide us. The first was our belief that it is in the area of psychological movement through people that individuals with autism are especially handicapped. Not only are they often unmoved by other people's expressions of emotion, but more generally they seem to remain stuck in one-track modes of thought and feeling and are often unresponsive to the influence of the people around them. We reasoned that any abnormality would perhaps have something to do with this in the context of imitation too. Second, we had already conducted the dots-of-light experiment I described in a previous chapter. You will recall that the children with autism were quite able to perceive and interpret the actions of the point-light figures depicted in motion on videotape, but they were much less able to perceive and understand expressions of emotion and other subjectively experienced states such as itchiness or coldness presented in this way. This also seemed to be relevant for what the children might or might not imitate. Finally, our view is that in autism there appears to be a weakness in identifying with others, one feature of which is a failure to assume the orientation of someone else. The fault is in the means by which self and other are at the same time connected and differentiated.

Therefore we reasoned as follows. Perhaps children and adolescents with autism are able not only to perceive but also to imitate the goal-directed actions of other people. They can watch and understand what is happening when someone else adopts a certain strategy to achieve a goal. If they then want to achieve the same goal themselves, they can copy the means to attain it. This is not a problem. What is a problem is identifying with someone else.

The challenge we faced was to devise a way of testing this hypothesis. What we did was to formulate our ideas in a rather crude and preliminary way as the basis for an experiment. Other workers had made the distinction between the goal of an action to be imitated, or *what* is to be done, and the means by which the goal is to be achieved, or *how* it is to be done. We now drew a further distinction between two senses of how an action is imitated. The first sense is that emphasized by others and concerns the behavioural strategy by which the goal is achieved, the means to the end. The second sense is more difficult to define, but we called it the 'style' which someone adopts in executing a strategy. For example, two people may do the same thing to accomplish a goal, yet differ in the style with which they conduct themselves. Their movements may look different, they may or may not show accompanying gestures, and they may convey different attitudes in their actions. For the purposes of the study, we gave special emphasis to whether actions were done in a harsh or a gentle manner.

To begin with, we gathered together our task materials. I dug out an old pipe-rack which had a ledge with slots in it for the pipe-stems. We also found a ten-inch wooden stick that had been part of a children's construction kit. Together these would serve for the first part of the experiment. My colleague Tony would demonstrate the action to be imitated: he would pick up the pipe-rack and hold it against his shoulder like a violin, and strum the stick along the slotted part of its length, to produce a rat-a-tat sound.

As we continued to rummage through the junk in our respective households, I came across a bean-filled cloth frog. That seemed a friendly thing to use in a task for children. I also found an unused present from long ago – a wooden foot-massager with a handle and some rollers that were supposed to relax one's feet when drawn along the sole (I was too ticklish). What should we do with these? We decided that Tony would rest the frog in the palm of his right hand and bring it to his forehead in order to wipe his brow three times. Then he would place the frog on the table, pick up the roller, and flatten the frog with it.

Next I remembered that a Japanese visitor had given me a small ivory block with a raised, intricate design on one end, together with an accompanying inkpad. This stamp and pad could be used to transfer a copy of the design onto paper. We thought it unlikely that the children in our study would have done this before, so that would be our next action.

For our final imitation, Tony borrowed one of his children's toys. This was a six-inch-high plastic policeman that stood on hidden wheels. When the policeman was standing on a table, you pressed down on the head and the policeman moved along under his own steam.

Those were our materials. Now to the experiment itself. We tested sixteen children and adolescents with autism (they were aged between nine and nineteen years), and sixteen children and adolescents without autism who were similar in age and in verbal ability. The first thing we needed to do was to check that they would not spontaneously use the materials in the ways we were going to demonstrate. If they did, then what would look like imitation might not be imitation at all – the children might simply be doing what they would have done anyway. So, in a preliminary session a week before the testing proper, we gave each set of materials to our children and asked them to 'Use this.' In the event, not a single participant performed an action that was similar to what Tony was going to model later on. So, if in the task proper they produced the actions that Tony demonstrated, this must have occurred because they had copied him.

For the demonstration session, the child was seated across the table from Tony. Tony produced the pipe-rack and stick and said, 'Watch this.' He put the pipe-rack to his shoulder and drew the stick along its slotted edge three times. He put the materials away, brought out the frog and roller and, repeating his instruction to 'Watch this', wiped his brow in three brief movements and then flattened the frog with the roller. The approach was the same for the stamp-and-pad and rolling-policeman tasks, except that the actions for each were performed once only. Note that the children were not informed that they were going to be given the materials to use at a later point. They were simply told to watch.

I have omitted one crucial detail from this description of the tasks. We know the kinds of goal-directed action that the children were being shown, but what had happened to the matter of style? The answer is that in his demonstrations Tony employed two different styles of action. Half the children in each group saw Tony strum the pipe-rack in a harsh way, making a staccato sound, and half saw him use a graceful and gentle strumming action. Half the children saw Tony wipe the frog across his brow with abrupt, harsh movements, and half saw him using gentler, caressing movements. Half saw him bring the stamp down upon the inkpad and then the paper in a forceful way, and half saw him employ a careful rolling motion. Finally, in the rolling-policeman task, half saw Tony use two outstretched fingers to depress the top of the policeman, and half saw him use the front of his cocked wrist (as in the photograph below). Over the series

FIGURE 24

of demonstrations, each participant saw a mixture of harsh and gentle versions of the actions (or, in the case of the policeman, one or other of the styles of pressing down), although they were shown only one version of any one action.

There was then a period of ten minutes during which the children were given a language test that was not related in any way to imitation. After this break, Tony produced the pipe-rack and stick and gave them to the child, saying merely, 'Use this.' Participants were given time to use the materials in whatever way they chose. After a while Tony would give a prompt if necessary, by saying, 'Can you remember exactly how I used it?' This was just to make sure that a child was not failing to respond because he or she did not know what was expected. It turned out that this prompt made very little difference to the responses, so I shall not discuss it further.

The videotapes of the experiment were edited so that we could give excerpts to judges, who assessed the styles of the children's responses without knowing which style had been modelled to each child. Our prediction was that the children and adolescents with autism would be able to copy the goal-directed actions, but they would not imitate the style with which those actions were performed.

The results were as follows. Nearly all the children of each group applied the stick to the pipe-rack to make a sound. They used the stamp and pad to transfer an imprint to the paper. And they depressed the head of the policeman in order to make him move. (I shall come to the case of brow-wiping with the frog in a moment.) This established that almost everyone taking part was attentive to what Tony was doing and was interested and motivated to achieve the goal in each task.

When it came to imitating the different styles of action, the large majority of the non-autistic children performed each action in the same way that Tony had done. Eleven out of sixteen adopted the same harsh or gentle strumming of the stick on the pipe-rack, for example, and thirteen out of sixteen pressed the head of the toy policeman in just the manner they had seen Tony adopt. This last test was perhaps the most striking, because it was often with great care that a child cocked back his wrist or extended his fingers before pressing down on the policeman's head, even though it was totally unnecessary to use these unnatural postures. These children and adolescents seemed to have an investment in performing the action exactly as Tony had done, almost always without the need for prompting.

In the case of the children with autism, the results were quite different. Only a small minority of these children and adolescents imitated the style with which the actions had been demonstrated, even though they were perfectly able to copy the strategy needed to achieve a goal. For example, only two out of sixteen children with autism strummed the pipe-rack in the harsh or gentle way that Tony had demonstrated (remember that the style of Tony's actions was not known to the people who rated the videotapes); and only four imitated Tony's style of action in depressing the head of the policeman. A majority of the children with autism pressed down the policeman's head in the simplest way possible, by using the palm of their hand. They did not need to copy the style of Tony's actions to achieve the goal of setting the policeman in motion, and so they ignored it.

How do we understand these results? As I have already suggested, the children without autism watched Tony carefully and seemed motivated to perform each of the actions just as Tony had done. They were imitating the *person* of Tony, and in order to do so they assumed his style as well as his approach to accomplishing each goal. The situation was different for the children with autism. It appeared that they too were attentive and motivated to achieve the goal that was demonstrated – but they watched and imitated the *action* rather than the person doing the action. This may sound bizarre, because how can you watch and imitate an action without watching and imitating the person who is acting? In a way, you can't. Yet perhaps even a non-autistic person may adopt rather different orientations to what is happening. Suppose I ask you to copy *me*. Suppose I then ask you to copy *my action*, and I do something that reveals how a particular technique is effective in achieving a goal. Here the difference is probably one of degree, but I hope it illustrates how the orientation of a child with autism seems closer to the latter situation than to the former. There is something impersonal about the way they imitate.

If this interpretation is speculative, the findings themselves are not. The fact is that the children with autism did not copy the style of the person whose goal-directed actions they were perfectly able to copy. By the way, we could ascertain from other ratings of their behaviour that this was not because they were especially clumsy or because they were unable to perform actions gently or harshly.

Moreover, there was another feature of the results that I have not told you. This proved to be the icing on the cake of our experiment. It emerged not because we had planned for it – we had not – but because we had given ourselves licence to play around with various kinds of action that seemed interesting. By chance, two of those actions involved an orientation to the body of the person who was acting. Tony positioned the pipe-rack against his own shoulder before strumming the stick against it. He also wiped the frog against his own brow.

Why should this matter? It has nothing to do with style. No, but it does have special importance for something else that is at the heart of our concerns. In the area of imitation, just as in the area of emotional responsiveness, we have been giving a lot of emphasis to the notion of movement through persons. Just as one person's expressions of feeling can move someone else to feel things in sympathy, so a person may identify with someone else in the act of imitation. This, too, involves a kind of movement into the other person's position. The person who imitates assumes something of the mental orientation of the other person.

The crux for our experiment is that we should see one thing if a child identifies with Tony and something else if the child merely copies 'behaviour' without reference to the person (Tony) who is behaving. Recall that the child sees Tony placing the pipe-rack against him*self*, and wiping him*self* across the brow with the cloth frog. Only if the participant identifies with Tony will he subsequently place the pipe-rack against *him*self, or wipe his *own* brow. It is only through such role-taking that the child will adopt Tony's self-orientated action as something he can now perform in relation to a quite different body, namely his own. In other words, he copies the action *as* a self-orientated action. In this case, he imitates not only the action but also the self-orientation of the action. Someone who is only copying the action will not notice or bother with the self-orientation part of this.

The results were as follows. About two-thirds of the *non*-autistic children copied Tony's self-orientation in the pipe-rack and brow-wiping tasks by orienting the actions to their own bodies. Yet only two of the sixteen children and adolescents with autism held the pipe-rack against their own neck or upper arm. Even when prompted, there were only three others who held the pipe-rack against their own bodies at all (and not in the way Tony had done). In the brow-wiping task, fourteen of the sixteen non-autistic children but only five of the sixteen children with autism applied the frog to their own brows. Even more startling in the case of brow-wiping, where not only the action but also the goal of the action was self-orientated, was the fact that only nine of the sixteen children with autism (as against fifteen of the sixteen non-autistic children) took hold of the frog at all – and this despite the fact that all but one proceeded to flatten the frog with the roller. It was as if the self-orientated brow-wiping did not register with the autistic children, even though they had no problem in copying the other actions.

In two respects, then, the children with autism were not moved to adopt the orientation of the person they were watching. They did not adopt the style with which Tony executed the actions, nor did they identify with him and copy his self-orientated actions so that these actions became orientated towards themselves. On the other hand, they were perfectly able to perceive and copy the strategies by which he achieved the goals in each demonstration. So they were able to learn something from watching what Tony did. They were also motivated to use what they had learned when their own turn came round. Yet what they learned seemed to be available from their position as a kind of detached observer of actions and goals. They were not moved.

This has important implications for our understanding of the self. Identifying with someone means recognizing the someone as a person with characteristics that one can make one's own — characteristics that come to enrich one's self. The process may seem rather unsubtle in an experiment on imitation, but if one imagines that this kind of identification is going on all the time, mostly invisibly, one can appreciate that it represents a deeply influential mode of cultural transmission. A child is learning through repeated shifts into the roles of others, doing things and seeing things and adopting attitudes towards the world as 'they' do. Which returns us to an aspect of language learning that is especially relevant for our exploration of the self in autism. This concerns the personal pronouns 'I' and 'you'.

I have already discussed the peculiarities of the personal pronouns 'I' and 'you'. A child who is just two years old hears her mother say: 'I do it!' If the child learns to say 'I do it!' when the child wants to do something, then something rather remarkable has happened. The child has learned that the word 'I' does not refer to mother — or at least not always. The word 'I' refers to the child herself — or at least it does when she uses it. Similarly with the word 'you' — or 'mine' and 'yours', come to that. The words are not like names, stuck to particular individuals. They shift in meaning according to who is speaking.

As we have seen, the child learns to comprehend and use such terms by identifying with the person who speaks. She recognizes that her mother's insistent 'I do it!' expresses her mother's attitude, and that her mother's 'That's mine!' expresses her mother's claim to possession. So, when the child herself has that attitude, then all she has to do is use the utterance which expresses that attitude for herself. She does what her mother does, and insists 'I do it!' or 'Mine!' Therefore if it is the case that children with autism have a weakness in identifying with others, one might expect that personal pronouns would present special difficulty for them. This would not be because personal pronouns present a complex bit of grammar for a child to learn, but because these words are deeply embedded in particular interpersonal processes. They show that 'you' and 'I' are concepts with a grounding in self–other relations that are deeper than language itself.

Beginning with the earliest descriptions of children with autism, one can find accounts of abnormalities in their use of personal pronouns. Kanner noted how some of the children seemed to repeat pronouns just as they had been heard, without the alteration that comes with the shifting of roles I have described. He reported how they appeared to echo what another person had said, so that the personal pronouns were associated not with what the person expressed from a particular vantage-point but rather with the impersonal context of what was happening. If the mother were to say 'Do you want a bath?', then the child with autism might express his wish for a bath in just the same terms: 'Do you want a bath?'. In fact the abnormalities may be more subtle than this, as when a child with autism may refer to himself as 'he', or fail to assert himself or his wishes at all.

A study by Tony Lee, Shula Chiat and myself may be used to illustrate how partial is autistic children's grasp of personal pronouns.[5] It is not that they always use 'I' and 'you' incorrectly, but rather that they seem less firmly anchored in what it means to be 'I' or what it means to address a 'you'. We took two groups of adolescents, one composed of individuals with autism and one of individuals who did not have autism, and as usual the groups were selected so that the children were similar in age and verbal ability. We asked two separate teachers whether these adolescents ever got into a muddle over personal pronouns. Not a single non-autistic adolescent had such a problem, but seventeen out of the twenty-five adolescents with autism sometimes made mistakes. In fact we happened to capture an example on video-tape, when one of the adolescents departed with the remark 'Thank you for seeing you, Tony.'

The principal finding from our study was that, in naming photographs, the children with autism seemed to have a rather detached attitude towards both themselves and the person (Tony) who was testing them. Our method consisted of presenting pairs of photographs – for example, one of Tony wearing a scarf alongside one of the child without a scarf – and asking simple questions such as 'Who is this a picture of?' or 'Who is wearing the scarf?' The large majority of lower-ability children with autism consistently referred to themselves and to Tony by proper names, whereas the children who did not have autism would often refer to themselves as 'me' and to Tony as 'you'. A similar result emerged when Tony simply offered each adolescent a pile of photographs of their peers, and asked, 'Tell me who they are.' Mixed in among the photographs was one of the child himself and another of Tony. Here the main result was that the children with autism were unusual in saying that the photo of Tony was of 'Tony', rather than referring to Tony (who was sitting alongside) as 'you'.

So, overall, there seemed to be something missing in the autistic children's sense of me-ness and you-ness in their responses. If I were to show you a photograph of myself and say that this is a photo of Peter, you would find it a bewildering experience; if I then produced a photo of yourself and referred to this using your proper name, you would wonder if I was aware that the person depicted was in fact you. In the case of autism, then, it is almost as if the child is not committed to his experience of himself, as well as being relatively detached from the other person present. If we follow the drift of my earlier argument, we could say that the child with autism does not even identify with the photograph of himself, he does not seem to care about the fact that this person is 'me'. In our study, it was as if the photographs existed out of the context of the current goings-on between two people, the child and the experimenter.

In the case of self-awareness, then, we have a variation on a familiar theme: what happens between people is intimately connected with what happens within the individual. If the child with autism is not engaged with other people, and especially with the attitudes of others, then he is not going to be very concerned with other people's attitudes towards himself. More than this, he does not identify with others, so in the extreme case (and this is not true of all people with autism) he may not even move to the position of taking *any* attitude towards himself. We noted L's lack of self-consciousness as he would walk naked through the house without a care for the feelings of others. It seemed that in his own mind there was no position from which he imagined himself through the eyes – or, more important, through the mind – of someone else.

Yet, for all this, anyone who has in-depth experience of children with autism knows that the picture is more complex. It is even the case that some of the children have a very painful and moving awareness that they are not like other people. As an autistic person known to Michael Rutter once remarked, he felt he differed from other people because he couldn't mind-read. So Tony Lee and I decided we should find out how more able adolescents with autism do think about themselves.

It hardly needs saying that most adolescents are deeply preoccupied with how they compare with their peers. They constantly draw parallels with others, and they may spend hours ruminating on whether they are as attractive or as strong, have as many friends, or otherwise measure up to their friends and classmates. Self and other are two sides of the same coin. Given their lack of engagement with the attitudes of others, we anticipated that this would not be so for adolescents with autism.

In order to find out what adolescents with autism think about themselves, it seemed most sensible to ask them. What we needed was an approach that allowed us to ask questions in a systematic but natural way. Even though this study was not intended as an experiment, we could still compare individuals with and without autism who were similar in age and language ability. In fact it was even more important than usual to establish that, if there was anything special about the responses of people with autism, this reflected something unusual about their self-concepts and not merely something about their lack of fluent speech. So we were very careful to make sure that the two groups were very similar with respect to aspects of language productivity and complexity.

Tony gave our subjects an interview that had been designed by William Damon and Daniel Hart to examine the self-concepts of young children.[6] The interview proceeds in a semi-formal way, but with flexibility about the ordering of questions and the gentle encouragement that may be given to elicit more elaborate replies. It begins with questions such as 'What are you like?' and 'What kind of person are you?', and then attempts to draw out why the person thinks these features are important; then the interviewer asks what the person is proud of about himself, how he thinks he will be the same or different in five years' time, what kind of person he would want to be, how he changes from year to year, how he became the person he is, and what makes him different from anyone he knows. In each respect, the interviewer provides help in drawing out what the person can say about himself.

We videotaped the interviews and had them transcribed. The next task was to identify 'chunks', which were the sections of the interview in which a person mentioned and elaborated upon a particular characteristic. These could then be abstracted from the interviews so that, when they came to rate them, the judges did not know if a given chunk was from an interview with someone with autism. Each chunk was rated according to the kind of characteristic described, and here there were four main categories: (a) physical characteristics, which had to do with an individual's body and material possessions, (b) features to do with the person's activities, (c) social characteristics, including attributes related to social interactions, and (c) psychological characteristics, which concerned the person's emotions, thoughts and preferences. Each of the four categories was also rated for a number of 'levels of description'. At the more sophisticated levels, for example, even physical or active attributes could be described in the context of social interactions. The question was whether the adolescents with autism were in any way different from those who did not have autism – and, in particular, whether their thinking about themselves was less embedded in interpersonal experience and in social comparisons.

What emerged was that the two groups were very similar in the ways they described their physical characteristics, whether involving reference to their bodies or their abilities in activities like sport. More surprisingly, they were also similar in the numbers of their responses that made reference to psychological states. In this case, however, the *quality* of the responses was different in the individuals with autism. They gave more emphasis to their preferences rather than their emotions or intellectual capacities. Moreover, the statements by the adolescents with autism that referred to emotions made reference only to being wound up, happy, excited, upset, and enjoying things, and in two cases the statements were more about behaviour than feelings ('I had little tears coming down here' and 'I do funny things. Screaming and shouting'). The emotional statements by non-autistic adolescents were far more varied, for example, including references to being mad, uptight, ashamed, angry, anxious, having a vicious temper, having feelings, and crying because of missing someone.

The main group difference was that very few of the statements made by the autistic adolescents referred to social relations, and many of those that did merely implied social awareness (for example, with reference to themselves as 'good' or 'nice'). This was true not only in the specifically social category, where they made about a quarter as many statements as the adolescents who did not have autism, but also in those levels of description of physical, active and psychological categories that concerned social appeal and social interactions. Compared to those without autism, half as many of the autistic adolescents mentioned their families, but, most striking of all, not a single individual with autism mentioned a friend except in passing (and even this happened only once), whereas 70 per cent of the non-autistic adolescents did so. Only a quarter of the adolescents with autism but as many as 90 per cent of those without autism made explicit social statements of other kinds, for example, about helping others, being bullied by others, and membership of social groups such as scouts.

Here are some illustrative examples, where 'I' stands for the interviewer and 'A' for the adolescent. The first three instances are from interviews with mildly retarded adolescents who do not have autism, and the second three involve adolescents with autism who are comparable to the first three in age and verbal abililty. I should stress that in the course of the interview all the adolescents received exactly the same questions, and these excerpts are selected to give a sense of the ground covered.

First adolescent without autism

I: What sort of person are you?

A: A girl.

I: Why is it important for me to know that you are a girl?

A: I hate being a girl – yuk!

I: You hate being a girl?

A: Yes.

I: You'd rather be a boy?

A: Mm.

I: What difference would it make if you were a boy?

A: Well, I like being a boy because you get all interested, you hang around with boys, hang around with friends and like my brother does.

I: When you said 'hang around', what does that mean?

A: Like hang around with a lot of people.

I: Just be with them.

A: Mm. When I am a girl I don't get on with people.

I: You don't get on with people? That's very surprising.

A: Only, only, two people that I get along with. That's Susan and Mike. Five people I get along with. That's Susan, Mike, Peter, James – no, Susan, Mike, Peter, Anne, Maria – no. That's the five people I get along with.

Second adolescent without autism

I: What are you proud of about yourself?

A: Getting on with the girls in my dormitory.

I: Is it important to get on?

A: Yeah. One of my friends, my best mate, is Mary.

I: Yes.

A: She's one of my best mates.

I: She's your best mate and you get on with her?

A: Yes.

I: Why is it important to get on with people?

A: To make friends.

I: Right. So it's important to have friends?

A: Yeah.

I: And could you tell me why?

A: If y'don't get on with people you row and everything.

Third adolescent without autism

I: Are there things about yourself that you don't like?

A: People winding me up all the time.

I: Right. And why does that happen?

A: I don't know why. They just get at me and I fall into their trap and get really wound up. I got a vicious temper on me.

I: So, having a temper on you: is that something you're not proud of?

A: Yeah.

I: So how do you control that?

A: I'm not sure. The only one who can calm me down is my brother. If I really lose my temper he's the only one who can calm me down.

First adolescent with autism

I: How are you different now to, let's say, five years ago? How old are you now?

A: Ten.

I: You're ten. So when you were five years old how were you different?

A: No, I've been one. When I was one I couldn't stop screaming.

I: Right. So you don't scream any more.

A: And I used to have epilepsy.

I: Right.

A: I had tablets.

I: Right. Are you on tablets now?

A: No. Because I don't scream so much.

I: Do you remember why you screamed?

A: I expect it was because I had epilepsy.

I: Right. How did the epilepsy make you feel?

A: Well, I just couldn't stop screaming.

Second adolescent with autism

I: What sort of person do you want to be like?

A: I like to be a man.

I: Right. Why is that important? Why do you want to be a man?

A: To saw things.

I: To saw things?

A: Saw wood.

I: Right. And why is that important, to saw wood?

A: Because it is.

I: Right. Any other reasons why you want to be a man?

A: Eh ... screw-drive.

I: Right. So you can use all these different tools?

A: Yeah.

I: Right. Why is it important to use tools?

A: Because it is.

Second adolescent with autism (later)

I: Is there anyone who is exactly like you in the world?

A: It's mummy.

I: Mummy?

A: Yeah.

I: In what ways is she like you?

A: Eh, because ... she did. She walks like me.

Third adolescent with autism

I: We were talking about getting bigger, and you had said earlier
on that when you get older you are going to have to start doing
things by yourself. What sort of things will you have to do for
yourself when you are eighteen?

A: Y'have to go in pubs and that, 'cause you're allowed to go in
pubs when you're that age.

I: And what would you do in the pub?

A: You have ... you'd have a drink of beer or whisky or brandy or
bitter.

I: And why do people drink?

A: 'Cause they want to. They're thirsty.

I: Why don't they just drink water then?

A: 'Cause they don't do water in pubs, and in pubs y'have to just drink beer.

I: I see. So will you go into pubs when you get older?

A: Yes I will.

I: Apart from going in because you're thirsty to have a drink, are there any other reasons why it's maybe important to go into a pub?

A: Yes, 'cause you want dinner.

It is clear that able adolescents with autism can talk about themselves, but when they do so they reveal just how similar and different they are to adolescents who do not have autism. They are similar in so far as they can describe their bodies and their activities, and even their preferences and (to a limited degree) their feelings. They are different in so far as they do not talk about more subtle feelings, and, most especially, they hardly make reference to family, friends or peers. They rarely compare or contrast themselves with others.

Adolescents with mild mental retardation but without autism carry in their minds a richly social world in which they themselves have a place, both affecting and being affected by family and friends. Adolescents with autism seem to carry in their minds a world that is thinly populated, one in which they themselves seem to be portrayed without colour and substance. It was not at all uncommon for the adolescent with autism to begin to speak about himself, but then to trail off as if there was little more to be said. My colleague Tony felt that, however hard he tried, often he could not get hold of what this person with autism really meant to himself, as well as what he felt he meant to others. It was a haunting experience to try to enter the autistic person's world, only to discover that one felt lost and uncertain where to turn.

Yet still we should be careful in concluding too much from an interview study. The study has revealed what adolescents with autism are able to say about themselves, but then we know that they struggle with language. Even though we took pains to check that in many respects these particular individuals were fluent and productive in speaking to the interviewer (whom they knew well), we cannot be sure how far the language demands of the interview set limits to what they could express. Then of course there are our own limitations in being sensitive to the experiences of people who have a very different existence from our own, and we may simply have overlooked or bypassed the most important things they were needing to convey.

With these concerns in mind, we decided to try another approach. Suppose we asked children with autism to draw themselves?

There have been long-running disputes over the significance one should attribute to children's drawings of people. For example, there have been disagreements over the usefulness or otherwise of human-figure drawings as indicators of children's emotional disturbance, including distortions in self-image. Here, features such as the omission or unusual inclusion of body parts, or drawings of people with atypical body proportions, have sometimes been interpreted as reflecting maladjustment. There have also been conflicting views about the drawings of mentally retarded people, and whether they are simply delayed in comparison with the drawings of typically developing individuals (which they probably are). In our own approach to the matter, we took as our principal focus the degree to which children with and without autism would highlight the individuality of themselves in relation to others – the very issue on which the self-understanding interviews had thrown up suggestive evidence.

The groups of children and adolescents we tested had language ability at about the level of normal youngsters between three and nine years old.[7] We began by establishing that the two groups were equivalent in their ability to copy abstract designs. When the children were asked to draw a house, the groups were also similar in the number of details they included, for example, giving it a roof, windows, doors, and so on. It also turned out that the children with autism included as many details in their drawings of a person, for example, depicting a head, hair, eyes, nose, mouth, neck, trunk and limbs.

However, there seemed to be a contrast in how the two groups produced their human-figure drawings. As expected, the non-autistic adolescents who did best in IQ tests were also those who provided the greatest detail and accuracy across the range of drawing tasks. At the same time, the patterning of their scores indicated that their skill in drawing human figures was partly separable from that involved in other kinds of drawing, because these abilities did not always correspond. In each respect, the adolescents with autism appeared to be different: firstly, their scores in drawing both people and things were often out of keeping with their verbal ability, and, secondly, the amount of detail in their drawings of people seemed to reflect a general skill that also applied to their drawings of non-personal objects.

So we decided to test two new groups of children. They were asked to draw three different humans: a person, a person of the opposite sex to the first, and lastly themselves. They were also asked to draw three different houses: a house, a different house, and then their own house. Half our children completed the human figures first, and then drew the houses, and half the children completed these two tasks in the opposite order.

Our plan was to add up the number of features that distinguished the first and second human figures (supposed to differ in sex) and compare this with the number of features that distinguished the first and second houses; and we could also compare the number of features that distinguished the drawing of the same-sex figure from that of the child's self with the number of features that distinguished the first drawing of a house from the drawing of the child's own house. If it turned out that the children with autism were able to draw distinctive houses, but were repetitive and stereotyped in their drawings of different people and themselves, this would show there was something special about the lack of individuality in their mental pictures of people.

Here are some examples of what the children drew. First we have the drawings of a non-autistic child aged nine and a half years whose language ability was equivalent to that of a normal six-and-a-half-year-old. Here one can see that the child is able to draw houses that are distinctive, and also people who are distinctive. The child's drawing of himself has qualities that set him apart from just 'a person'.

Now we can compare the drawings of a child with autism who was similar in age and ability to the individual whose drawings we have just considered. Once again the child shows flexibility and creativity in making the drawings of the houses. It is very impressive and important that in this respect the child is just as able and creative as the first

FIGURE 25

child. The drawings of people are also very accomplished, technically speaking, and they also seem more mature than those of the first child. Yet, despite this, there is strikingly little to distinguish the drawing of 'a person' from the drawing of the child himself.

The contrast between these two children was typical, as can be seen from the following figure. The numbers on the vertical part of the graph indicate the average numbers of features used by each child in distinguishing (a) a house from their own house, and (b) the drawing of a person from that of the self. In other words, the heights of the columns show how distinctive were the drawings of houses on the one hand, and the drawings of people on the other. The thing to notice is how the pattern of results is strikingly different in the two groups. It is not that one group is better than the other overall. On the contrary, the two groups are very similar in their ability to produce distinctive drawings. One can see this by adding up their scores on the drawings of houses and their scores on the drawings of humans. What makes the difference is that the non-autistic adolescents are best at

FIGURE 26

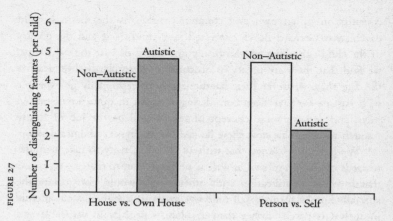

FIGURE 27

distinguishing humans, including themselves, whereas the adolescents with autism are best at distinguishing houses. What those with autism do not do is give special characteristics to drawings of themselves. It was also the case that many failed to draw clear distinctions between male and female figures.

In our earlier interviews on the self, we discovered that adolescents with autism do not describe themselves in the context of their relationships. Nor do they give special importance to family and friends. In the present experiment on drawings, we have found that they do not represent themselves as distinctive. In each case, we have found that a vital something is missing in their mental picture of themselves in relation to others.

Autism has shown us things both about thinking and about the self's embeddedness in personal relations with others. We have seen what thinking is like when it is not grounded in shared perspectives on the world, and we have seen a kind of thinness to the self when it is not rooted in the forms of self-evaluation that come with being engaged with the attitudes of others. We have been made aware of the contrast between our own world, steeped in the interpersonal and the intersubjective – a world where both the qualities and the perspectives of self and other are constantly brought into relation with one another – and the detached and lonely world of the person with autism. Without 'the constitution of an own and common world', as the German child psychiatrist Gerhard Bosch expressed it, a child's self and the quality of the child's thinking are drastically impoverished.[8] At the same time, we find that there are plenty of obscurities yet to clarify. Not least is the fact that, whatever their handicaps, the exceptionally able people with autism we have been considering *do* think in quite sophisticated ways, and *do* have some concept of self. It will be the job of future research to determine how these limited but impressive abilities develop.

We have also learned that without the propensity to take attitudes towards one's own mental as well as physical characteristics — a process that involves identification with others — we would not acquire the specially human form of self-reflective awareness. Although the picture in autism is patchy rather than absolute, especially in very able and articulate individuals with autism, it teaches us something about the Jamesian distinction between the consciousness of humans and the consciousness of animals.

> I never saw a wild thing
> sorry for itself.
> A small bird will drop frozen dead from a bough
> without ever having felt sorry for itself.
>
> D. H. Lawrence, 'Self-Pity'

What remains to be solved is an enigma at the very core of human consciousness and thinking: how we know that selves, and more fundamentally persons, are a class of thing with both bodies and minds. This conundrum provides a fitting challenge for the final chapter.

NINE

Understanding Minds

As a very young child comes to understand more about the mind, her own mind is transformed. This is a rather curious thing. It is especially curious because the complementary claim is also true: a child's understanding of the mind is transformed by changes that are taking place in her own ability to think about things.

The clearest example of this is when a child starts to use symbols. If my argument is correct, a young child begins to use symbols because she grasps the fact that people have the mental ability to attribute meanings to things. She begins to anchor particular meanings in what are otherwise meaningless sounds and squiggles (words) or objects that can mean something else (the materials of play). This shows that she understands the mind as a meaning-conferring property of human beings. She has grasped that we each have a subjective perspective, a personal way of experiencing the world, that we can apply to things. Her new insight that people can have alternative takes on things has led to revolutionary changes in the form of her intellectual life: she can make one thing stand for another, and she picks up what another speaker is meaning in such a way that she can adopt the other's expressions and words for what she herself wants to express and communicate.

At the same time, her new-found grasp of symbols allows her to locate and anchor aspects of her interpersonal understanding. In a way, she can arrive at true concepts or thoughts about the mind — and about self and others, come to that — only when she can use words or other symbols to encompass those thoughts. So, at just the time when she apprehends something deeper about people with minds, she acquires a new intellectual device for stabilizing and clarifying that understanding. Symbols, and especially words, help her to sort out and refine what she has gleaned from her engagements with others.

Even very young children cannot pull themselves off the ground by tugging at their own feet. So it is just as well that there are other people to lift them into the realms of symbolic thinking. It is also just as well that other people provide the means for them to understand what is involved in having a mind.

Thus far, we have concentrated on the facts of early social development. What we have not done is to focus on how, out of her experiences of interpersonal engagement, the child is moving towards our adult way of thinking about human beings. In particular, she is coming to think of people as a special class of thing, with minds as well as bodies. How is it that before long, as her words show very clearly, she has acquired a concept of something so seemingly obsure as the mind?

It is a daunting challenge to explain how anyone, never mind a child of two years, comes to understand that people have minds as well as bodies. After all, there is a long tradition of philosophical dispute about the basis for our knowledge of 'other minds'. The controversies have been fuelled rather than quelled by the recent advent of cognitive science and the attempt to fashion an account of human psychology on the model of computers. Among many points of contention are the following issues. How can we arrive at the idea of something so hidden and private as the mind? How do we see bodies but then ascribe invisible mental events to these same bodies? How do we come to suppose that other people have their own subjective experiences just as we do? Why do we take the view that there are specific kinds of mental event such as feelings, intentions, wishes, beliefs, and so on?

These questions provide a meeting ground for philosophy and developmental psychology. On the one side there is philosophy, with its concern to clarify how we use concepts. On the other side there is developmental psychology, with its task of elucidating how children come to acquire concepts in the first place. The greatest developmental psychologist of them all, Jean Piaget, characterized his own body of research on child psychology as 'genetic epistemology', which means an account of what makes knowledge and the acquisition of concepts possible.[1] It will be little wonder if, in attempting to understand the basis for children's understanding of the mind, we find ourselves embroiled in philosophy. Philosophical considerations should alert us to what exactly children come to understand, and developmental considerations should help us to see how they do so.

There are many people who think that human beings perceive bodies as things. They also think that, as a quite separate matter, we have awareness of our own minds. There can be no disputing that bodies *are* things, and that we *do* have experience of our own minds, so these people cannot be completely mistaken. The only problem, it seems, is why we believe that other bodies have minds as we do.

An argument that is commonly used to support such a view goes something like this. We can see other people's bodies, but not their minds. By contrast, we have direct access to our own minds. Indeed, we are the only ones who have. Therefore we must reason that, because other people have bodies which look like our own bodies, they have minds too. We arrive at our knowledge of minds through a process of inference, starting from our own case. There it is: an account that maintains our common-sense distinction between bodies and minds and explains how we see bodies but ascribe minds.

There are a tangle of difficulties with this argument. The most penetrating analysis of those difficulties was presented by the philosopher Ludwig Wittgenstein.[2] Unfortunately, Wittgenstein's own arguments are not easy to summarize. Perhaps it is best if I confine myself to a couple of pointers to where the difficulties lie.

There are several reasons why it cannot be the case that one arrives at knowledge of other minds by applying an analogy from what one knows of one's own mind. For example, one's experience of a mind would be the most prominent thing to strike one about one's own case. One would begin by knowing about one's own mind (so the argument goes), but not about that of anyone else. Now suppose one's experiences of other people were as neutral as one's experiences of a stone, say, or a tree. A stone or a tree seems so very different from oneself that the last thing one would do is to draw an analogy that it has a mind. You may think that this misses the point, because stones and trees do not have bodies like ours. That is true, but if one simply 'noticed' that other bodies have hands and legs and heads like one's own body does, this would provide a very fragile basis for drawing an analogy about those bodies having a *mind* like oneself. They would still seem so very, very different from oneself. Other people would seem almost (but not quite) alien from oneself, precisely because they would lack all those qualities of mental existence that one has oneself. Note how much stranger it is to think of ascribing minds to bodies than to think of ascribing minds to people.

Second, and even more telling, we are supposed to accept the idea that one can arrive at a concept of one's own mind all by oneself. This would be necessary if one only subsequently applied that concept to other bodies. But, to have and to use a concept, one needs to have it and use it consistently and appropriately. In order for this to be possible, one needs to be able to check that the concept is being used correctly and not at whim. For this one needs a way of checking, and here other people come into the picture.

To take one simple example, a child learns the meaning of the word 'happy' (and the concept of what it means to be happy) when other people use the word both about the child's own experiences and about people other than the child. If the child starts using the word about herself and/or others when they are manifestly unhappy, she will be corrected. It is when she starts to use the word appropriately that she has the concept. No, one might object: her using the word appropriately is just a sign that she has the concept. She could have a concept for her own case to begin with, and only subsequently apply it to others. This objection runs into trouble because it makes no sense to think of having a *concept* of anything if it can be applied to only one case. The whole point of having a concept is that it can be applied to different instances – and the child has acquired the concept of happiness only when she can correctly apply it to herself and others.

The upshot is that one needs experience of other people (with minds) in order to acquire concepts of mind in the first place. In addition, one needs to have the capacity to respond to correction as correction. It really does not make sense that one could, all by oneself, derive and apply concepts of mind correctly. And, if the case that I have been making in this book carries any weight, one certainly could not think in conventional symbols – whether about the mind or anything else – without first engaging with the minds of others.

I apologize if these ideas are overcondensed. In the notes I provide references to writings in which they are elaborated in detail.[3] I have wanted to outline the philosophical arguments for two connected reasons. The first reason is that I find them utterly persuasive. The second reason is that they make a big difference to how we should explain the basis for children's understanding of minds.

Consider all the developmental evidence we have been gathering. Is it in fact the case that infants experience bodies in the same way that they experience other physical objects? Can we find evidence that the ways in which they perceive and respond to other people's bodies differ from the ways in which they perceive and respond to non-personal objects? The answer is that we have found abundant evidence. Infants perceive and respond to people's bodies in very special ways. Those ways seem to suggest that they apprehend feelings *through* the bodily expressions of others. The European philosopher Maurice Merleau-Ponty quoted his fellow philosopher Edmund Husserl as saying that a person's perception of others is like a phenomenon of coupling. That is a wonderful way of putting it – that when we perceive someone, we become coupled with the person. Merleau-Ponty himself expressed something similar when he stressed the fact that 'I live in the facial expressions of the other, as I feel him living in mine.' The way we apprehend another person involves us with that person's subjective life.

The writings of Wittgenstein helped me to get hold of this idea, and here are three quotations from his two volumes of *Remarks on the Philosophy of Psychology* that I find especially illuminating:

> 'We *see* emotion.' – As opposed to what? – We do not see facial contortions and *make the inference* that he is feeling joy, grief, boredom. We describe a face immediately as sad, radiant, bored, even when we are unable to give any other description of the features. Vol. II, 570.

> One may note an alteration in a face and describe it by saying that the face assumed a harder expression – and yet not be able to

describe the alteration in spatial terms. This is enormously important. – Perhaps someone now says: if you do that, you just aren't
describing the alteration of the face, but only the effect on yourself ... Vol. I, 919.

'I see that the child wants to touch the dog, but doesn't dare.' How
can I see that? – Is this description of what is seen on the same level
as a description of moving shapes and colours? Is an interpretation
in question? Well, remember that you may also *mimic* a human being
who would like to touch something, but doesn't dare. Vol. I, 1066.

The first of these passages shows us that we have a kind of direct
route into the minds of others. We do not perceive a smile as an
upturned configuration of the mouth and by an intellectual process
decide that this configuration means the person is happy. When you
last experienced a three-month-old give you a broad smile, for instance,
I bet you did not even notice the shape of the baby's mouth – but
such a smile can affect one very strongly. Which is the point of the
second passage: the effect on yourself is what makes the perception of
emotion the kind of perception that it is. The third quotation is
perhaps the most abstruse, but it suggests that the way in which we are
able to imitate and identify with others' physically expressed attitudes
is critical for understanding their minds. In each of the examples
Wittgenstein selects – our ability to perceive a bored person, or a
harder facial expression, or a child wanting but not daring to touch
a dog – we see how subtle the processes involved can be.

Philosophy is not for everyone. Someone once said that philosophy
is common sense in a dress suit. Other people feel just the opposite,
and would agree with Bertrand Russell's self-effacing statement that
the point of philosophy is 'to start with something so simple as to
seem not worth stating, and to end with something so paradoxical that
no one will believe it'. Just now I presented the problem of how we
know other minds to my young teenage son. With some nudging from
me, he managed to solve it, but he also added, 'So get a life!'

There is a very different way to sharpen our thinking about the
perception of bodies, which is to revisit the most serious disorder of
'coupling' that exists: childhood autism. Through children with autism,

we get a sense of how different life would be if we could neither see nor hear feelings in the expressions of other people. I want to describe one final experiment on this topic. I hope that this study will complement others I have already described and ground our philosophical speculations in concrete facts about autism.

My colleagues Janet Ouston and Tony Lee and myself wanted to devise a task in which success depended on the children perceiving emotional meanings in the face.[4] At the same time, we needed a control task to assess the perception of faces when emotions were not involved. Here we thought it would be an idea to see if the children could identify different people by differences in their faces. If they could do this, but they had difficulty in recognizing emotional expressions, then this would indicate that such expressions pose special problems.

The task we employed is complicated to describe in detail, but its essence was to sort photographs of happy, unhappy, angry and afraid faces to match these same emotions in photographs of new individuals.[5] The happy face of person A was supposed to go with the happy face of person B, the angry face of A with the angry face of B, and so on. The control task was to sort photographs of the faces of four different individuals – persons A, B, C and D – to match photographs of these same individuals when they had different emotional expressions. The happy face of person A was to go with the angry face of person A, the happy face of B with the angry face of B, and so on.

The first result was that both autistic and non-autistic children could accomplish these tasks. They had no difficulty in matching either emotions or people's identities. They could put happy faces with happy faces, despite these being on different people; and they could put a photo of a person with another photo of the same person, despite the two photographs differing in emotional expression. This showed something, but not much. It showed that all the children could do a fairly simple matching task very proficiently. The question remained: were they doing it in the same way? Did the emotional expressions really have the same meaning for the children with autism? Might a photographed smile have amounted to an upturned mouth? If you and I can sense emotions by the slightest changes in the feel of what a face conveys, can children with autism do the same?

To test this, we blanked out parts of the photographs to be sorted.

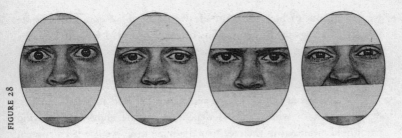

FIGURE 28

To begin with we blanked out the mouths, then we blanked out the foreheads as well, leaving only the eyes by which to judge emotion. In the control condition, the same blanking-out procedure was used to increase the difficulty of judging people's identities. The photographs above show the emotions portrayed in the blank-mouth-and-forehead condition.

The prediction was that non-autistic children would be able to sort the photographs of emotion even when there was little of the face to go by. The eyes should be enough to give them a feel of what was being expressed. We predicted that children with autism would find this task very difficult, but still be as good as the non-autistic children at sorting identities, where they were at no special disadvantage.

And so it proved. When sorting the photographs by the people's identities, the performance of each group showed a steady decline as the faces were increasingly blanked out. There was no group difference in this respect: the children in each group found it more difficult to recognize individuals A, B, C and D when there was only a small section of the face to go by. On the emotions task, by contrast, the non-autistic children were still able to match emotions by using the feel of the part-faces. Here the children with autism showed a much steeper decline in performance — and they were no longer able to sort the emotions in the faces with blanked out mouths and foreheads.

Then we did something that might have been inspired by Wittgenstein, who remarked:

> Hold the drawing of a face upside-down and you can't tell the *expression* of the face. Perhaps you can see that it is smiling, but you won't be able to say what *sort* of smile it is. You wouldn't be able to

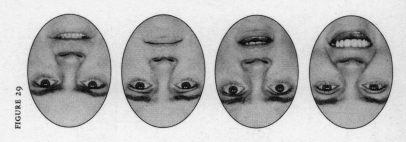

FIGURE 29

imitate the smile or describe its character more exactly ... And yet the upside-down picture may represent the object extremely accurately. Vol. I, 991.

As a final test, therefore, we placed the four target full-face photographs upside-down. Then we gave the children upside-down full-face photographs to sort. Still they had to match emotions across different individuals, and still they had to match photographs of the same individual when that person's emotion differed – but all with upside-down faces.

The difference between the groups was startling. The following graph represents the results from the emotions part of the task. It was hardly surprising that the performance of the non-autistic children slumped on the upside-down faces: the task was beyond them. What *was* surprising was that the performance of the children with autism substantially improved over the blank-mouth-and-forehead condition. Although they had performed poorly in sorting the partly obscured upright faces, they scored significantly higher than the comparison children in sorting upside-down emotions. This result was similar for upside-down identities as well.

In fact, of course, the 'emotions' were no longer recognizable *as* emotions when the faces were presented upside-down. Effectively, the task was reduced to one of pattern or feature recognition. Once the task was meaningless from an emotional point of view, the children with autism performed better than the children without autism. These results brought home to us just how different other people must appear to children with autism. They can detect fine detail in faces,

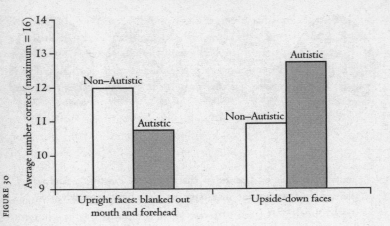

FIGURE 30

but they cannot see emotional meanings. They do not pick up the emotional dimension of another person's bodily features.

Most of us do not have autism. We are moved by someone else's pain or joy. We find ourselves relating to other people in ways that are special to people. This is true of infants as well as young children as well as older children as well as adults. For us, to perceive a living body is more than to perceive a thing – it is to become engaged with a person. A person has a subjective, mental, dimension: we see it and we feel it. Thus we come to know what a mind is – what thoughts are, what feelings are, what intentions are, what beliefs are – on the foundation of our direct experience of other persons as having a subjective dimension behind their behaviour. We perceive bodies and bodily expressions, but we do so in such a way that we perceive and react to the mental life that those physical forms express. Forms of feeling (the title of a book by my late father, Bob Hobson) constitute the primary source of mental contact between one human being and another.[6]

The upshot is that our experience and knowledge of *persons* is primary. Our knowledge of minds as distinct from bodies comes later. We know what a person is because a person offers us emotional contact and emotional interchange; what we experience with persons but not things are mutual mental connections. We do not size up people's behaviour, and then work out that people have minds. We do not have 'a theory' that a person has a mind, because we do not need one. It is the person with autism who demonstrates what it might be like to have recourse to theory. The highly intelligent adult with autism I quoted in the first chapter said almost as much: 'I then suddenly realized that there were people. *But not like you do. I still have to remind myself that there are people.*'

I accept that for many of us it seems awkward and unfamiliar to imagine that very young children distil out the idea of the mind, on the one hand, and of the human body, on the other, on the basis of their experience of this strange hybrid thing called a person. In contrast, it is so natural for us to imagine that infants first perceive and react to bodies, and then discover or theorize that there are minds at a much later period and on a quite different basis. It is easier to think in terms of persons being constructed in children's minds, as they glue body and mind together. And it requires quite an effort to turn such reasoning on its head.

Once again, it was someone with autism who helped me to achieve this shift in perspective. The person was an eighteen-year-old man who had difficulty in grasping a particular concept. In his case, the difficulty was with the concept of 'friend'. What is so interesting is why he could not grasp this simple idea.

It was certainly not because he lacked the ability to use language. On the contrary, he had passed higher school exams in both English and German. It was only in particular areas that he could not understand what most people find simple. Foremost among his pre-occupations was his inability to grasp what a friend is. He would ask again and again, 'Are you a friend?', 'Is he a friend?', and so on. When he spent some time in hospital, the ward staff made every effort to teach him what a friend is. They even found him a befriender to accompany him to the local shops and to talk with him in a personal way. Yet all this was to no avail. He simply could not fathom what a friend is.

Why not? What is so peculiar, and in this case so elusive, about the concept of friend? The answer is that the concept of friend cannot be defined by features that may be observed by one who stands outside and merely watches behaviour. One has to experience the kinds of sharing and arguing and competing and so on that make up friendship.

Because most children experience these things, they do not find it difficult to learn the meaning of the word 'friend'. They already know the kind of thing that is being referred to, even though this thing is impossible to describe in terms of its physical characteristics. The situation was different for this man with autism. He made almost no emotional contact with the people around him. He simply did not have the kinds of experience of others that would have enabled him to know what a friend is.

I suggest that exactly the same kind of account might be given of our experiences of persons-with-minds. It explains why people with autism have such difficulties in understanding minds. In a way, it is not just understanding minds that presents a problem for individuals with autism. The problem is understanding people and the expressions of people *as* expressive of their inner, subjective, mental and emotional life. And in my view it is in autistic children's deficient experience of mutual relations with people that the source of their difficulties is to be found.

Just imagine for a moment that you are faced with a computer that talks intelligibly. It even talks about its feelings. But it has a body like a postbox. Perhaps you could begin to imagine that it is human-like, an old-fashioned and rather dumpy android, a kind of paralysed Dalek ... But now compare your reaction to someone throwing this lump of electronics out of the window with your reaction to someone trying to throw a person out of the window. It is simply not possible for one to have the same feelings of respect and concern for a computer, however articulate, that one has for a person. Only to the extent that it begins to look like, act like and feel like a human being, do you come to treat it as such.

Now imagine something else: that you were born without respon-siveness to persons. Another body would still have its usual bodily form, but in your experience this form would not have the capacity to express attitudes, nor evoke person-appropriate attitudes in you. It would be more interesting than a postbox, in that it would have physical properties like the ability to move itself and do things and make sounds. But it would be no more or less engaging than ... an interesting object. What could possibly lead you to have empathy for such a body, or relate to it as a centre of consciousness? The fact is that, if you always experienced people as things, you could not arrive at the concept of a person. You simply would not know what 'a person' means, just as the autistic man I described did not know what 'a friend' means. Nor would you have any idea of what a mind is. Although the situation is not quite like this for people with autism, who after all can perceive and copy actions, it is not so very different either.

For those of us who do not have autism, it is natural to become engaged with people. We do not have concern or hatred for others because we think they have a mind. It is the other way round: we come to think people have minds because we find we are involved with them. What we begin with is our attitudes towards persons. That is how it is in early childhood and how it is throughout life. As Wittgenstein put it, 'My attitude towards him is an attitude towards a soul. I am not of the *opinion* that he has a soul.'[7] It is a mistake to think that opinions or knowledge about minds are at the root of empathy. Knowledge of how people tick and insights into the perspectives of others certainly make us more sensitive, but these things are icing on the cake. Such knowledge and insight and role-taking develop on the basis of our natural emotional reactions to one another. They would not be there at all were it not for the social interplay of attitudes that precede them early in life.

I hope that by now two things are clear. First, if we are to understand that other people have subjective experiences (that is, a mind), we need to relate to people with feelings. Second, in relating to people we get access to minds directly, not via a convoluted route of inferences, deductions and analogies. Minds are neither so hidden nor so abstract as they may seem.

Some arguments are difficult to grasp, and others seem difficult to keep hold of. The ones that are difficult to keep hold of are the ones that contradict our usual ways of thinking. We slip back to our old assumptions, and lose the thread. For many people, the arguments I am making may fall into this category. When I face a situation like that, I try to find a pithy summary of the main point – preferably a summary that appeals to my common sense. It helps me to grip those new threads. Perhaps this quote from the philosopher Woodruff Smith will serve for the present purposes: 'I not only see "her", I also see that "she is feeling sad" ... Such an experience we feel intuitively is a direct awareness of the other's grief ... And such is our acquaintance with others.'[8]

The infant finds herself relating differently to people and things. So far, so good. But there is still a long way to go before she will *understand* the difference between people and things. To react to other people as persons is the foundation for understanding minds, but concepts about the mind still have to be built upon these foundations. An infant does not yet know what a thought is, or what a feeling is, or (until much later on) what a belief is. Indeed, it is only with progress towards such understanding that she will be able to think. These further developments depend on the infant having the support and mind-enhancing containment of an interpersonal cradle.

The critical thing is that the infant has the experience of sharing experiences with someone else, as well as experiences of being separate and her own person.[9] She registers when she is in tune with her caregiver, and she registers when she is out of tune. It is very significant that the human infant and her caregiver spend so much time exchanging smiles and other facial expressions, coos and other sounds, caresses and various forms of touch, and a veritable rainbow of communicative gestures. These days, psychologists have taken to calling such things 'behaviours', a term that makes me vaguely nauseous. The acts, the gestures, the expressions are part of deep interpersonal engagement.

The point is that the infant needs to share experiences in order to come to understand what it is to share. She needs to find that sharing experiences is something that happens and then stops, but is also something that can start again and stop again. It can be sought and achieved. She is learning what it means to be connected and separate from someone else; she discovers that the experience of being with someone is special in kind. In order for this to happen, she has to be endowed with the capacity to respond with feelings to the feelings of others. This is the first step towards understanding minds.

The second step is to relate to the outer-directed attitudes and behaviour of other people. The infant seeks out and responds to the attitudes of others towards objects and events that exist in a shared world.[10] Still this does not really amount to the child understanding that a person has a mind: it is simply that she is coming to register and respond to other people in increasingly complex ways. In this stage of secondary intersubjectivity, it is not just that other people have entered the picture in a new guise, as sources of attitudes with their own take on objects and events. It is not just that the world has changed, now that it has come to have meanings-for-the-other. It is also that the baby has gained a self with a new kind of status. There is still a way to go before the child can think of herself as an individual in relation to other individuals, but already there is a boundary between self and other. The baby shows things to others, for example; she realizes there is a need to do so, to engage a person who may be orientated to something else. Self and other, as two sides of the same coin, are becoming distinct in the baby's mind. And, because knowledge of the self is grounded in awareness of persons, the self, too, is a body-and-mind kind of thing.

A major advance in research on this period came with the discovery by workers such as Katherine Bates that there are two distinct classes of communication in the stage of secondary intersubjectivity.[11] In one of these, the infant requests or demands that an adult does something such as get a sweetie or start up a toy. In the other, the infant shows things to the adult or follows into whatever is the focus of the adult's attention.

It is this latter kind of relatedness that is most important for our concerns. The reason is that one can make a request to someone without having to get far beneath that person's skin. One simply needs the person to act on one's behalf, and therefore all the infant needs is to realize that another person can do things. Making a request often involves more than this, in fact, because the infant will sometimes look to the person's face when doing so, but nevertheless the contact is aimed at eliciting action. It is a different matter when the child shows things to someone, or otherwise shares her experiences with another person. Here, the whole point of the exercise is to become engaged with the other. The infant seeks out expressions that convey how the adult is attentive towards and emotionally engaged with her and what she is doing and showing. In other words, the infant is tapping into the subjective dimension of the other person – and this subjective aspect is manifest in the person's expressions of interest and delight.

It is no coincidence that *sharing* is what we find to be lacking in children with autism. Young children with autism very rarely show things or point things out to other people, and they rarely follow the eye gaze or the pointing of others. They do not share things or experiences with others. Nor do they change their feelings towards the world in accordance with the feelings of others. They do not look to an adult when they are confronted with something that may provoke anxiety or curiosity; they are unaffected by another person's attitude of fear towards something. Although they can imitate goal-directed actions, they often fail to attend to and engage with another person, and so they carry on regardless of what other people are doing. There are all manner of ways in which they should be learning about the world through others – how to feel about things, how to act upon things, how to represent one thing by another in play – but often they seem oblivious to these opportunities.

Then there is the third and final step into the realm of thinking. The child not only changes her attitudes to accord with those of others, she not only registers and reacts to the expressions and behaviour of others, she not only utters sounds that seem to refer to objects and events around her – she also knows that she does so. Not only does she take roles and adopt perspectives because that is how people affect her, but also she can choose to put herself into the shoes of someone else. She has insight into the other's perspective *as* another person's perspective. She not only names things, but also comments on things for the other. For many children, there is a quantum leap in the rate of learning words as every word uttered by someone else becomes a candidate word for the child's own use. The child realizes that a word used by the other towards herself has a meaning which holds when she uses the same word for the other. She grasps that she herself can attribute meanings and can shift meanings from one thing on to another in symbolic play.

This is what thinking is. Our child who is not yet two years old has achieved mental space. She can move in that space, and relate to her own attitudes and actions. She can hold symbols in mind, and think with them. She can hold other selves in mind, and relate to the desires and feelings and intentions of others. She can begin to adopt alternative perspectives, to choose among alternative courses of action.

In the field of symbolic play, she can represent events that have happened in the past or that might happen in the future.

In order for this to happen, certain things need to have crystallized in her mind. She is aware of herself as a self among other selves. She is a source of perspectives and attitudes that are both connected with and separated from the perspectives and attitudes of others. Accordingly, she understands that meanings are person-centred, in the sense that people can give meanings to things. Therefore attitudes (and now thoughts) can be detached from context, and things like arbitrary sounds and written squiggles that have no intrinsic meaning may be given meaning. She can intend to symbolize, and make one thing stand for something else. In the context of language, she finds that words have consistent meanings for others and for herself. She finds that there are correct ways of using words, and she follows the leads that others provide.

But *how* has all this happened so miraculously? I get cold feet whenever I get to this point in the argument. There is little evidence, never mind proof, to indicate how these revolutionary changes take place. But where angels fear to tread...

It seems to me that we do not need to invent innate mechanisms to explain the third step into thought. This is what others have done. They have suggested that the brain, acting like a computer, develops a new switch that allows the child to represent her own representations of the world. This is a fancy way of saying that she can think of her own thoughts. In a way, that is close to what I have described, even though my emphasis is on having attitudes to one's own attitudes, rather than thoughts about thoughts (the importance of this distinction being that attitudes are what thoughts develop *out of*). But why do I not accept the easy alternative, and admit that probably brain growth and computational mechanisms hold the key to explaining how we come to symbolize? Mainly, because it is too easy. If one sees a radical change in a child's mind, then of course one can say that the change is caused by an innate mechanism. This is not a very inspiring explanation. It may be the correct explanation, of course, but it should be an explanation of last resort. Especially when it is an explanation that creates as many developmental obscurities as it resolves.

I will not get embroiled in what the obscurities are. I have done that in dusty academic papers, using arguments that do not bear repeating here. And, to be forthright, why on earth should we invent innate switches for which we have absolutely no evidence? Early social development provides the mechanisms that we need, and the settings we need, to bring the child to the brink of discovering what she needs to discover.

The acts of discovery I have detailed are no more or less mysterious than any other discovery. What the infant discovers is herself as a mental being with the capacity to think. Which is a succinct and provocative way of summarizing all those things I listed a few paragraphs ago, about self-awareness, perspective-taking, using symbols, and so on. The discovery may not be an all-at-once or an everywhere-at-once event, but it does happen. It is a discovery about the nature of minds – which is why I am justified in recapitulating my points about symbolizing in a chapter on understanding minds. The mechanisms that are needed to prompt this discovery have to do with responding to others' attitudes as these are directed to the world and towards the child herself – the kind of responding that involves being moved in feeling. All the child needs is the ability to read the directedness of attitudes in the expressions and bodily orientation of the other, and to respond by identifying with the other. These abilities and processes are the stuff of relatedness triangles. Relatedness triangles constitute the settings within which the discovery takes place.

What I have tried to do in my description of relatedness triangles is to show that they involve a set of experiences which are just like any other set of experiences that lead to discovery. Once a child is relating in these ways, then one expects that sooner or later the penny will drop. What gives the final nudge is not clear. Perhaps it is a matter of having enough experience of relating to others' relations to shared objects and events; perhaps it is that the child needs to be guided towards shifting meanings herself; perhaps the rate-limiting process is the child's adopting others' attitudes to her own attitudes, so that she starts to do this all by herself. And, yes, perhaps her brain has to grow too. What I doubt is that the nature of any brain growth involves the specific kind of switch-on mechanism that others have proposed. All we would need is some general increase in the brain's capacity. The mechanisms of identification and role-taking should do the rest.

So, to return full circle to the ability to symbolize: a child symbolizes only when she understands something of what a symbol is – *and* when she understands something of what she herself is choosing to do in making one thing stand for another. I would state this even more strongly: what leads a child into being able to symbolize in a creative way is neither an increase in the computing hardware of her brain nor a new-found information-processing strategy in her general cognitive repertoire. It is nothing more nor less than her realizing that symbolizing is something she already has the potential to do.

What a curious idea – that a child becomes able to do something by realizing that she can do it. The idea is more complicated than it first appears, because of what it means to 'realize' something about one's own abilities. In most contexts, this would mean adding something new to one's repertoire. In the present case, it means acquiring a new repertoire altogether. Or is the idea so curious? Are there not many things in life for which this is true? What about the many times one coaxes a child with the statement 'You can do it!' – especially in situations where what the child can do (but does not yet know she can do) involves her applying old skills in a novel context, or where her seemingly limited skills are amplified and transformed by the use of a new tool? In the present instance, the new tool is a simple intellectual trick: you make this stand for that. The only problem is that you cannot do this until you know that you can.

There is a final reason why I fight against the innateness hypothesis. This is that there seems to be a wide-ranging developmental process at work which subsumes much that I have just described. It is a process that may explain what we need to explain: the newly appearing qualities of thinking *and* the new kinds of self- and other-awareness. This is the process of interiorization described by Lev Vygotsky and central to psychoanalytic accounts of development. It is the process by which things that happen between people become things that happen within the individual's own mind.

'There are two kinds of people in the world. Those who divide the world into two kinds of people and those who don't.' A similar aphorism could apply to the kinds of people who try to explain phenomena in development. Either you can start with abilities that are separate, and try to say how they become linked; or you can start with abilities or aspects of mental functioning that are yoked together or even mixed in with each other, and say how they become separated out. I am now going to oppose the joining-together and differentiating-out approaches in several of the areas with which we have been concerned. Either explanation will have to allow for the emergence of new abilities that arise as the brain develops.

The joining-together account says that the baby's mind is carved up into a cognitive aspect (thoughts or their precursors), a motivational aspect (the will) and a feeling aspect (the emotions). For example, an infant can feel certain things like shame or coyness only when she has the kinds of concept that underpin these feelings, and, in particular, concepts about the self. The differentiating-out approach says that there are quite complex feelings like coyness that may manifest themselves as more primitive expressions of the relatedness between the individual and her world. These do not necessarily depend on sophisticated concepts. More fundamentally, infants derive thoughts and feelings from something composite – again, modes of relatedness. In the account I have given, thoughts are only gradually distilled out of the attitudes and intentions that are fundamental to relatedness between the infant and the world. One implication of this is something that Vygotsky stressed: every thought contains a transmuted element of feeling.

The joining-together account says that the baby perceives bodies and then infers the existence of minds. Then bodies and minds have to be welded together. The differentiating-out approach says that children derive concepts of body and mind from something composite, an awareness of persons. From a 'primordial sharing situation' between infant and caregiver (as it was called in a classic text by Werner and Kaplan), the infant comes to distil out self and other as persons-with-minds.[12] Children acquire concepts of their own minds in parallel with their concepts of other minds.

The joining-together account says that children begin with their own thoughts, and learn how to communicate these thoughts to others. The differentiating-out approach says that children begin with an ability to communicate with others, and through communication they distil out thoughts-for-themselves. It is this developmental grounding that dissolves the mystery of why it is possible to convey thoughts from one person to another. Symbols *begin* life between people, and only as a secondary development do they become vehicles for an individual's thoughts.

It is worth emphasizing how genuine communication could not take place without a background of sharing. True, an individual could utter sounds in order to make things happen, just as one might imagine oneself making 'requests' to a robot. But this is not real communication. Communication involves affecting and being affected by someone else. The transaction involves the transmission of feelings, thoughts or whatever between two minds. Therefore sharing — and, if my argument is correct, sharing implicates feelings — is at the root of *all* communication and all intentions to communicate. Or, to put this more simply, feelings that can link one person to another are what underpin a child's wish to convey something to someone else, and her understanding that someone else may be trying to communicate something to herself. In fact, communication involves more complex processes in which one person needs to appreciate that the other is intending to communicate, and moreover intending that the listener appreciates that she is intending to do just that (recall Magritte's pipe and Hamlet bamboozling Polonius). But these complexities can look after themselves.

Finally, we come to an overarching principle: whereas the joining-together account says that children begin as individuals and become social, the differentiating-out approach says that certain very important psychological abilities begin in the interpersonal sphere and become features of the individual's mental functioning.

The oppositions I have presented are too polarized. Most fundamentally, we need to recall that a child's own experiences are a vital part of what goes into her interpersonal awareness in the first place. More than this, it is very important that, once a child has acquired insights into her own mind, these *do* inform her ability to put herself into someone else's shoes; and, once a child has become able to symbolize, then her thinking *can* become a partly private and invisible process. The important thing from a developmental view is where the infant starts from so that these things are made possible.

I need hardly restate that my own position is that a child's understanding of the mental and the physical is an understanding of two different aspects of the same thing – persons – and that no account that attempts to glue these things together will succeed.

> Sweet is the lore which nature brings;
>   Our meddling intellect
> Misshapes the beauteous forms of things
>   —We murder to dissect.
>
> Wordsworth, 'The Tables Turned'

I have emphasized that understanding develops slowly. This is true about the child's ideas about the functioning of minds. We adults are so used to thinking in terms of feelings, wishes, intentions, beliefs, and the like, that it is easy to underestimate how these concepts are hard-won over the early years of life. Some are more difficult to acquire than others. I do not intend to map these developments in detail, but it is worth illustrating how, having gained access to this realm of knowledge through their experience of interpersonal relations, children come to think of the mind as having its own distinctive characteristics.

One way to study a young child's understanding of the mind is to listen to what she says. In a study by Inge Bretherton and her colleagues, mothers were asked to say when their young children first used words to refer to internal states such as feelings and thoughts.[13] A large proportion of twenty-month-olds applied words like 'kiss' and 'cry' both to themselves and to others, and a small number of the children already used psychological words such as sad, mad, scared and hungry. When presented with pictures of emotionally expressive faces of children, a number of toddlers spontaneously referred to pictures of sad children as 'he cry', 'crying', 'baby cry', 'oh-oh, cry', sometimes with wiping of tears, imitation of crying noises, and kissing of the baby picture. Children who had just turned two years were beginning to reason about mental states. For example, one child of twenty-five months said, 'I'm sad I popped it' about a balloon, and another said, 'Those ladies scare me.' Home recordings have confirmed that by twenty-four months of age children take an active part in talking about feeling states such as those of sadness, distress, happiness, affection and tiredness.

Another investigator, Henry Wellman, asked two-year-olds to make judgements about the actions and emotional reactions of story characters in each of three types of situation.[14] In the first, a doll character wanted something that might be in one of two locations, searched in one location, and found it. In the second, the character found nothing in the place she searched. In the third, the character found an attractive object, but not the one she wanted. The children were asked how the character would act — and here the critical issue was whether or not she would go on searching — and how she would feel: happy or sad. The children solved these simple tasks with ease — for instance, saying that the character who found nothing or a substitute object would be sad.

Even more explicit evidence for children's abilities to distinguish mental and physical things comes from interviews with slightly older children. Three-year-olds can be asked about the difference between a boy who has a cookie and one who has a thought about a cookie: which of these — the cookie or the thought about the cookie — could be seen by someone else, could be touched, or could be transformed at will? Or one can ask similar questions about dreamed, remembered or pretended events: 'Can you touch a dreamed tree with your hand?' 'Why not?' When such questions were put to three-year-olds, the replies included 'No, 'cause it's in his mind', 'No, because he's just dreaming about it', 'No, because he's thinking it and he can't see it.' Children of this age can be quite explicit about the ways in which mental events differ from physical ones.

Finally, Wellman and his colleagues asked three-year-olds what a story character does if she 'thinks' that a desired object is in one place whereas it is really in another. Or they were required to reason backwards from a person's actions to that person's underlying beliefs and desires: 'Jane is looking for her kitten. The kitten is hiding under a chair, but Jane is looking for her kitten under the piano. Why do you think Jane is doing that?' Children as young as three years often seemed to understand that a person's beliefs and desires combine to produce actions. Even so, another year must pass before the children fully grasp what it means to have a false belief, as we saw in an earlier chapter.

The picture that emerges from these studies is that, from the middle of the second year of life, children become increasingly adept in thinking and talking about the life of the mind. As children's understanding of minds deepens, the flexibility of their thinking – and especially their ability to reflect on their own mental processes – increases too.

There is a complementary approach to the developmental perspective I have been taking on the nature of thinking. This is to re-examine some of our assumptions about what happens when adults think. It is especially illuminating to observe circumstances where the distinctions between movements in thought and movements in attitude, and between thoughts that are hidden and thoughts that are manifest, are not so clear. These circumstances afford a picture of thinking-in-action that is quite different from our usual image of people who are lost in their own private and inscrutable thoughts.

Consider this account of Tom, an adult who moves from one stance to another in relation to a particular topic. Tom thinks about an apple: at first he thinks it looks tasty, then he thinks it is not yet ripe. When such thinking occurs within a single individual's mind, it looks as if the person simply passes from thought to thought. Even so, we can see that the thought is not so abstracted from feelings, in that Tom's attitude is bound up with his feelings about the apple.

Now consider how Tom might move to the psychological position of another person who is related to that same object of thought in a different way. If we stick to the case of Tom thinking about the apple, we can imagine the effects when his friend Simon expresses another thought in words. Simon handles the apple and says that it feels hard. Tom reacts to this statement by entertaining a thought of the apple as hard. He changes from thinking the apple looks tasty to thinking it looks unripe. Here we have an instance in which Tom's movement in thought occurs through someone else. The change takes place because Simon's words, expressing his thoughts, change what Tom has in mind. Or, to be more accurate, the words spoken by Simon in context have this remarkable effect of introducing new thoughts into Tom's mind.

In this case, what I have called Tom's stance amounts to his having a thought-with-feeling about an apple. Then Simon introduces a new thought into Tom's mind by the use of language. Simple enough. But, if we are trying to explain the very beginnings of thought and language, this cannot be the place to start. We cannot explain the origins of thought by saying that a baby can already discern someone else's thoughts; nor can we explain the origins of language by suggesting that the child already understands another person's words. There needs to be something prior to thought and language that does the trick of introducing the child to what thinking and speaking are all about. Are there kinds of psychological stance that do not yet amount to thinking and do not yet involve language, but that can nevertheless be adopted and changed through interpersonal contact?

If we revisit Tom and his apple, we have already pictured Tom having different feelings about the apple or different intentions towards it. He begins by desiring the apple and having pleasure anticipating its juiciness. He is intending to take it. Those feelings and those intentions could have been changed by Tom's observing that Simon is looking at the apple with disgust or is about to grab the apple for himself. Here we see that, without the mediation of thought and language, Tom's attitude to the apple could have been altered through his perceiving Simon's attitude to the apple. Once again, one person's psychological stance can be changed through another person.

In this new scenario, we do not need to describe what happens in terms of the thoughts of Tom and Simon. We might reflect that what we observe is not sufficiently specific or so precisely formulated as to justify a description in terms of Tom thinking such-and-such. All we see is a change in Tom's reactions to the apple. However, it does not make sense to suppose that any thoughts that take place in Tom's mind are completely separate from feelings. They are not just grey, disembodied thoughts. They are coloured by feelings. Or, as I would prefer to put it, the feelings are partly shaped into thoughts.

It is striking how easily we can pass between the two kinds of description in our account of Tom and Simon. On the one hand, we describe changes in Tom's mental orientation that are brought about by Simon's statements. On the other hand, we describe changes that are brought about by Simon's expressed attitudes. The two descriptions no longer seem different in kind. In this context at least, a person's words and a person's attitudes appear similar in the effects they have on another person's thoughts. And note that what Tom and Simon are thinking is, by and large, perfectly visible. Thoughts are not always hidden. Which is just as well if infants need to read them.

Of course it is no coincidence that my scenario involves the kind of interchange that can occur between a twelve-month-old and other people. In the case of the twelve-month-old, we would be right to avoid talking about the infant thinking, because the infant does not yet have the concepts to think about the apple in this way or that. Nor could the infant articulate her thoughts, nor would she understand the stated opinions of someone else. Tom and Simon have intellectual equipment that is not available to twelve-month-olds. The equipment consists of symbols that are grounded in very basic forms of human interaction that continue throughout life. That is why the pattern of interaction between Tom and Simon maps on to a pattern of interaction observable in one-year-olds. Symbols are first conceived between people through the coordination of attitudes that take place in such interactions. Only from this starting point do they become the means to thinking inside one's own head.

Now at last we come full circle to the issue I raised at the beginning of Chapter I. If we have arrived at a picture of the development of thinking in early childhood, have we also gained insight into the development of thinking in the evolution of primates? I think we have.

Primates such as chimpanzees and baboons may have their own ways of thinking, but, with the possible and partial exception of a select group of chimpanzees brought up by human beings, they do not think symbolically. In asking ourselves why not, it is appropriate to examine their non-social mental abilities and then their social abilities in order to see whether there are clues to the sources of their intellectual strengths and limitations.

According to an authoritative review of the evidence by Michael Tomasello, chimpanzees' impressive abilities to find, identify and obtain food (even food that is hidden and needs retrieving) are not unique among mammals.[15] It is even doubtful whether their ability to use tools to forage for food is especially well developed. The only kind of intellectual task on which they outperform other non-human animal species involves the recognition of relations among objects — for example, when they learn to choose the odd one out of three objects. It would seem that if we are looking to non-human primates for something that reveals the final steps towards human thinking, this something does not reside in their non-social intelligence.

If we now turn our attention to comparisons between chimpanzees and humans, the differences in practical, non-symbolic understanding of the world — in the ability to grasp that objects have permanent existence in a space, for example, and in the ability to form mental maps of the spatial layout of the environment — are again far from striking. The one possible exception is that chimpanzees may fail to understand how forces act when one thing causes another. For example, they need lots and lots of learning trials before they can select which one of a number of sticks has the right dimensions to push food out of a transparent tube. This seems to be something they cannot work out in their heads. This is unsurprising if abstract thinking about unseen forces needs mental symbols to hold such ideas in mind. It may tell us more about the effects of a lack of symbolizing than about the reason for that lack in non-human primates.

In order to find the missing link in the story of the evolution of thinking, we may need to examine other aspects of chimpanzee mentality. One fruitful place to look might be in their social intelligence. Chimpanzees do seem to show sensitivity to other chimpanzees, and they appear to have human-like awareness of social relations. Again we should note that chimpanzees are not alone in forming relationships with their peers. The cooperative hunting of lions and wolves is well known, for example. Despite this, Tomasello argues that there is something distinctive about primates, and this is their ability to understand something of the relationships between other individuals, not merely the relationships between themselves and others. For example, if one animal (A) is attacked by another (B), then A may attack a relative of B, revealing its knowledge of the relationship between the two; or A may select an ally (C) that outranks B, indicating its awareness of the relative ranking of B and C; or A may try to interfere with B's attempt to form alliances. From a complementary perspective, another chimpanzee (D) may intervene to try to lower the heat between A and B. These kinds of interaction attest to an especially rich social fabric within primate groups. They may also suggest that, if chimpanzees are one step closer to thinking than other animals, their involvement in and appreciation of social relations may hold the key.

Yet what is critical for the story of the development of thinking is the matter of social *learning*. What can one chimpanzee pick up from other chimpanzees? Does a chimpanzee acquire new understandings through its social interactions? If so, in what ways? Do these ways have the power to transform a chimpanzee's means of relating to things, the very intellectual processes that can be applied in its dealings with the world?

Like other animals such as rats, chimpanzees can certainly learn a lot from watching the behaviour of others. For example, a young chimpanzee may observe its mother pushing over a log and notice there are insects beneath it. The young chimpanzee may then follow suit. Is it imitating its mother? From a careful analysis of such situations, both in the wild and in more controlled situations, Tomasello proposes that the chimpanzee is learning more about the world than about the ways one can act upon it. The chimpanzee merely applies its own skills and strategies to capitalize on what the other chimpanzee's behaviour has shown. In the case of the mother pushing the log, what the young chimpanzee learns is that there are insects under the log. What the chimpanzee does not do is to attempt to reproduce the actual behaviour or behavioural strategy of another chimpanzee. It does not imitate; it merely emulates. It attempts to reproduce the end result of the other's actions, but according to its own methods.

So, too, when a chimpanzee appears to copy the communicative gestures of another chimpanzee, it is not in fact copying, but rather having its behaviour shaped by what is successful or unsuccessful in eliciting desired behaviour. When Tomasello and his colleagues gathered together all their observations of shared and non-shared gestures among the group of chimpanzees they had studied at the Yerkes Primate Center over a period of twelve years, they found that the prevalence of gestures shared among the individuals in a group was no greater than in unrelated chimpanzees. Nor could they find evidence that, when one chimpanzee acquired a new gesture, this was imitated by others.

The differences between chimpanzees and humans in the use of gestures is especially telling, because the differences highlight those relational characteristics that are already familiar from our account of secondary intersubjectivity. Chimpanzees use gestures towards each other – for example, to regulate their play and sexual behaviour – but they do not use them to refer to objects and events in the world. Even in face-to-face contexts, gestures are used for getting other chimpanzees to do things, rather than for showing things and sharing things. Moreover, as Tomasello also stresses, the gestures are unidirectional rather than intersubjective. The infant chimpanzee touches its mother's rear end to make her lower her bottom so it can get aboard, but would not understand being touched in this same way by another chimpanzee. Even apes that have been trained to point to direct humans to food do not understand human pointing when this is directed to them.

Finally, there is only very little (and highly controversial) evidence that chimpanzees have any concept of the minds of other chimpanzees or humans. It seems very likely that, when they seem to have such understanding, this is explicable in terms of much simpler principles of behavioural shaping. For example, Daniel Povinelli and Timothy Eddy carried out a series of experiments to determine whether young chimpanzees understand seeing as a mental event.[16] They found that chimpanzees would gesture no more towards a human who could see them than towards one whose sight was occluded (for example, by a bucket on his head). Experiments to test for chimpanzees' ability to adjust to the beliefs of others have given similarly equivocal findings.

However, there is a complication to the apparently clear division between non-human primates and humans. This is that chimpanzees brought up by humans can display special forms of learning that are not evident when they grow up in the wild or when reared by their natural mothers in captivity. Tomasello and his colleagues tested imitation in three 'enculturated' chimpanzees who had been raised from infancy with humans as well as other chimpanzees.[17] As part of their everyday lives, they had been encouraged to take part in a number of human activities that facilitated joint attention and action towards objects. They were also exposed to human speech and a manually operated device that displayed symbols. Three mother-reared chimpanzees with much less human input were also tested, along with groups of eighteen- and thirty-month-old human children. An experimenter modelled actions with a series of test objects, for example demonstrating how to reel in an object and how to employ a lever. In each case, either immediately following the demonstration or after a two-day gap, the participant chimpanzee or human was presented with the object and prompted to imitate what the experimenter had done.

The results were that human-reared chimpanzees were much more likely to copy the behaviour of the human demonstrator than were mother-reared chimpanzees. For example, the best-performing mother-reared chimpanzee reproduced both the ends and means of novel actions much less often than the poorest-performing enculturated chimpanzee. By contrast, the enculturated chimpanzees were quite similar to young children in their ability to imitate the actions on objects. There was still some indication that they were inclined to emulate rather than to imitate the experimenter's actions, because in the tests of immediate imitation they were more likely than the children to reproduce the ends but not the means of the actions. Yet, compared with their mother-reared peers, they were able to pick up much more from the human demonstrations.

Several mechanisms could account for these results. For example, the enculturated chimpanzees had a history of receiving praise for imitating their human caregivers, whereas the mother-reared chimpanzees had not. This might have influenced the readiness with which they attended to and copied the experimenter. Having noted such possibilities, Tomasello and his colleagues preferred the explanation that a human-led upbringing had had the effect of 'socializing the attention' of the chimpanzees in contexts of joint attention to objects and events.

I have quoted from Tomasello at some length, partly because of the sophistication of his own research and theory and partly because we share much common ground in our emphasis on the importance of symbolic thinking in young children and the lack of symbolic thinking in non-human primates. We also agree in our emphasis on the social origins of what is distinctive about human thinking and, in particular, on the importance of humans learning through each other. But there is a critical point on which we part company. Although Tomasello has stressed that human beings differ from non-human primates in achieving joint attention with others, his primary emphasis has been on the reading of others' goals and the means to achieving those goals. For example, in concluding the review from which I have been selecting examples, he states that humans differ from non-human primates in understanding others 'as beings that have goals, behavioral means to attain those goals, and perceptual/attentional/mental processes with which to monitor progress towards goals'.

What seems to be lacking is a view of how the human infant comes to grasp that others have a mental orientation of their own. 'Joint attention' actually means engaging with another individual's psychological engagement with the world, and I do not think that reading goals and copying the strategies to achieve those goals is enough to yield jointness in this respect. In my view, what we need is an account of the mechanism by which individual human beings, but not individual chimpanzees, come to link in with each other in such a way as to understand both themselves and others as beings who have subjective experiences. I think that only this kind of account will explain why non-human primate gestures differ from those of human one-year-olds, in the ways described earlier. Only this kind of account will explain the origins of creative symbolizing.

Let us accept that chimpanzees do not think symbolically, either in language or in play, and also that they lack concepts about the minds of others. The question arises, Why this should be so? Is it merely that the outer layer of the chimpanzee brain – the neocortex that seems so well developed for supporting intellectual activity in man – needs to be bigger or better at what it does? And, even if this is the case, what is it that has led to the super-brain of humans?

I think the answer is this. What chimpanzees lack is the *capacity to identify with others through emotional engagement* – an ability that, as we have seen, transforms the intellectual life of a baby. My bet is that, if chimpanzees acquired this ability, their intellectual life would be transformed, too.

I once visited the Yerkes compound for chimpanzees in Atlanta, by courtesy of Michael Tomasello. I sat gazing at a chimpanzee who sat on the other side of a fence, gazing at me. As a psychoanalyst, I have been taught to analyse the countertransference, which means that I try to formulate how this individual is making me feel. So I sat there and tried my very hardest to do just that. I felt ... something missing.

I could not connect. I was reminded of the experience one sometimes gets when relating to a child with autism, if one is not filling the void by saying things or doing things. It was as if this chimpanzee was not at home, mentally speaking. Or at least I was not entering a home, in his mind. I wondered if this was because we belonged to different species. Would it be different if I were a chimpanzee? I seriously doubt it.

Primatologists tell me that chimpanzees indulge in a lot of rough and tumble together, just as children with autism often do with their caregivers. What they do not do is to spend time gazing into each others' eyes, or engaging in the kinds of intense face-to-face interpersonal communication that we see in human infants. They do not dwell in each other's expressions. This is on the level of primary intersubjectivity. On the level of secondary intersubjectivity, too, they do not enter the subjective lives of their fellow chimpanzees. They never (or almost never) show things to each other, nor do they appear to share experiences of the world with others.

Yet social referencing abounds. Chimpanzees are very acute in picking up when another chimpanzee is interested in something, or is showing fear towards an object or event. There can be no doubt that they perceive meanings in actions and expressions of emotion, therefore, and no doubt that they can read the directedness of what is being done and expressed. The difference from humans is in the depth and strength of emotional contact with others. It is a difference that begins at the level of primary intersubjectivity – the pull towards sharing experiences and engaging in mutually coordinated mental states – and it is a difference that continues into the level of secondary intersubjectivity and the sharing of experiences about the world. The fact that chimpanzees' attention is not 'socialized' is only partly because they are brought up differently from humans. It is also because their attention is itself less social in nature. This difference proves to be critical for subsequent mental development.

Chimpanzees see and hear other chimpanzees' actions and expressions, and they react in accordance with what they see and hear. And yet ... they are mostly reacting to what is on the surface. They do not apprehend the surface as expressive of something else – of a dimension of life that we call subjective experience. They neither notice nor explore nor understand 'what it is like' for the other chimpanzee to experience the world. This is something that human infants *do* apprehend. Humans relate to the 'bodies' of others as more than objects with surfaces. The human infant is drawn into the mental life of her caregiver *through* her perception of and responsiveness to the bodily expressed attitudes of the adult. See how the baby attends to a person, engages with a person, even struggles with a person in face-to-face contact. And see how, by the end of the first year of life, the baby is focused on *the person* when she shows her things, points things out to her, and imitates her actions.

This fact – the fact that the human infant is drawn into the feelings and actions of the other – is one that has profound implications. It leads to what we have called 'identifying with' other people. Identifying with people is what leads to mental perspective-taking. Mental perspective-taking leads to insight into what it means to have a subjective perspective. And, once the infant understands that, symbolizing becomes possible. Because chimpanzees are not drawn into the feelings and actions of others, they do not identify with other chimpanzees, they do not take or understand perspectives, and they fail to symbolize. At root, their intellectual limitations are social limitations.

The difference between chimpanzees and humans can be illustrated by the case of social referencing. Consider the relatedness triangle as this applies to chimpanzees. As in the case of humans, the chimpanzee can relate to another chimpanzee's way of relating to something in the world. The difference is that for chimpanzees the focus is on the world, not on the other chimpanzee. The chimpanzee who watches learns about the world through the reaction of the other, but the other might as well be flashing a green light for 'go for it' and a red light for 'hold back'. The other is *merely* an indicator of what the object means. The object is what matters, and it is the object that occupies centre-stage in the triangle. The chimpanzee does not use the object as a way of getting access to the subjective state of the other chimpanzee, even though objects may be employed to alter another chimpanzee's behaviour. The chimpanzee does not use the object as a way of exploring relations with the other chimpanzee, or of finding out about chimpanzee minds. And in all of this, the chimpanzee is using the other chimpanzee simply as a waystation to the object.

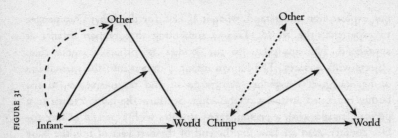

FIGURE 31

As a result, the chimpanzee does come to construe the object in a new way, for example, as something to be feared. In *this* sense there is a shift in attitude via the other. Yet for the chimpanzee this is little different from shifting in attitude simply because it has an opportunity to examine the object more closely and discovers something about it. There is not the experience of identifying with the other, of moving to the other's mental stance. There is simply a change in the chimpanzee's own stance. It is a shift that occurs *by means of* the other, but not *through* the other. There is no developmental dynamic; there is nothing to be learned about minds in relation to the world.

If this is so, then why do enculturated chimpanzees do so much better in tests of imitation than their peers who grow up in chimpanzee society? Surely this suggests that it is in the cultural settings created by humans — all those game-like interchanges and all that deliberate coaxing and teaching — that we should locate the critical difference. Perhaps the *individual's* capacity for identifying with others is not the issue, but the opportunities for the elaboration of experience.

To some extent, this is a matter of chicken and egg. It is only when the infant can identify with someone else that she can make full use of the modes of human exchange leading to thought. It is only when the wonderfully fashioned and coordinated structures of social interaction are available, that the infant's capacity to identify with the other is plumbed for its developmental potential. Almost certainly, evolution elaborated the individual and the social in tandem, as each tiny increase in the primate's ability to respond to and identify with the other led to enrichment in the exchanges that took place between individuals. What we see from the evidence on enculturated chimpanzees is that those species which benefit from intensive human input are very, very close to having what it takes. Sure enough, they may also lack those additional computational brain resources that evolved to capitalize on the symbol-using potential of our ancestors. Sure enough, they do not completely lack the resources to move towards human social engagement and therefore human symbolic functioning. It is just that their resources are insufficient to complete the journey — even with energetic input from their human friends.

As we come to the end of the book, it seems fitting to draw comparisons between two of our special cases — chimpanzees and children with autism. What these two groups have in common is the difficulty in apprehending and responding to the attitudes of others in typically human ways. Neither chimpanzees nor children with autism gesture to others to share experiences, because neither are sufficiently engaged with the emotional dimension of others' experience; neither chimpanzees nor children with autism identify with others, and thereby recognize the correspondences and contrasts between meanings-for-me and meanings-for-others. Where the two groups differ is in their accompanying abilities (rather than disabilities) in the non-social and social domains. These differences may highlight which aspects of intelligence and interpersonal engagement are insufficient for the achievement of symbolizing.

In certain respects, chimpanzees appear to be more affected by others' expressions of emotion than are children with autism. They are also more sensitive to other aspects of social interchange, and probably have greater awareness of other individuals' relations with each other. Although this has not been demonstrated experimentally, it is likely that they are more affected by others' emotional reactions to objects and events in the environment. Yet still they do not identify with others. Their emotional engagement is shallow. As a result, even basic forms of human perspective-taking, and all the understandings that arise out of perspective-taking, are deficient.

Many children with autism have computational hardware in the brain to achieve impressive intellectual feats that are way beyond the abilities of chimpanzees. More strikingly, they also have social abilities that seem to exceed those of chimpanzees — most notably in their ability to copy the actions of others, and in acquiring quite a lot of language. In our own experiments on imitation, for example, children with autism would notice and imitate another person's strategy to achieve a goal in a way that does not happen in most chimpanzees. In this respect, children with autism could assume the other person's actions for themselves. This almost certainly contributes to the development of their many impressive abilities – for example, in learning language to a far more sophisticated level than chimpanzees can achieve. Yet, when it comes to identifying with the attitudes of others, and when it comes to understanding the nature of subjective perspectives and therefore of people's minds, children with autism – like chimpanzees – have serious limitations.

In each case, the abilities to understand minds and to engage in creative symbolizing are nearly within reach. Yet in each case this potential is largely unrealized. Without the right kind of social engagement, intellectual development can proceed only so far.

We have arrived at a new perspective on the intimate connection among three developmental achievements: the child's growing awareness that she is aware, her knowledge that she is a self among other selves, and, last but not least, her capacity for symbolic and imaginative thought.

Only when an infant understands that she has a mind (which goes with an understanding that other people have minds) does she acquire for herself a mind that is distinctive to human kind. To understand that one has a subjective perspective – a mind of one's own – is to open the door on a world of meanings that can be given to the objects of symbolic play, anchored in the verbal symbols of language, or captured in other symbolic forms. Symbols crystallize and then protect a child's ideas, so that the ideas can be thought with and thought about. Along with these changes in the child's mind, there dawns the insight that she is but one self among many. From this time on she does more than react to the attitudes of others. She also thinks about other people as individuals with subjective perspectives of their own.

At this point, she leaves infancy behind. Empowered by language and other forms of symbolic functioning, she takes off into the realms of culture.

The infant has been lifted out of the cradle of thought. Engagement with others has taught this soul to fly.

Notes

The purpose of these notes is to signpost where readers may find details of the studies cited in the text, and to indicate further reading that may be of interest.

PREFACE

1. R. P. Hobson, *Autism and the Development of Mind* (Hove, Erlbaum, 1993).

ONE: JUST THINK...

1. A paper that attempts to integrate biological and psychological perspectives on autism with psychological research (and provides plenty of secondary references) is A. Bailey, W. Phillips and M. Rutter, 'Autism: towards an integration of clinical, genetic, neuro-psychological, and neurobiological perspectives', *Journal of Child Psychology and Psychiatry*, 37 (1996), pp. 89–126.

2. For rather different versions of autism as an interpersonal disorder see R. P. Hobson, 'What is autism?' in M. Konstantareas and J. Beitchman (eds), *Psychiatric Clinics of North America*, 14 (1991), pp. 1–17. R. P. Hobson, 'Understanding persons: the role of affect', in S. Baron-Cohen, H. Tager-Flusberg and D. Cohen (eds), *Understanding Other Minds: Perspectives from Autism* (Oxford University Press, 1993), pp. 204–27. S. J. Rogers and B. F. Pennington, 'A theoretical approach to the deficits in infantile autism', *Development and Psychopathology*, 3 (1991), pp. 137–62.

3. R. P. Hobson, 'Developmental psychopathology: revolution and

reformation', in M. Bennett (ed.), *Developmental Psychology: Achievements and Prospects* (Philadelphia, Psychology Press, 1999), pp. 126–46.

4. L. Kanner, 'Autistic disturbances of affective contact', *Nervous Child*, 2 (1943), pp. 217–50. The excerpts come from the numbered cases in the paper; the quotation is on p. 250.

5. D. J. Cohen, 'The pathology of the self in primary childhood autism and Gilles de la Tourette syndrome', *Psychiatric Clinics of North America*, 3 (1980), pp. 383–402. The quotation is from p. 388.

6. R. P. Hobson, 'Methodological issues for experiments on autistic individuals' perception and understanding of emotion', *Journal of Child Psychology and Psychiatry*, 32 (1991), pp. 1135–58.

7. R. P. Hobson, J. Ouston and A. Lee, 'Emotion recognition in autism: coordinating faces and voices', *Psychological Medicine*, 18, (1988), pp. 911–23.

8. P. Ekman and V. W. Friesen, *Pictures of Facial Affect* (available from Paul Ekman, University of California, 1976).

P. Ekman and V. W. Friesen, *Unmasking the Face. A Guide to Recognizing Emotions from Facial Cues* (Englewood Cliffs, NJ, Prentice-Hall, 1975).

9. R. P. Hobson, J. Ouston, and A. Lee, 'Naming emotion in faces and voices: abilities and disabilities in autism and mental retardation', *British Journal of Developmental Psychology*, 7 (1989), pp. 237–50.

10. The principles of psychoanalysis were established by Freud and elaborated and modified by his many successors. He gives a succinct account and illustration of transference in the postscript on p. 116 et seq in S. Freud, 'Fragment of an analysis of a case of hysteria', in *Standard Edition of the Complete Works of Sigmund Freud*, vol. 7, tr. A. and J. Strachey (London, Hogarth Press, 1953), pp. 15–122.

A helpful paper in describing the interplay between internal and external relationships is J. and A. M. Sandler, 'On the development of object relationships and affects', *International Journal of Psycho-Analysis*, 59 (1978), pp. 285–96.

11. An impressive discussion of the structure and development of symbolizing is in C. Sinha, *Language and Representation* (New York, Harvester, 1988).

Two: Before Thought

1. G. Kugiumutzakis, 'Neonatal imitation in the intersubjective companion space', in S. Braten (ed.), *Intersubjective Communication and Emotion in Early Ontogeny* (Cambridge University Press, 1988), pp. 63–88. The concluding quotation is from p. 80.

2. A. N. Meltzoff and M. K. Moore, 'Imitation of facial and manual gestures by human neonates', *Science*, 198 (1977), pp. 75–8.

   T. M. Field, R. Woodson, R. Greenberg and D. Cohen, 'Discrimination and imitation of facial expressions by neonates', *Science*, 218 (1982), pp. 179–81.

3. T. B. Brazelton, B. Koslowski, and M. Main, 'The origins of reciprocity: the early mother-infant interaction', in M. Lewis and L. A. Rosenblum (eds), *The Effect of the Infant on its Caregiver* (New York, Wiley, 1974), pp. 49–76.

4. C. Trevarthen, 'Communication and cooperation in early infancy: a description of primary intersubjectivity', in M. Bullowa (ed.), *Before Speech*, pp. 321–72. (Cambridge University Press, 1979). The quotation is from pp. 336–40.

5. C. Trevarthen, 'Conversation with a two-month-old', *New Scientist* (2 May 1974). The quotation is from p. 232.

6. E. Tronick, H. Als and L. Adamson 'The structure of face-to-face communicative interactions,' in M. Bullowa (ed.), *Before Speech* (Cambridge University Press, 1977), pp. 349–70. The quotation is from p. 369.

7. E. Tronick, H. Als, L. Adamson, S. Wise and T. B. Brazelton, 'The infant's response to entrapment between contradictory messages in face-to-face interaction', *Journal of the American Academy of Child and Adolescent Psychiatry*, 17 (1978), pp. 1–13.

   J. F. Cohn and E. Z. Tronick, 'Three-month-old infants' reaction to simulated maternal depression', *Child Development*, 54 (1983), pp. 185–93.

8. N. Kogan and A. S. Carter, 'Mother-infant re-engagement following the still-face: the role of maternal emotional availability in infant affect regulation', *Infant Behavior and Development*, 19 (1996), pp. 359–70.

9. E. Z. Tronick, 'Emotions and emotional communication in infants', *American Psychologist*, 44 (1989), pp. 112–19.

   M. K.Weinberg and E. Z. Tronick, 'Infant affective reactions to the resumption of maternal interaction after the still-face', *Child Development*, 67 (1996), pp. 905–14.

10. L. Murray and C. Trevarthen, 'Emotional regulation of interactions between two-month-olds and their mothers', in T. M. Field and N. A. Fox (eds), *Social Perception in Infants* (Norwood, NJ, Ablex, 1985), pp. 177–97.

11. J. M. Haviland and M. Lelwica, 'The induced affect response: 10-week-old infants' responses to three emotion expressions', *Developmental Psychology*, 23 (1987), pp. 97–104.

12. A. S. Walker, 'Intermodal perception of expressive behaviors by human infants', *Journal of Experimental Child Psychology*, 33 (1982), pp. 514–35.

13. J. S. Bruner, 'The ontogenesis of speech acts', *Journal of Child Language*, 2 (1975), pp. 1–19.

   J. S. Bruner, *Child's Talk* (Oxford, Oxford University Press, 1983).

14. D. C. Wimpory, R. P. Hobson, J. M. G. Williams and S. Nash, 'Are infants with autism socially engaged? A study of recent retrospective parental reports', *Journal of Autism and Developmental Disorders*, 30 (2000), pp. 525–36.

15. T. Charman, J. Swettenham, S. Baron-Cohen, A. Cox, G. Baird and A. Drew, 'Infants with autism: an investigation of empathy, pretend play, joint attention, and imitation', *Developmental Psychology*, 33 (1997), pp. 781–9.

16. L. Kanner, 'Autistic disturbances of affective contact', *Nervous Child*, 2 (1943) pp. 217–50.

17. R. P. Hobson and A. Lee, 'Hello and goodbye: a study of social engagement in autism', *Journal of Autism and Developmental Disorders*, 28 (1998), pp. 117–26.

18. S. Story, 'August Rodin and his work', in *Rodin* (London, Phaidon, 1964), pp. 5–17. The quotation is from p. 16.

19. D. Moore, R. P. Hobson and A. Lee, 'Components of person perception: an investigation with autistic, nonautistic retarded and

normal children and adolescents', *British Journal of Developmental Psychology*, 15 (1997), pp. 401–23.

R. P. Hobson, 'Apprehending attitudes and actions: separable abilities in early development?' *Development and Psychopathology*, 7 (1995), pp. 171–82.

20. G. Johansson, 'Visual perception of biological motion and a model for its analysis', *Perception and Psychophysics*, 14 (1973), pp. 201–11.

21. B. I. Bertenthal, D. R. Proffitt and J. E. Cutting, 'Infant sensitivity to figural coherence in biomechanical motions', *Journal of Experimental Child Psychology*, 37 (1984), pp. 213–30.

THREE: THE DAWN OF THINKING

1. C. Trevarthen and P. Hubley, 'Secondary intersubjectivity: confidence, confiding and acts of meaning in the first year', in A. Lock (ed.), *Action, Gesture and Symbol: The Emergence of Language* (London, Academic Press, 1978), pp. 183–229.

2. V. Reddy, 'Playing with others' expectations: teasing and mucking about in the first year', in A. Whiten (ed.), *Natural Theories of Mind* (Oxford, Blackwell, 1991), pp. 143–58.

3. J. F. Sorce, R. N. Emde, J. Campos and M. D. Klinnert, 'Maternal emotional signaling: its effect on the visual cliff behavior of one year olds', *Developmental Psychology*, 21 (1985), pp. 195–200.

R. Bakeman and L. B. Adamson, 'Coordinating attention to people and objects in mother-infant and peer-infant interaction,' *Child Development*, 55 (1982), pp. 1278–89.

4. R. Hornik, N. Risenhoover and M. Gunnar, 'The effects of maternal positive, neutral and negative affective communications on infant responses to new toys', *Child Development*, 58 (1987), pp. 937–44.

5. T. A. Walden and T. A. Ogan, 'The development of social referencing', *Child Development*, 59 (1988), pp. 1230–40.

6. J. S. Bruner, *Child's Talk* (Oxford, Oxford University Press, 1983).

7. I. Bretherton, S. McNew and M. Beeghly-Smith, 'Early person knowledge as expressed in gestural and verbal communication: when do infants acquire a "theory of mind"?'in M. E. Lamb and

L. R. Sherrod (eds), *Infant Social Cognition: Empirical and Theoretical Considerations* (Hillsdale, NJ, Erlbaum, 1981), pp. 333–73.

8. M. Tomasello, A. C. Kruger and H. H. Ratner, 'Cultural Learning', *Behavioral and Brain Sciences*, 16 (1993), pp. 495–552.

9. There are a number of theories concerned with children's abilities to play symbolically. Key references are J. Huttenlocher and E. T. Higgins, 'Issues in the study of symbolic development,' in W. A. Collins (ed.), *Minnesota Symposia on Child Psychology*, vol. 11 (Hillsdale, NJ, Erlbaum, 1978), pp. 98–140. H. Werner and B. Kaplan, *Symbol Formation* (Hillsdale, NJ, Erlbaum, 1963/1984). E. Bates, 'The emergence of symbols: ontogeny and phylogeny,' in W.A. Collins (ed.), *Children's Language and Communication, Minnesota Symposia on Child Psychology*, vol. 12 (Hillsdale NJ, Erlbaum, 1979) pp. 121–55. D. Wolf and H. Gardner, 'On the structure of early symbolisation,' in R. L. Schiefelbusch and D. D. Bricker (eds), *Early language: Acquisition and Intervention* (Baltimore, University Park Press, 1981), pp. 287–327.

10. C. Bühler, *From Birth to Maturity* (London, Kegan Paul, 1937). The quotation is from pp. 66–7.

11. J. Kagan, 'The emergence of self', *Journal of Child Psychology and Psychiatry*, 23 (1982), pp. 363–81.

12. G. G. Gallup, 'Mirror-image stimulation', *Psychological Bulletin*, 70 (1968), pp. 782–93. Further research on self-consciousness is discussed in G. G. Gallup, 'Self-awareness and the emergence of mind in primates', *American Journal of Primatology*, 2 (1982), pp. 237–48, and M. Lewis and J. Brooks-Gunn, '*Social Cognition and the Acquisition of Self* (New York, Plenum, 1979).

13. M. L. Hoffman, 'Developmental synthesis of affect and cognition and its implications for altruistic motivation', *Developmental Psychology*, 11 (1975), pp. 607–22.

   M. L. Hoffman, 'Interaction of affect and cognition in empathy', in C. E. Izard, J. Kagan and R. B. Zajonc (eds), *Emotions, Cognition and Behaviour* (Cambridge, Cambridge University Press, 1984), pp. 103–31.

14. J. S. Bruner, 'From communication to language – a psychological perspective', *Cognition*, 3 (1975), pp. 255–87.

J. S. Bruner, *Child's Talk* (Oxford, Oxford University Press, 1983).

15. D. C. Wimpory, R. P. Hobson, J. M. G.Williams and S. Nash, 'Are infants with autism socially engaged? A study of recent retrospective parental reports', *Journal of Autism and Developmental Disorders*, 30 (2000), pp. 525–36.

For the groundbreaking research that demonstrated limited joint attention in children with autism see K. A. Loveland and S. H. Landry, 'Joint attention and language in autism and developmental language delay', *Journal of Autism and Developmental Disorders*, 16 (1986), pp. 335–49. P. Mundy, M. Sigman, J. Ungerer and T. Sherman, 'Defining the social deficits of autism: the contribution of non-verbal communication measures', *Journal of Child Psychology and Psychiatry*, 27 (1986), pp. 657–69. B. M. Prizant and A. M. Wetherby, 'Communicative intent: a framework for understanding social-communicative behavior in autism', *Journal of the American Academy of Child and Adolescent Psychiatry*, 26 (1987), pp. 472–79.

16. S. Baron-Cohen, J. Allen and C. Gillberg, 'Can autism be detected at 18 months? The needle, the haystack, and the CHAT', *British Journal of Psychiatry*, 161 (1992), pp. 839–43.

S. Baron-Cohen, A. Cox, G. Baird, J. Swettenham, N. Nightingale, K. Morgan, A. Drew and T. Charman, 'Psychological markers in the detection of autism in infancy in a large population', *British Journal of Psychiatry*, 168 (1996), pp. 158–63.

17. T. Charman, J. Swettenham, S. Baron-Cohen, A. Cox, G. Baird and A. Drew, 'Infants with autism: an investigation of empathy, pretend play, joint attention, and imitation', *Developmental Psychology*, 33 (1997), pp. 781–9.

18. M. D. Sigman, C. Kasari, J.-H. Kwon and N. Yirmiya, 'Responses to the negative emotions of others by autistic, mentally retarded, and normal children', *Child Development*, 63 (1992), pp. 796–807.

19. S. B. Wulff, 'The symbolic and object play of children with autism: a review', *Journal of Autism and Developmental Disorder*, 15 (1985), pp. 139–48.

C. B. Riguet, N. D. Taylor, S. Benaroya and L. S. Klein, 'Symbolic play in autistic, Down's, and normal children of equivalent mental age', *Journal of Autism and Developmental Disorders*, 11 (1981), pp. 439–48.

V. Lewis and J. Boucher, 'Spontaneous, instructed and elicited play in relatively able autistic children,' *British Journal of Developmental Psychology*, 6 (1988), pp. 325–39.

L. Wing and J. Gould, 'Severe impairments of social interaction and associated abnormalities in children: epidemiology and classification', *Journal of Autism and Developmental Disorders*, 9 (1979), pp. 11–29.

20. G. Dawson and F. C. McKissick, 'Self-recognition in autistic children', *Journal of Autism and Developmental Disorders*, 14 (1984), pp. 383–94.

21. C. Kasari, M. D. Sigman, P. Baumgartner and D. J. Stipek, 'Pride and mastery in children with autism', *Journal of Child Psychology and Psychiatry*, 34 (1993), pp. 353–62.

22. H. Tager-Flusberg, 'What language reveals about the understanding of minds in children with autism', in S. Baron-Cohen, H. Tager-Flusberg and D.J. Cohen (eds), *Understanding Other Minds: Perspectives from Autism* (Oxford, Oxford University Press, 1993), pp. 138–57.

23. M. A. Dewey and M. P. Everard, 'The near-normal autistic adolescent', *Journal of Autism and Childhood Schizophrenia*, 4 (1974), pp. 348–56.

D. M. Ricks and L. Wing, 'Language, communication and the use of symbols in normal and autistic children', *Journal of Autism and Childhood Schizophrenia*, 5 (1975), pp. 191–221.

C. A. M. Baltaxe, 'Pragmatic deficits in the language of autistic adolescents', *Journal of Pediatric Psychology*, 2 (1977), pp. 176–80.

FOUR: THE CAST OF THOUGHT

1. D. W. Hamlyn, *Experience and the Growth of Understanding* (London, Routledge and Kegan Paul, 1978)

2. M. Warnock, *Imagination* (London, Faber and Faber, 1976). The quotation is from p. 171.

3. K. Clark, *Civilisation* (London, British Broadcasting Corporation, 1969). The quotation is from pp. 284–5.

4. M. Warnock, *Imagination* (London, Faber & Faber, 1976). The quotation is from p. 197.

5. M. Buber, *I and Thou*, 2nd edn, tr. R. G. Smith (Edinburgh, Clark, 1937/58).

6. There is nothing quite like reading the work of a genius in the original, but when it comes to the writings of Piaget, one may find oneself either immersed in wonderful but highly detailed observations of children, or confronted with impenetrable theory. Two relatively reader-friendly books are J. Piaget, *The Principles of Genetic Epistemology*, tr. W. Mays (London, Routledge and Kegan Paul, 1972). J. Piaget, *The Origins of Intelligence in the Child* (London, Routledge and Keegan Paul, 1953).

   Someone who wants to tackle Piaget for the first time might begin with an overview that places Piaget's theory in the context of contemporary approaches, for example, K. Richardson, *Models of Cognitive Development* (Hove, Psychology Press, 1998).

   A chapter of my own that attempts to characterize Piaget's approach appears in an edition of a book that has now been superceded, and therefore only available from a library: R. P. Hobson, 'Piaget: on the ways of knowing in childhood', in M. Rutter and L. Hersov (eds), *Child and Adolescent Psychiatry: Modern Approaches*, 2nd edn (Oxford, Blackwell, 1985), pp. 191–203.

   For a more detailed exposition of Piaget's work, I can recommend M. Chapman, *Constructive Evolution* (Cambridge, Cambridge University Press, 1988).

7. G. H. Mead, *Mind, Self and Society* (Chicago and London, University of Chicago Press, 1934).

   H. Werner and B. Kaplan, *Symbol Formation* (Hillsdale, NJ, Erlbaum, 1963/1984).

8. R. P. Hobson, 'The grounding of symbols: a social-developmental account', in P. Mitchell and K. J. Riggs (eds), *Reasoning and the Mind* (Hove, Psychology Press, 2000), pp. 11–35.

9. R. Britton, 'The missing link: parental sexuality in the Oedipus complex', in R. Britton, M. Feldman and E. O'Shaughnessy (eds), *The Oedipus Complex Today* (London, Karnac, 1989), pp. 83–101.

   R. P. Hobson, 'Symbols, social relations and psychoanalysis', *Social Development*, 3 (1994), pp. 172–6.

10. S. K. Langer, *Philosophy in a New Key*, 3rd edn (Cambridge, Mass., Harvard University Press, 1957).

C. K. Ogden and I. A. Richards, *The Meaning of Meaning* (London, Routledge, 1923/1985).

11. G. H. Mead, *Mind, Self and Society* (Chicago and London, University of Chicago Press, 1934).

12. D. W. Hamlyn, *Experience and the Growth of Understanding* (London, Routledge and Kegan Paul, 1978).

D. W. Hamlyn, *In and out of the Black Box* (Oxford, Blackwell, 1990).

13. D. Hammerskjold, *Markings* (London, Faber, 1964). The quotation is from p. 101.

14. M. Tomasello, *The Cultural Origins of Human Cognition* (Cambridge, Mass, Harvard University Press, 1999).

M. Tomasello and M. Barton, 'Learning words in nonostensive contexts', *Developmental Psychology*, 30 (1994), pp. 639–50.

15. W. James, *The Principles of Psychology*, vol. I (New York, Dover, 1890).

16. R. Charney, 'Speech roles and the development of personal pronouns', *Journal of Child Language*, 7 (1980), pp. 509–28.

17. K. Kaye, *The Mental and Social Life of Babies* (London, Methuen, 1982).

18. L. S. Vygotsky, *Thought and Language*, tr. E. Hanfmann and G. Vakar (Cambridge, Mass, M.I.T. Press, 1962). The quotation is from p. 8.

Five: The Fragile Growth of Mind

1. C. Trevarthen and P. Hubley, 'Secondary intersubjectivity: confidence, confiding and acts of meaning in the first year', in A. Lock (ed.), *Action, Gesture and Symbol: The Emergence of Language* (London, Academic Press, 1978), pp. 183–229.

2. L. E. Crandell, M. P. H. Patrick, R. P. Hobson, R. M. García Pérez and A. Lee, 'Mothers with borderline personality disorder and their two-month-old infants', paper presented to the Tavistock Clinic, July 2001.

3. R. P. Hobson, M. P. H. Patrick, L. E. Crandell, R. M. Garcia-

Perez and A. Lee, 'Infant triadic communication in the context of maternal borderline personality disorder' (submitted).

4. L. Murray, A. Fiori-Cowley, R. Hooper, and P. J. Cooper, 'The impact of postnatal depression and associated adversity on early mother-infant interactions and later infant outcome', *Child Development*, 67 (1996), pp. 2512–26.

   L. Murray and P. J. Cooper, 'The role of infant and maternal factors in postpartum depression, mother-infant interactions, and infant outcome', in L. Murray and P. J. Cooper (eds), *Postpartum Depression and Child Development* (New York, Guilford, 1997), pp. 111–35. The quotation is from p. 129.

5. D. Sharp, D. Hay, S. Pawlby, G. Schmucker, H. Allen, and R. Kumar, 'The impact of postnatal depression on boys' intellectual development', *Journal of Child Psychology and Psychiatry*, 36 (1995), pp. 1315– 36.

6. M. Tomasello and M. J. Farrar, 'Joint attention and early language', *Child Development*, 57 (1986), pp. 1454–63.

   D. A. Baldwin, 'Infants' contribution to the achievement of joint reference', *Child Development*, 62 (1991), pp. 875–90.

7. L. E. Crandell and R. P. Hobson, 'Individual differences in young children's IQ: a social-developmental perspective', *Journal of Child Psychology and Psychiatry*, 40 (1999), pp. 455–64.

8. H. Wimmer and J. Perner, 'Beliefs about beliefs: representation and constraining function of wrong beliefs in young children's understanding of deception', *Cognition*, 13 (1983), pp. 103–28.

9. J. Perner, S. R. Leekam and H. Wimmer, 'Three-year-olds' difficulty with false belief', *British Journal of Developmental Psychology*, 5 (1987), pp. 125–37.

10. J. H. Flavell, E. R. Flavell and F. L. Green, 'Development of the appearance-reality distinction', *Cognitive Psychology*, 15 (1983), pp. 95–120.

11. E. Meins, C. Fernyhough, J. Russell and D. Clark-Carter, 'Security of attachment as a predictor of symbolic and mentalising abilities: a longitudinal study', *Social Development*, 7 (1998), pp. 1–24.

SIX: THE INNER AND THE OUTER

1. M. B. Ainsworth and B. A. Wittig, 'Attachment and exploratory behaviour of one-year-olds in a Strange Situation', in B. M. Foss (ed.), *Determinants of Infant Behaviour*, Vol. 4 (London, Methuen, 1969), pp. 111–36.

    M. D. S. Ainsworth, M. C. Blehar, E. Waters, and S. Wall, *Patterns of Attachment* (Hillsdale, NJ, Erlbaum, 1978).

    E. A. Carlson and L. A. Sroufe, 'Contribution of attachment theory to developmental psychopathology', in D. Cicchetti and D. J. Cohen (eds), *Developmental Psychopathology. Theory and Methods* (New York, Wiley, 1995), pp. 581–617.

2. C. George, N. Kaplan and M. Main, *The Attachment Interview for Adults* (unpublished ms., University of California, Berkeley, 1985).

3. P. Fonagy, H. Steele and M. Steele, 'Maternal representations of attachment during pregnancy predict the organisation of infant–mother attachment at one year of age', *Child Development*, 62 (1991), pp. 891–905.

4. M. Patrick, R. P. Hobson, D. Castle, R. Howard and B. Maughan, 'Personality disorder and the representation of early social experience', *Development and Psychopathology*, 6 (1994), pp. 375–88.

5. S. Freud, 'Mourning and melancholia', *Standard Edition of the Works of Sigmund Freud*, vol. 14, tr. J. Strachey (London, Hogarth, 1957), pp. 243–58. The quotation is from p. 246.

6. L. S. Vygotsky, 'Internalization of higher psychological functions', in M. Cole, V. John-Steiner, S. Scribner and E. Souberman (eds), *Mind in Society: The Development of Higher Psychological Processes* (Cambridge, Mass, Harvard University Press, 1978), pp. 52–7.

7. Two good introductions to Kleinian theory are S. Isaacs, 'The nature and function of phantasy', *International Journal of Psychoanalysis*, 29 (1948), pp. 73–97, and H. Segal, *Introduction to the Work of Melanie Klein* (London, Hogarth, 1973).

8. R. P. Hobson, M. P. H. Patrick and J. D. Valentine, 'Objectivity in psychoanalytic judgements', *British Journal of Psychiatry*, 173 (1998), pp. 172–77.

9. R. P. Hobson, 'Psychoanalysis and infancy,' in G. Bremner, G.

Butterworth and A. Slater (eds), *Infant Development: Recent Advances* (Hove, Sussex, Psychology Press, 1997), pp. 275–90.

T. H. Ogden, 'The concept of internal object relations', *International Journal of Psycho-Analysis*, 64 (1983), pp. 227–41.

10. R. P. Hobson, 'Self-representing dreams', *Psychoanalytic Psychotherapy*, I (1985), pp. 43–53.

SEVEN: FETTERED MINDS

1. L. Kanner, 'Autistic disturbances of affective contact', *Nervous Child*, 2 (1943), pp. 217–50. The quotation is from pp. 247–8.
2. R. P. Hobson, *Autism and the Development of Mind* (Hove, Erlbaum, 1993). The evidence that underpins my summary account of autistic children's thinking is given in this book, and the quotation is from pp. 179–80.
3. R. P. Hobson and A. Lee, 'Emotion-related and abstract concepts in autistic people: evidence from the British Picture Vocabulary Scale', *Journal of Autism and Developmental Disorders*, 19 (1989), pp. 601–23.
4. S. Baron-Cohen, A. M. Leslie and U. Frith, 'Does the autistic child have a "theory of mind"? *Cognition*, 21 (1985), pp. 37–46.
5. S. Baron-Cohen, 'Are autistic children "behaviourists"? An examination of their mental-physical and appearance-reality distinctions'. *Journal of Autism and Developmental Disorders*, 19 (1989), pp. 579–600.
6. The debate between myself and a colleague who takes a computational approach appeared in the following: A. M. Leslie, 'Pretense and representation: the origins of "theory of mind"', *Psychological Review*, 94 (1987), pp. 412–26; R. P. Hobson, 'On acquiring knowledge about people and the capacity to pretend: response to Leslie', *Psychological Review*, 97 (1990), pp. 114–21; A. M. Leslie and U. Frith, 'Prospects for a cognitive neuropsychology of autism: Hobson's choice', *Psychological Review*, 97 (1990), pp. 122–31, and A. M. Leslie, 'The Theory of Mind impairment in autism: evidence for a modular mechanism of development?' in A. Whiten (ed.), *Natural Theories of Mind* (Oxford, Blackwell, 1991), pp. 63–78.

7. S. Fraiberg, *Insights From the Blind* (London, Souvenir, 1977), ch. xi.

8. For evidence that children with autism are able to co-ordinate visual perspectives see R. P. Hobson, 'Early childhood autism and the question of egocentrism', *Journal of Autism and Developmental Disorders*, 14 (1984), pp. 85–104.

9. M. Bishop and R. P. Hobson, 'Patterns of social interaction in congenitally blind children' (unpublished manuscript, 2000).

10. R. Brown, R. P. Hobson, A. Lee and J. Stevenson, 'Are there "autistic-like" features in congenitally blind children?' *Journal of Child Psychology and Psychiatry*, 38 (1997), pp. 693–703.

    R. P. Hobson, A. Lee and R. Brown, 'Autism and congenital blindness', *Journal of Autism and Developmental Disorders*, 29 (1999), pp. 45–56.

11. E. S. Andersen, A. Dunlea and L. S. Kekelis, 'Blind children's language: resolving some differences' *Journal of Child Language*, 11 (1984), pp. 645–64.

12. Minter, M., R. P. Hobson and M. Bishop, 'Congenital visual impairment and "theory of mind"', *British Journal of Developmental Psychology*, 16 (1998), pp. 183–96.

    Our own studies on blind children are summarized in R. P. Hobson, R. Brown, M. Minter and A. Lee, '"Autism" revisited: the case of congenital blindness' in V. Lewis and G. M. Collis (eds), *Blindness and Psychological Development in Young Children* (Leicester, British Psychological Society, 1997), pp. 99–115.

13. M. Rutter, L. Andersen-Wood, C. Beckett, D. Bredenkamp, J. Castle, C. Groothues, J. Kreppner, L. Keaveney, C. Lord, T. G. O'Connor and the English and Romanian adoptees study team, 'Quasi-autistic patterns following severe early global privation', *Journal of Child Psychology and Psychiatry*, 40 (1999), pp. 537–49. The quotation at the end of this section is from p. 538.

14. *Ibid.*

Eight: Self and Others

1. M. Scheerer, E. Rothmann and K. Goldstein, 'A case of "idiot savant": an experimental study of personality organisation', *Psychological Monographs*, 58, 4, 269 (1945), pp. 1–63.

2. A very interesting but complex discussion of pathology of the self in autism is in G. Bosch, *Infantile Autism*, tr. D. and I. Jordan (New York, Springer–Verlag, 1970).

3. S. J. Weeks and R. P. Hobson, 'The salience of facial expression for autistic children', *Journal of Child Psychology and Psychiatry*, 28 (1987), pp. 137–52.

4. R. P. Hobson and A. Lee, 'Imitation and identification in autism', *Journal of Child Psychology and Psychiatry*, 40 (1999), pp. 649–59.

5. A. Lee, R. P. Hobson and S. Chiat, 'I, you, me and autism: an experimental study', *Journal of Autism and Developmental Disorders*, 24 (1994), pp. 155–76.

6. W. Damon and D. Hart, 'The development of self-understanding from infancy through adolescence', *Child Development*, 53 (1982), pp. 841–64.

   W. Damon and D. Hart, *Self-understanding in Childhood and Adolescence* (New York, Cambridge University Press, 1988).

   A. Lee and R. P. Hobson, 'On developing self-concepts: a controlled study of children and adolescents with autism', *Journal of Child Psychology and Psychiatry*, 39 (1998), pp. 1131–41.

7. A. Lee and R. P. Hobson, 'Self-depiction: a controlled study of children and adolescents with autism' (submitted, 2001).

8. G. Bosch, *Infantile Autism*, tr. D. and I. Jordan (New York, Springer-Verlag, 1970).

NINE: UNDERSTANDING MINDS

1. J. Piaget, *Genetic Epistemology*, tr. E. Duckworth (New York and London, Columbia University Press, 1970).

2. An excellent introduction to Wittgenstein's contributions to philosophy of mind is in N. Malcolm, 'Wittgenstein's philosophical investigations' in V. C. Chappell (ed.), *The Philosophy of Mind* (Englewood Cliffs, NJ, Prentice-Hall, 1962), pp. 74–100.

   L. Wittgenstein, *Philosophical Investigations*, tr. G. E. M. Anscombe (Oxford, Blackwell, 1958).

   L. Wittgenstein, in G. H. von Wright and H. Nyman (eds), *Remarks on the Philosophy of Psychology*, vol. 2, tr. C. G. Luckhardt and M.A.E. Aue (Oxford, Blackwell, 1980).

D. W. Hamlyn, *In and out of the Black Box* (Oxford, Blackwell, 1990).

3. Arguments that underpin my approach to knowing other minds may be found in P. F. Strawson, 'Persons', in V.C. Chappell (ed.), *The Philosophy of Mind* (Englewood Cliffs, NJ, Prentice-Hall, 1958/1962), pp. 127–46.

D. W. Hamlyn, 'Person-perception and our understanding of others', in T. Mischel (ed.), *Understanding Other Persons*, (Oxford, Blackwell, 1974) pp. 1–36.

R. P. Hobson 'Concerning knowledge of mental states', *British Journal of Medical Psychology*, 63 (1990), pp. 199–213.

R. P. Hobson, 'On the origins of self and the case of autism', *Development and Psychopathology*, 2 (1990), pp. 163–81.

R. P. Hobson, 'Against the theory of "Theory of Mind"', *British Journal of Developmental Psychology*, 9 (1991), pp. 33–51.

R. P. Hobson, 'The emotional origins of social understanding', *Philosophical Psychology*, 6 (1993), pp. 227–49.

R. P. Hobson, 'Perceiving attitudes, conceiving minds', in C. Lewis and P. Mitchell (eds), *Origins of an Understanding of Mind* (Hillsdale, NJ, Erlbaum, 1994), pp. 71–93.

M. Merleau-Ponty, 'The child's relations with others', tr. W. Cobb, in M. Merleau-Ponty, *The Primacy of Perception* (Evanston, IL, Northwestern University Press, 1964), pp. 96–155. The quotation is from p. 146.

L. Wittgenstein, in G. E. M. Anscombe and G. H. von Wright (eds), *Remarks on the Philosophy of Psychology*, vol. 1, tr. G. E. M. Anscombe (Oxford, Blackwell, 1980).

L. Wittgenstein, in G. H. von Wright and H. Nyman (eds), *Remarks on the Philosophy of Psychology*, vol. 2, tr. C. G. Luckhardt and M.A.E. Aue (Oxford, Blackwell, 1980).

4. R. P. Hobson, J. Ouston and A. Lee, 'What's in a face? The case of autism', *British Journal of Psychology*, 79 (1988), pp. 441–53.

5. P. Ekman and W. F. Friesen, 'Pictures of facial affect', available from Paul Ekman, copyright 1976.

6. R. F. Hobson, *Forms of Feeling* (London, Tavistock, 1985).

7. L. Wittgenstein, *Philosophical Investigations*, tr. G. E. M. Anscombe (Oxford, Blackwell, 1958). The quotation is from p. 178.

8. D. Woodruff Smith, *The Circle of Acquaintance* (Dordrecht, Kluwer Academic, 1989). The quotation is from p. 134.

9. R. P. Hobson, 'On sharing experiences', *Development and Psychopathology*, I (1989), pp. 197–203.

10. R. P. Hobson, 'The intersubjective foundations of thought', in S. Braten (ed.), *Intersubjective Communication and Emotion in Ontogeny* (Cambridge, Cambridge University Press, 1998), pp. 283–96.

11. E. Bates, L. Camaioni and Volterra, 'The acquisition of performatives prior to speech', *Merrill-Palmer Quarterly*, 21 (1975), pp. 205–26.

12. H. Werner and B. Kaplan, *Symbol Formation* (Hillsdale, NJ, Erlbaum, 1963/1984).

13. I. Bretherton and M. Beeghly, 'Talking about internal states: the acquisition of an explicit theory of mind', *Developmental Psychology*, 18 (1982), pp. 906–21.

14. H. M. Wellman, *The Child's Theory of Mind* (Cambridge, Mass, Bradford, 1990).

15. M. Tomasello, 'Uniquely primate, uniquely human', *Developmental Science*, I (1998), pp. I–16.

16. D. J. Povinelli and T. J. Eddy, 'What young chimpanzees know about seeing', Monographs of the Society for Research in Child Development, Child Development Publications, Serial 247, vol. 61, No. 3. (The University of Chicago Press, Chicago, 1996). This monograph also contains my commentary on the research, under the title 'On not understanding minds'.

17. M. Tomasello, S. Savage-Rumbaugh and A. C. Kruger, 'Imitative learning of actions on objects by children, chimpanzees, and enculturated chimpanzees', *Child Development*, 64 (1993), pp. 1688–705.

Index

Index

Visit **www.panmacmillan.com** to read more about all our books and to buy them. You will also find features, author interviews and news of any author events, and you can sign up for e-newsletters so that you're always first to hear about our new releases.